ANALYZING ECONOMIC MAN: KEY ISSUES.

STANLEY J BASS

Abstract

This is a philosophical study of economics and cognitive psychology as sciences of human behaviour. Boundaries and interactions of the two sciences are examined with a close look at the experimental studies on judgement and decision making, and on strategic interaction in games. I argue, against conceptual scepticism, that not only is a science of human behaviour possible, but it is exemplified by both economics and psychology, which have been striving to measure decision-relevant psychological quantities and explain the behavioural anomalies that have emerged as a result of theoretical and empirical progress in measurement and experimentation. The dialectics of 'crises and responses' involved in this process reveals various ways in which representations, models and experiments are employed in the laboratory. I emphasize the precision of measurement and the severity of test as important methodological values in scientific progress, and argue that these values are the basis of theoretical progress. I explore alternative ways in which economic models of rational choice can be informed by psychology, and argue that a successful model should incorporate empirical findings from social and cognitive psychology, instead of maintaining familiar economic modelling strategies while relying on folk psychological intuitions. I propose that, in addition to modelling human behaviour as utility maximization, explicitly modelling human reasoning *qua* cognitive process may be the key to success. I point out two metaphysical stances—mechanistic and functional—implicit in the debates over the prospect of neuroeconomics, and consider their methodological implications to the study of human cognition and behaviour. I argue that it is unlikely that neuroscience will radically eliminate constructs of economic theory such as beliefs and preferences, based on the observation that recent brain-imaging studies of individual decision making largely presuppose constructs of cogntive psychology.

Contents

List of Figures   7

List of Tables   7

1   Introduction   **8**

    1.1   Economics as a Separate Science   11

    1.2   The Birth of Contemporary Decision Theory   17

    1.3   The Emergence of Behavioural Economics   18

    1.4   Summary of the Following Chapters   22

2   Measurement and the Progress of Empirical Decision Theory   **25**

    2.1   Introduction   25

    2.2   From Folk Psychology to Decision Theory   27

    2.3   Holism of the Mental, Circularity, and Indeterminacy   30

       2.3.1   Circularity   31

       2.3.2   Indeterminacy   35

    2.4   Incompleteness, Externalism, and Causation   38

    2.5   The Argument from Normativity   41

       2.5.1   The Principle of Charity as a Heuristic   41

       2.5.2   The Principle of Invariance and Measurement   45

    2.6   Conclusion   49

3   Unification and Causal Analysis: Inconsistency Anomalies   **51**

    3.1   Introduction   51

    3.2   The Unificationist Approach to Anomalies   52

       3.2.1   'Ptolemaic' Science and Ad Hocness   53

       3.2.2   The Standard Model of Discounted Utility and its Rivals   55

    3.3   The 'Ptolemaic' Critique and its Problems   60

    3.4   Decomposing the Compatibility Hypothesis   62

       3.4.1   History   62

       3.4.2   Separating Causes   66

    3.5   The Procedural Approach   68

    3.6   Can 'Wider Theoretical Considerations' Help?   72

    3.7   Conclusion   74

4   Testing Game Theory with Repetition: Cooperation Anomalies   76

4.1   The Prisoner's Dilemma   77

4.2   Public Goods Experiments: Testing Game Theory?   81

     4.2.1   Environment   82

     4.2.2   Institution   84

     4.2.3   Game Theory as a Model of Behaviour   88

4.3   Measuring Preferences with Game Theory   89

     4.3.1   Is Game Theory a Tautology?   89

     4.3.2   Altruism and its Refutation   94

     4.3.3   The Argument from Unnatural Habitat: Is There a Dilemma?   100

4.4   Conclusion   106

Appendix: Results of a 'Casual' Classroom Experiment   108

5   From Social Preferences to Cognitive Rational Choice   110

5.1   Limits of the Payoff Respecification Approach   110

     5.1.1   Models of Social Preference   111

     5.1.2   Sharpening the Tools: Ultimatum, Dictator, and Trust Games   114

     5.1.3   Empirical Assessment   116

     5.1.4   Path Dependency and Norm Exogeny   117

5.2   Social Norms   123

5.3   Group Identification   126

5.4   Team Reasoning   130

     5.4.1   The Independence Hypothesis   130

     5.4.2   The Reasoning Effect and Agency Transformation   132

     5.4.3   Experimental Tests of Team Reasoning   135

5.5   Conclusion   143

6   Neuroeconomics and the Unity of Science   144

6.1   The Metaphysical Turn in the Unity of Science Debate   145

6.2   The Neuroeconomics Controversy   146

     6.2.1   The Promise of Neuroeconomics   146

     6.2.2   Gul and Pesendorfer's Conceptual Critique   148

     6.2.3   Harrison's Methodological Critique   153

  6.3   Metaphysics That Matters to Science   157

     6.3.1   The Mechanistic Stance   157

     6.3.2   The Functional Stance   160

     6.3.3   Implications for Neuroeconomics   163

  6.4   The Functional Stance at Work in Cognitive Neuroscience   166

     6.4.1   Framing   166

     6.4.2   Compatibility   169

     6.4.3   The Functional Stance on What?   171

  6.5   Conclusion   174

7   Conclusion   176

Bibliography   180

List of Figures

1.1	Indifference Curve Analysis	14
3.1	Exponential and Hyperbolic Discount Curves	57
4.1	Schelling Diagram	79
4.2	Extensive-Form Representation of the Repeated Prisoner's Dilemma	86
4.3	Subject Heterogeneity in a Public Goods Game	100
4.A	Results of a 'Casual' Classroom Experiment	108
5.1	Ultimatum Game and Dictator Game	118
5.2	Cognitive Mapping from Context to Norm	124
5.3	Five PD Games	139
5.4	C-Choice vs. E-Choice in Five Experiments	140
6.1	Comparison between Two Experimental Paradigms	173

List of Tables

2.1	Types of Measurement	29
2.2	Bets on the Roulette	44
3.1	Percentage of Responses Favouring the H bet over the L bet for Four Different Elicitation Procedures	65
4.1	The Prisoner's Dilemma	77
4.2	A Payoff Respecification of the Prisoner's Dilemma	90
4.3	PD-material Game Played by Pure Altruists	94
4.4	PD-material Game Played by Warm-Glow Altruists	95
4.5	(M)PD Experiments with 2 by 2 Designs	101
5.1	PD-material Game Played by Inequality-Averse Players	111
5.2	PD-material Game Played by Social-Welfare Players	112
5.3	PD-material Game Played by Reciprocally-Fair Players	113
5.4	The Rectangular Field Assumption	120
5.5	Cooperation in Three Conditions	128
5.6	Hi-Lo Game	133
5.7	Hi-Lo-material Game Played by Social-Welfare Players	134
5.8	PD-material Game Played by *SWDF* Players	135
5.9	Strategy-Profiles 'Customized' for Different Types of Individuals	137
5.10	Results of Experiment 1	138
5.11	Results of Experiment 2	140

Chapter 1

Introduction

Where does one science end, and another begin? How do the sciences interact at their boundaries, if there are boundaries at all? And if different sciences tell us different things on the same subject matter, how can we tell which is/are right? Most abstractly put, these are the questions I shall address in this thesis. Of course, these questions are partly historical and sociological, and must be answered as such. However, my project is philosophical. That is, I want to learn some methodological, epistemological as well as metaphysical lessons in attempting to answer these questions. Specifically, I will be exploring the boundaries of two branches of behavioural and social science, namely, economics and psychology.

Why economics and psychology? Why not, say, edaphology and phycology? Are the samples representative of all science? Most likely not, but my aim is not to make universal claims that are also applicable to the sciences of soils and seaweeds. Rather, I want first and foremost to make claims that are relevant to economics and psychology. Ultimately my interests differ from those of economists and psychologists only in the level of abstraction, not in subject.

I choose economics and psychology in part because these sciences, and behavioural and social science in general, have been relatively underrepresented in the standard philosophy of science, compared to the natural and biological sciences. Surely economics has been studied more than psychology (e.g., Hausman 1992; Rosenberg 1992; Mäki 2001; 2002, among others), but it is only recently that philosophers started to examine economists' practices with more respect, care and rigor (e.g., Hoover (2001) for macroeconomics; Guala (2005) for experimental economics). Psychology has always been of great interest for philosophers, but typically to the extent that it is relevant to issues concerning the metaphysics of the mind, such as consciousness, reduction, mental causation, etc. Bermúdez (2005) distinguishes philosophy of psychology from philosophy of mind, and focuses on cognition and behaviour. Somewhat surprisingly, however, in his textbook there is virtually no discussion of experimental methods in psychology. The relevance of psychology, in particular of cognitive psychology, has been discussed by some epistemologists (e.g., Goldman 1992; Stich 1990), and Bishop and Trout (2005) even claim that psychology can drastically reform normative epistemology, or the study of what constitutes good reasoning. A related movement called *experimental philosophy* (Knobe and Nichols 2008) applies experimental methods in testing folk intutions that are relevant to philosophical questions. But these naturalistic movements tend to take for granted psychologists' process of knowledge production itself. They lack a careful examination of the methodology of experimental psychology, and without such caution, naturalism may result in just another philosophical *Sprechchor*.

Philosophers' relative neglect of behavioural and social science is not without reason. After all, philosophers of science since Carnap and Popper have been fascinated by the combination of modern science's extraordinary (i.e., non-folk) theoretical claims and its immense success in prediction and application. By contrast, the behavioural and social sciences might be viewed rather unimpressive in both respects: although they have developed technical concepts such as 'Nash equilibrium', 'stimuli-response compatibility', etc., these sciences have not revolutionalized our conceptions about humans and society as Newtonian mechanics or Einstein's relativistic theory changed our worldviews. And the success of these sciences is not as impressive as sending humans to the moon, or making clone pigs. So it is in a way understandable that philosophers do not feel compelled to take such seemingly mediocre sciences seriously. But this evaluation needs reconsideration at least for three reasons. First, it is becoming a mainstream consensus among philosophers of science that practice is as important as theory in understanding science, and the study of experimental practice has yielded important contributions to the discussion of scientific realism (Hacking 1983), causation (Cartwright 1989), reductionism (Wimsatt 2007), etc. One of the common themes emerging from this study is a relative autonomy of practice (in particular experimental practice) from theoretical development (Galison 1987; Chang 2004). In light of this theme, the practice of behavioural and social scientists deserves more philosophical attention, even if their theories are not so impressive. Trout (1998), for example, gives a realist twist to this theme and argues for 'measured realism'—the thesis that reliably measurable quantities suggest that they really exist (see chapter 6)—based on the observation that the measurement of psychological attributes and social variables has been remarkably stable despite the lack of powerful psychological and sociological theories. While he is right in pointing out the relevance of these sciences to metaphysical debates in philosophy, Trout (1998) glosses over considerable differences among psychology, sociology, political science and history, with a curious total neglect of economics, which occupies an important place in social science and is increasingly becoming influential in behavioural science as well. I suspect that this selective bias was partly caused by the metaphysical view Trout endorses: if one wants to argue that scientists are studying the 'same things', it is natural to de-emphasize disciplinary diversity and to neglect 'theory-loaded' disciplines such as economics. In this thesis, in contrast, I shall not start from a preferred metaphysical viewpoint. My discussion will not be biased in favour of scientific realism, nor against the theory-ladenness of experimental practice. By focusing on the boundary between economics and psychology, I hope to provide a more realistic (though far from comprehensive) picture of behavioural and social science.

A second reason why philosophers of science should reexamine their views about behavioural and social science concerns diverging criteria of success. The mobilization of science and technology during and after World War II has affected behavioural and social science profoundly, creating multidisciplinary research programmes such as Operations Research, Artificial Intelligence, and Management and Policy Sciences (see Mirowski (2002) for a critical history of the relationship between economics and these new disciplines).[1] These research programmes made salient the gap between success in prediction/explanation, on the one hand, and success in application, on the other. That is, these programmes have been employed to intervene on reality, before it is established that they sufficiently predict or explain phenomena in question based on some criteria. Such a gap is typical of economics and psychology, and its investigation may yield important implications for e.g., social ontology. Hacking's (1995) study of the 'looping effect' of psychological research and MacKenzie's (2006) study of the 'performativity' of financial theory provide good examples.[2]

Finally, and perhaps most importantly, the behavioural and social sciences have, as a matter of fact, enjoyed considerable progress during the last couple of centuries. Since it is my task in the next chapter to concretely argue for this claim, here I shall motivate my investigation by pointing out two historical perculiarities that make this progress particularly interesting from a methodological point of view. The first one concerns the separation of economics from the rest of behavioural and social science, and the second one concerns the interactions of economics and psychology since the middle of the 20th century. I will discuss them in turn. The purpose is to provide a

---

[1] This development also made obsolete the conventional dichotomy between natural and social sciences as well as the distinction between science and technology. Simon ([1969] 1996) provides a useful perspective to see these research programmes as the 'sciences of the *artificial*'.
[2] See Guala (2007) for a survey of recent trends in social ontology.

context for the following chapters, not to write a proper history of economic thought (for that see e.g., Mandler 1999; Weintraub 2002).

1.1 Economics as a Separate Science

Political economists, or 'classical' economists of the 18-19th centuries were mainly motivated to explain the process of Western industrialization that was changing people's life and society irreversibly. Although Adam Smith—who had much wider interests in human nature and society (see Sugden 2002; Ashraf et al. 2005)—is officially recognized as the father of economics, it was John Stuart Mill who took a crucial methodological step, namely to focus on a narrow but well-defined set of human motives which are presumed to be relevant to the explanation of economic phenomena. Thus Mill proposed a model of man—later to be known as 'economic man', or *homo economicus*:[3] "Political Economy", he contends,

> does not treat of the whole of man's nature as modified by the social state, nor of the whole conduct of man in society. It is concerned with him solely as *a being who desires to possess wealth, and who is capable of judging of the comparative efficacy of means for obtaining that end.* It predicts only such of the phenomena of the social state as take place in consequence of the pursuit of wealth. It makes entire abstraction of every other human passion or motive; except those which may be regarded as perpetually antagonizing principles to the desire of wealth, namely, aversion to labour, and desire of the present enjoyment of costly indulgences. (Mill [1836] 2000: 97; my italics)

The core of economic man consists of material interests and cognitive capacities to satisfy those interests. This model of man was the basis of Mill's deductive approach, or the 'method a priori', according to which one first abstracts a few relevant causes (based on introspectively valid 'laws of human nature') and their effects, and then modifies these by adding extra causes in an analogous way as the vector analysis in Newtonian mechanics. Mill's deductive approach was put forward explicitly against August Comte's vision of historical, inductive, comprehensive, and unified social science; for

---

[3] Persky (1995: 222) notes that Mill himself used neither the term 'economic man', nor its Latin version; the former was used by one of Mill's critics, John Kells Ingram, and the latter by Vilfredo Pareto. Persky also points out that the term was widely used among Cambridge economists such as John Neville Keynes and Alfred Marshall.

Mill, economics was a 'distinct and separate, though not independent' (Mill 1843: 6.9.3) branch of social science.[4]

From the vantage-point of modern economics, however, Mill's model is unsatisfactory at least in two respects. First, the motives of economic man are directed towards objective values such as 'wealth', '(less) labour', and 'costly indulgences'. But how could we know what heterogeneous people value, and how exactly each individual attaches different values to different objects? Second, the focus on these narrow material values also considerably limits the proper domain of economics. Indeed, Mill admitted that material motives were predominant only in his contemporary Great Britain and in the United States, noting 'how apparently small a motive often outweighs the desire of money-getting, even in the operations which have money-getting for their direct object' in Continental Europe (Mill 1843: 6.9.4). But economics would be far too parochial a science if it could explain only two countries at a particular time in history.

The theoretical innovations of so-called 'neoclassical' economists can be understood as an attempt to overcome these problems. First, these economists replaced Mill's objective notion of values with Jeremy Bentham's subjective concept of *utility*, i.e., 'that property in any object, whereby it tends to produce benefit, advantage, pleasure, good, or happiness (all this in the present case comes to the same thing), or (what comes again to the same thing) to prevent the happening of mischief, pain, evil, or unhappiness to the party whose interest is considered' (Bentham [1789] 1843: 1.3). The principle of utility 'approves or disapproves of every action whatsoever, according to the tendency which it appears to have to augment or diminish the happiness of the party whose interest is in question' (1.2). Bentham's utilitarianism widened the potential domain of economics by enabling economists to talk about motivations *in general*, instead of those related to wealth, leisure, or some such specific objects. Economics was thus severed from historical and sociological questions concerning the genesis, development, and extinction of specific values. Now, all that had to be studied for economic analysis was utility.

Although completely subjective and one-dimensional, utility was still realistically interpreted as a psychic currency (sometimes referred to as 'utils') in the subject's head, and therefore how this unobservable quantity relates to observable choice behaviour had to be theoretically explicated. The principle of *marginal* utility (Jevons 1871; Menger 1871; Walras 1874) did exactly this: the principle states that an

---

[4] For a critical analysis of Mill's 'method *a priori*' see Hausman (1992: ch. 6). Persky (1995) notes that Mill's own empirical research was a little subtler than this simple methodology would suggest.

economic agent[5] will maximize her net utility, given her budget constraint, by consuming any one commodity until the marginal increment of utility from that commodity becomes equal to that from another. For example, given her pocket money £3, Anne's choice of one cup of coffee (£1.5) and one piece of cake (£1.5)—rather than two cups of coffee or two pieces of cake—can be explained by this principle: suppose her subjective utility for the first cup of coffee is 10 utils, that of the second cup 2 utils, that of the first piece of cake 8 utils, and that of the second piece 4 utils; then the observed choice gives her the maximum 18 utils, as opposed to the 12 utils she would receive from the other combinations; hence her observed choice. The concept of marginal utility is 'cardinal' in the sense that measuring the relative strengths of utility for the agent is crucial for the explanation of her choice behaviour. In particular, as in this example, it was presupposed that the marginal utility which the agent receives from one extra unit of any consumed good diminishes, other things being equal (the principle of *diminishing* marginal utility).

The principle of (diminishing) marginal utility was the early neoclassical answer to the problem of indirect measurement of an unobservable quantity, i.e., subjective utility.[6] Jevons (1871: I.17), for example, thought that hypothesizing such quantity was a legitimate scientific practice, comparable with hypothesizing 'gravity'—a similarly unobservable but fundamental quantity—in physics.[7] As it turned out, however, such a hypothesis is not necessary for the economic analysis of individual choice. Edgeworth (1881) and his followers (Fisher 1892; Pareto 1909; Hicks and Allen 1934) showed that a simple graphic analysis of the agent's *preferences* could dispense with the measurement of subjective utility altogether. First, take the quantity of coffee on the x-axis and that of cake on the y-axis, for instance (see Figure 1.1).[8]

---

[5] Instead of 'economic man', I will use the gender-neutral term 'agent'. Although I follow the convention to use it as a feminine noun, 'economic agents' may refer to non-individual human beings such as collective entities (e.g., households, firms and groups), or non-human beings (e.g., brain modules and bees). See chapter 3 for an explicit discussion of agent specification.

[6] 'I hesitate to say that men will ever have the means of measuring directly the feelings of the human heart. A unit of pleasure or of pain is difficult even to conceive; but it is the amount of these feelings which is continually prompting us to buying and selling, borrowing and lending, labouring and resting, producing and consuming; and *it is from the quantitative effects of the feelings that we must estimate their comparative amounts*' (Jevons 1871: I.17, original italics).

[7] This comparison with physics is characteristic of most modern decision theorists. See section 1.2 below.

[8] This is the exposition usually found in introductory microeconomics courses. In consumer theory, the objects of choice are 'consumption bundle', 'a complete list of the goods and services that are involved in the choice problem that we are investigating' (Varian 2003: 33). So if the choice problem we are investigating is general, a two-dimensional indifference curves graph represents the relation between one type of goods (or services) and the rest of all goods and services.

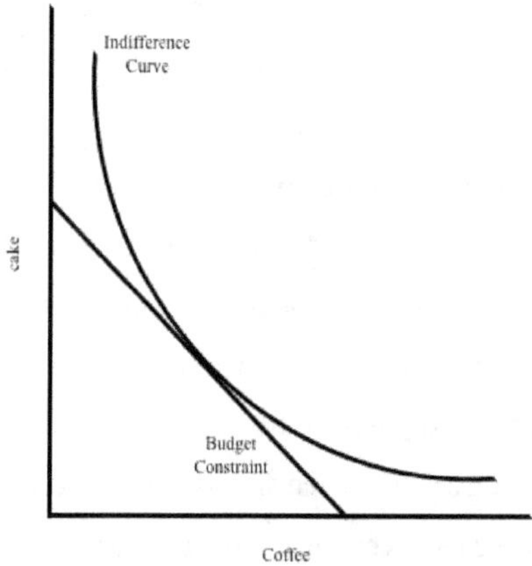

Figure 1.1: Indifference Curve Analysis

Then any point in the graph represents a combination of the two goods. For a given combination, we can think of other combinations which are equally preferred by the agent. Consider Anne's choice of one coffee and one cake: she may accept a smaller cup of coffee if we slice the cake a bit bigger; she may accept a smaller slice of cake if we offer her a 'grande' size coffee, and so on. If we connect all these points, then we obtain a line called an *indifference curve*. The slope of this indifference curve at a particular point expresses the *marginal rate of substitution* (MRS), the rate at which Anne is just willing to give up one good (coffee) for the other (cake). The agent then chooses the combination such that the MRS is equal to the ratio of the prices of the two goods. In our example, Anne's choice of one coffee and one cake is such a combination, given her budget constraint. Notice that we can, in principle, draw indifference curves from the observation of the agent's successive *indifference* judgement, without hypothesizing the underlying magnitudes of utility maximized by her. Such a psychological hypothesis becomes optional, instead of necessary.[9] Now the essential hypothesis is that the agent can rank bundles of goods according to her *preferences*, which are (1) complete (any two bundles can be compared); (2) reflexive (any bundle is as good as itself); and (3) transitive (if one bundle X is preferred to Y, and Y is prefered to Z, then X is preferred to Z).[10]

---

[9] Ross (2005: ch. 3) points out that what drove the early neoclassicists such as Fisher and Pareto was a pursuit of mathematical simplicity, elegance, etc., while later Robbins and Samuelson had more behaviouralistic motivations to eliminate all talk of unobservable entities such as subjective utility.

[10] Further assumptions are (4) monotonicity (more of any good is better than less) and (5) convexity (averages are preferred to extremes, roughly speaking). Preferences are said to be 'well-behaved' if (4) and (5) are satisfied in addition to (1) - (3). This makes any given indifference curve as a negative slope which is *convex* when seen from the origin. Our example of Anne's indifference curve shows such properties.

In addition, since preferences are no more directly observable than cardinal utility, we need a way to infer preferences from the observation of an agent's choice behaviour. *The principle of revealed preference* provides a simple way to operationalize the concept of preference: if one bundle X is chosen when another one Y is available and affordable, then it is inferred that X is preferred to Y.[11] This and the other assumptions (mentioned in the previous paragraph) about preferences were systematized by Samuelson (1938), Houthakker (1950) and Sen (1971) as Revealed Preference Theory, or RPT. In order to distinguish it from the principle of revealed preference, I shall refer to the whole theory of choice simply as *preference theory*.[12]

Although economists still use the concept of utility, it is now re-interpreted simply as a mathematically useful way of representing preferences as defined by preference theory. Specifically, 'utility' is defined as a *utility function*, for each agent, assigning a real value index to every consumption bundle; the agent is said to be 'maximizing her utility' (i) if her choice behaviour can be mapped onto (represented as) some utility function (this is guaranteed if the assumptions (1)-(3) are satisfied), and (ii) if the utility function thus identified describes the agent's choice behaviour in a meaningfully wide range of contexts (to see this we need to operationalize preference theory using something like the principle of revealed preference). The agent's choice behaviour is said to be 'rational' if and only if (i) and (ii) are satisfied. Now, rational economic man is defined neither by his specific material interests nor by his mental sensations, but by his *behavioural consistency* with preference theory. In sum, economics has achieved the separation from sociology and history by replacing objective values with subjective utility, and from psychology by replacing cardinal utility with ordinal preferences that are operationally inferred from choice.

The development of preference theory was accompanied by another important change from classical to neoclassical economics, i.e., the redefinition of the domain of economics. Robbins (1935: 16) famously defined the discipline as 'the science which studies human behaviour as a relationship between ends and scarce means which have alternative uses'. In this view, preference theory can be applied to *any* choice problem humans face, not just consumer choice. Instead of bugdet constraint, we can then talk of

---

[11] The weak axiom of revealed preference (WARP) states that if X is chosen over Y, and X and Y are not the same, then it cannot happen that Y is chosen over X. The strong axiom (SARP) extends WARP to bundles whose preference orderings are indirectly inferred by transitivity.

[12] Hausman (2000) and Ross (2005: ch. 3) both see the core of RPT as the *identification of preference and choice*, and respectively criticizes and defends the theory thus understood. My characterization of RPT here consciously avoids such characterization to remain uncontroversial. This is not unreasonable. For example, a standard textbook on microeconomics (Varian 2003: ch. 7) clearly denies such identification, emphasizing the operational character of the principle of revealed preference.

different kinds of constraints—time, mental effort, etc.—the key idea being that these are limited. Instead of consumption bundles, we can talk of different kinds of objects—such as fame, prestige, love, etc. Robbins' vision of economics as a general science of human behaviour has been implemented in a programmatic way by some economists (most notably by Gary Becker 1976; 1991), who have applied economic analysis to the family and other social phenomena which used to be considered as falling in the proper domain of sociology (hence the derogatory label "economic imperialism"). The expansion of the economic domain has caused lively debates on the boudaries between economics and the neighboring disciplines (see Swedberg (1990); Udehn (1996) for sociology and economics, Monroe and Downs (1991); Green and Shapiro (1994); Friedman (1996) for political science and economics). It is this combination of empirical ambition, on the one hand, and a preference theory detached from substantial psychological and sociological notions of human motivation and behaviour, on the other, that has made the scientific status of modern economics so controversial.

Struck by economics' theoretical sophistication and its apparent lack of empirical success, philosophers of economics have proposed various explanations. For example, Rosenberg (1992) argues that economics necessarily fails empirically because economic theory is untestable, while Hausman (1992) suggests that its empirical failure is due to its strategy (dating back to Mill) to separate itself from other sciences in order to retain its generality and wide scope. These accounts (typically based on a priori analysis of economic theory and methodology) seem to be getting increasingly obsolete in light of the two changes that took place in the last quarter of the 20th century: first, the experimental method has become a standard tool in economics, demonstrating that economic theory *can* be tested after all. Second, economists have begun to draw on social and cognitive psychology, and even on neuroscience in order to gain a better and deeper understanding of individual economic behaviour, thus making economics no longer a separate science. I shall attempt to explicate the implications of these new developments a posteriori, i.e., by critically engaging with the results and methods of economics and psychology. In particular, my focus in the present study will be the integration of these two sciences at their boundary, namely, the study of individual decision making. In the following I shall briefly describe how this integration is taking place.

1.2. The Birth of Contemporary Decision Theory

The integration of economics and psychology has been far from smooth, and it is incomplete even today. The economic profession officially recognized it with the 2002 Nobel Prize in Economics, awarded to the psychologist Daniel Kahneman 'for having integrated insights from psychological research into economic science, especially concerning human judgment and decision-making under uncertainty'.[13] The field which Kahneman and his colleagues pioneered is called *behavioural decision research* (BDR), a branch of psychology which investigates the cognitive mechanisms underlying human judgement and decision making. BDR has had a significant impact on economics for its implications to the theory of rational choice.[14] As suggested by the Nobel committee, the integration is often thought to be one-directional, economics being influenced by psychology. However, BDR has a root in contemporary decision theory, which developed in close relation with economics.

When preference theory reached maturity, another important theory was in its infancy: *game theory*, the study of decision making in strategic contexts, in which the consequence of one's action depends on others' actions (*and vice versa*). The Austrian economist Oscar Morgenstern saw the prevalence of such strategic interdependence in economic contexts, and collaborated with the mathematician John von Neumann to give full mathematical rigor to the analysis of interdependent decision making (von Neumann and Morgenstern [1944] 2004). Indeed, strategic uncertainty is a special case of uncertainty involved in economic decision making in general.[15] For example, Anne might choose to buy two cups of coffee (instead of one cup plus one slice of cake) if there is a sufficiently high probability (p) that coffee-drinking becomes illegal the next day. This may be unlikely, but the point is that uncertainty is the norm in everyday decision making, rather than the exception. In order to incorporate uncertainty (in this general sense) into economic analysis, von Neumann and Morgenstern developed Expected Utility Theory (EUT henceforth), according to which an economic agent maximizes a weighted sum of her utility function in each state of nature (e.g., coffee becomes illegal; or it doesn't), where the weights are given by the probability of each

---

[13] Press Release, 9 October 2002, The Royal Swedish Academy of Sciences. The other half went to the experimental economist Vernon Smith, 'for having established laboratory experiments as a tool in empirical economic analysis, especially in the study of alternative market mechanisms'. See Smith (1991; 2003) and Loewenstein (1999) for the differences between experimental economics and psychology-informed economics.

[14] I will use 'the theory of rational choice' or 'rational choice theory' to refer to both decision theory and game theory, which will be described in the next paragraph.

[15] Sometimes 'uncertainty' is distinguished from 'risk', which is presumed to be more amenable to quantitative estimation. I will not make such distinction and use risk and uncertainty interchangeably.

state (e.g., p; or $1-p$). Of particular importance was the 'axiomatization' of EUT provided in the appendix of the second edition (1947) of *Theory of Games and Economic Behavior*:[16] von Neumann and Morgenstern proved that if certain postulates about preferences are satisfied,[17] then the agent's preferences can be represented as an expected utility function which is unique up to positive affine transformation.[18] Although EUT was a digression in the context of game theory (its main concern being *strategic* uncertainty), it proved to be pivotal for economics as well as for decision theory, bringing back the concept of quantitative or 'cardinal' utility to economics in its modern form. In as early as 1948, Leonard Savage—the assistant of von Neumann at the Institute for Advanced Study, Princeton, during World War II—collaborated with the economist Milton Friedman, putting forward EUT as an economic hypothesis to explain the existence of insurance and lotteries (Friedman and Savage 1948). Savage further combined EUT with the idea that probability is a personal degree of belief (subject to the laws of probability calculus), and formulated subjective EUT, or SEUT (1954).[19] This was the birth of decision theory as we know it today.

1.3 The Emergence of Behavioural Economics

During the same period as Savage was establishing subjective EUT, the philosopher Patrick Suppes was developing an axiomatic approach to quantitative measurement in science, under the influence of Ernest Nagel and Alfred Tarski. The aspiration of Suppes's (1951; 1954) project was both logical and empirical: it was logical in trying to 'axiomatize' part of science, i.e., to build a system of a set of primitive propositions ('axioms') from which the rest of the theory deductively follows ('theorems'); but the project was at the same time empirical in trying to improve the accuracy of scientific measurement by providing a set-theoretic foundation of numerical ('quantitative') representations of empirical ('qualitative') observations (Michell 1999:193-211). While von Neumann and Morgenstern (1944) were well aware of the importance of

---

[16] The idea of expected utility itself was already proposed by the Dutch-Swiss mathematician Daniel Bernoulli in 1738. Bernoulli (1954) is an English translation of the original paper.

[17] There are different formulations of postulates. In addition to the ones already listed in section 1.1 (completeness, reflexivity, transitivity), important ones are continuity, independence, and monotonicity. Some of these are discussed in detail in chapter 2.

[18] A positive affine transformation simply means multiplying by a positive number and adding a constant. That is, a function $V(U)$ can be written in the form: $V(U) = aU + b$ where $a > 0$.

[19] Von Neumann and Morgenstern (1944) proposed the objective interpretation of probability (i.e., relative frequency of events in the long run), but anticipated SEUT, admitting that the subjective view of probability also 'leads to a satisfactory numerical concept of utility' (3.3.3, fn. 2). Since mostly EUT is interpreted subjectively nowadays, I will simply use 'EUT' rather than 'SEUT' unless the context requires such clarification.

axiomatizing decision theory to measure utility (see their discussion in chapter 1, section 3), it was Suppes and his colleagues who first attempted a systematic experimental measurement of utilities (Stanford Value Theory Project: see Suppes and Winet 1955; Davidson and Suppes 1957). This was a rather isolated, but in retrospect pioneering programme of behavioural economic experiments.[20]. Suppes's study led to a revolution in measurement theory (Suppes and Zinnes 1963; Luce and Tukey 1964), but to date it has not had a serious impact on mainstream quantitative psychology such as intelligence and personality research (see Michell (1999: 213-219) for diagnosis and critique). Behavioural decision research, however, is an exception in this respect.

Ward Edwards was one of the first psychologists to notice the relevance of EUT (in particular its subjective formulation by Savage) and introduce it to psychologists under the name of *behavioural* decision theory (Edwards 1954; 1961).[21] Edwards, the son of an economist, studied psychology at Harvard, where he wrote a Ph.D dissertation on people's preferences on gambles and the non-linear evaluation of probability, under the influence of the statistician Frederick Mosteller, who introduced Edwards to EUT (Phillips and von Winterfeldt 2007). In 1958 Edwards moved to the psychology department at the University of Michigan, Ann Arbor—then the world's biggest psychology department, with a growing crowd of graduate students including, among others, Amos Tversky, Paul Slovic and Sarah Lichtenstein. At Michigan Edwards and his student Harold Lindman collaborated with Savage, introducing Bayesian statistical inference as an empirical model of human information-processing (Edwards, Lindman and Savage 1963). With Edwards' support, Lichtenstein and Slovic conducted a series of experiments on people's risk assessment of gambling using real money, leading to the discovery of *preference reversals*, a serious anomaly for EUT (Lichtenstein and Slovic 1971; 1973, see the next chapter). Meanwhile, Tversky went back to Israel at the end of 1960s to teach at Hebrew University. There his faith in subjective Bayesianism was 'severely shaken' by conversations with Daniel Kahneman, who was establishing himself as a leading researcher in the field of mental effort (Kahneman 2003). Their subsequent collaborative work on 'cognitive illusions', or 'heuristics and biases' (Tversky and Kahneman 1974) in human judgment and decision making led to Prospect Theory (Kahneman and Tversky 1979) and the concept of *framing effects* (Tversky and

---

[20] Philosophers may remember the Stanford Value Theory Project as a failure, because of Donald Davidson's ([1974] 2001) negative comments on the Project. I will discuss Davidson's contribution and critique of empirical decision theory in chapter 2.

[21] The term 'behavioural' in here as elsewhere should not be confused with 'behaviourism' in psychology. Indeed, Edwards rejected behaviourism of B. F. Skinner—one of his teachers at Harvard— thinking that that is "what psychologists shouldn't do" (Phillips and von Winterfeldt 2007).

Kahneman 1981), which, together with preference reversals, gave rise to a branch of economics called *behavioural economics* (BE), also known as *economic psychology* or *economics and psychology*.[22]

It should be noted that in the 1950s and 60s, some acute economists had already challenged the empirical soundness of standard economic rational choice models such as EUT (Markowitz 1952; Allais 1953; Ellsberg 1961), the discount utility model of intertemporal choice (Strotz 1955) and some assumptions of game theory (Schelling 1960), based on introspection, casual observations and rudimentary experimental results. But it was only in the 1980s that the avalanche of the behavioural economics literature began under the direct influence of BDR. The phenomenon of preference reversals was taken up by the experimental economists Grether and Plott (1979), initiating a stream of publications on this topic in economic journals. Kahneman and Tversky's paper on Prospect Theory (1979) was published in *Econometrica*,[23] stimulating young economists such as Richard Thaler, who challenged the empirical as well as normative legitimacy of the standard models of rational choice. In 'Toward a Positive Theory of Consumer Choice' (1980), Thaler discussed various aspects of consumer behaviour (e.g., underweighting of opportunity costs, failure to ignore sunk costs, regret and self-control) that would become central themes in behavioural economics. These and other 'anomalies'—phenomena that do not conform to the standard models—are now compiled in Thaler (1992). Behavioural economists have tried to explain these anomalies by articulating cognitive mechanisms such as 'compatibility effects', 'framing effects', 'endowment effects', 'loss aversion', 'mental accounting', etc. But these explanations are often criticized by non-behavioural economists as 'ad hoc', mere empirical labeling rather than genuine explanation, irrelevant for economic phenomena, and so on. I will critically evaluate these criticisms in chapter 3.

In response, some behavioural economists have started to make their explanations more congenial to mainstream economics. Rabin (2002: 658) describes this new development as "second-wave behavioural economics", which 'moves beyond pointing out problems with current economic assumptions, and even beyond articulating

---

[22] Edwards himself pursued a different direction from his students. He devoted his career to develop usable tools to improve fallible human judgement and decision-making abilities. This research programme is called *psychological engineering*. See von Winterfeldt (1999).

[23] Kahneman (2003) recalls: 'The choice of venue turned out to be important; the identical paper, published in *Psychological Review*, would likely have had little impact on economics. But our decision was not guided by a wish to influence economics. *Econometrica* just happened to be the journal where the best papers on decision-making to date had been published, and we were aspiring to be in that company'. Kahneman and Tversky's paper was to become the most cited article in the history of that journal.

alternatives, and on to the task of systematically and formally exploring the alternatives with much the same sensibility and mostly the same methods that economists are familiar with' (see also Rabin 1998 for review). As an example, Rabin mentions so called 'social preference' models that try to explain apparent non-selfish behaviour in experimental games. In chapter 5 I will evaluate Rabin's proposal.

The emergence of *neuroeconomics* at the beginning of the 21st century (Breiter et al. 2001; McCabe et al. 2001 are among the first publications) may be considered the "third wave" of behavioural economics. Neuroeconomics is the study of brain functions and processes, in particular decision heuristics and the role of emotions underlying economic decision making. It is characterized by the use of neuroimaging technologies such as electroencephalography (EEG), magnetoencephalography (MEG), positron emission tomography (PET), and most prominently, functional magnetic resonance imaging (fMRI)[24] as well as the administration of chemicals and hormones. These technologies, mostly developed in clinical and cognitive science, are combined with the standard behavioural experiments, with the aim of providing "richer" evidence on the mechanics of human decision making (see Kenning and Plassmann (2005) for a careful survey). Neuroeconomics has caused heated debates among economists on the very relevance of psychology to the future of economic science. I will discuss neuroeconomics in chapter 6.

This is, briefly, how the separation between economics and psychology was challenged during the second half of the 20th century. As we have seen, the challenge was not primarily philosophical, but practical and empirical. However, scientific practice does raise important philosophical and methodological questions. The contribution of the present study is first of all to provide a systematic review of the episodes of the encounter of economics and psychology in individual and interactive decision making. Although I think this review is interesting in its own right, it is also useful because behavioural and social science is underrepresented in the philosophy literature, as I have mentioned above, despite the fact that the sciences of human behaviour are relevant to some of the issues in the philosophy of science such as demarcation, theory appraisal and scientific realism. In particular, a careful look at the *experimental* studies of decision making will turn out to be fruitful in informing philosophical and methodological debates that have been based mainly on

---

[24] The first two detects changes in electric activities in the brain, while the last two detects changes in cerebral blood flow/metabolism. There are several textbooks on fMRI, e.g., Jezzard et al. (2001) and Cabeza and Kingstone (2006). Huettel et al. (2009) contains a discussion of how fMRI differs from other imaging techniques.

interpretations of scientific *theories*. Of course, the proof of the pudding is in the eating, or in the following chapters. In the next section, I will summarize each chapter and its contribution.

1.4 Summary of the Following Chapters

The thesis is organized into seven chapters, of which the present introduction is the first. This is not a comprehensive study of behavioural economics. For that see Wilkinson (2008) (the first accessible textbook of behavioural economics); Camerer (2003) (the textbook of behavioural game theory); Camerer et al. (2003) and Loewenstein (2007) (anthorogies of important behavioural economic papers); Kahneman et al. (1982), Kahneman and Tversky (2000), Gilovich et al. (2002), Lichtenstein and Slovic (2006) (collections of important papers in behavioural decision research). Instead, I will adopt a controversy-based approach, i.e., focus on some philosophical debates surrounding behavioural economics, and evaluate these debates based on a detailed analysis of the relevant experimental studies (chapters 2, 3 and 6). I also venture to criticize some models proposed by behavioural economists, and discuss alternative models that exemplify (in my view) better ways of 'incorporating psychology into economics' (chapters 4 and 5). The summary of each chapter is provided below.

Chapter 2 discusses several preliminary issues concerning the scientificity of behavioural and social science in general. I will argue, against Rosenberg (1992) and Davidson ([1995] 2004), that EUT is testable and tested, and that normativity involved in the theory does not make this empirical test no less scientific. As an example I will illustrate the discovery of preference reversals—an anomaly in individual judgement and decision making under uncertainty—which will also be the basis of the discussions in chapters 3 and 6. This chapter will shed light on the persistent problem of demarcation between science and non-science, showing that a careful look at the experimental studies of individual decision making provides a strong case against the *a priori* argument to the effect that the sciences of human behaviour are impossible.

Chapter 3 evaluates Ross's (2005) critique that behavioural economists' explanations of preference reversals and other anomalous phenomena in the laboratory are *ad hoc*, or 'Ptolemaic'. I will argue that the explanatory strategy of BE is theoretically as well as empirically well motivated. In examining whether Ross's multiple-self model of intertemporal decision making will also explain intratemporal choice anomalies, I will introduce an alternative, procedural model; I also discuss the distinction between value-based and reason-based approaches in rational choice theory. This chapter examines the *abstract* methodological criteria of theory appraisal (such as unificationism and progressive researh programmes) in the *concrete* context of the experimental studies of individual decision making, in an attempt to identify the limits of such methodological criteria in evaluating the debate between psychologists and economists.

Chapter 4 turns to anomalies in game theory, in particular the existence of cooperation in the Prisoner's Dilemma and its multple-person variant, public goods games. I will argue that game theory is not a tautology, but can be tested together with preference theory. I will rebut two methodological arguments that try to insulate game theory from genuine tests, and review how models of altruism have tried to explain anomalies and failed. The contribution of this chapter is to show that some methodological problems concering theory testing (such as the alledged impossibility of testing game theory in the laboratory) are pseudo problems, and to draw attention to the real issues experimentalists face.

Chapter 5 compares several stylized social preference models that purport to explain cooperation in public goods games as well as other anomalies in Ultimatum, Dictator, and Trust games. I will point out two problems in trying to save game theory from these anomalies by 'getting the payoffs right'. One problem concerns measurement, and the other explanatory power. I will introduce economic models of cooperation informed by cognitive, social and evolutionary psychology. I will compare the cognitive-extension (Bicchieri 2006; Margolis 2007) and the rational-extension (Bacharach 2006) approaches to game theory, focusing on the different ways in which psychology can inform rational choice theory. I will evaluate both the cognitive-extension and the rational-extension models in light of some recent experimental results and end with some suggestions for future experiments that could inform this debate. Although this is not an empirical study in the sense of conducting experiments, this chapter aims to engage in the empirical studies of strategic interactions by way of methodological analysis, with some constructive proposals regarding novel experimental design.

Chapter 6 discusses the latest movement in BE, neuroeconomics. I will first revisit the unity of science and reductionism debates in philosophy of science, in order to make explicit the metaphysical assumptions involved in the arguments of both advocates and critics of neuroeconomics. I will identify mechanism and functionalism as the prominent metaphysical stances of both philosophers and scientists, and argue that functionalism is more congenial to the practice of neuroscientists, with some illustrations from the neuroscientific extension of behavioural decision research. This chapter contributes to the philosophical debates on scientific realism by identifying several distinct variants and components of realism implicit in the study of individual decision making, and by showing several ways in which such metaphysical assumptions may suggest different research strategies and influence scientific practice.

Chapter 7 summarizes the preceding arguments and concludes with a discussion of the illustrated empirical studies in economics and psychology and their implications for the concept of rationality.

Chapter 2

Measurement and the Progress of Empirical Decision Theory

In this chapter, I will address some fundamental worries concerning the very possibility of studying human behaviour in a scientific manner. Decision theory, in particular EUT, will be the case in point. I will argue for the following claims: (i) EUT is testable and has been tested; (ii) this process demonstrates progress of behavioural science both theoretically and empirically; and (iii) *a priori* arguments against the possibility of behavioural science generally fail.

2.1 Introduction

The problem of demarcation between science and pseudo-science has been central in the philosophy of science for much of the last century. Popper's falsifiability criterion is probably the best known attempt to solve the demarcation problem, not only among philosophers but also among economists and psychologists. Nevertheless, most philosophers of science now agree that many respectable scientific theories are not falsifiable in any straightforward sense. So lack of falsifiability should not make behavioural and social science any less scientific than their natural counterparts. Even Popper ([1967] 1995: 177-178) had to recognize the existence of at least one apparently unfalsifiable presupposition in social science, which he called *the rationality principle of the adequacy of our actions*, or the rationality principle for short. The principle states that people always act in such a way that we can make sense of their actions, given their situations. According to this principle, for example, a *kamikaze* pilot's suicidal attack is not incomprehensible, once we correctly identify his predicament: he didn't want to die, but abandoning his duty would have dishonoured not only himself but his ancestors, family and descendants, the consequences of which would have been grave in his society. Popper defended the rationality principle by arguing that it was a *sound methodological policy* not to blame the principle when some theory presupposing it failed to predict. His argument is that saving the principle from refutation is sound because (i) we know that this principle is not strictly true and (ii) we won't learn much by questioning the principle, while we learn more by questioning the other part of the theory under test. Although Popper's policy may be sound in the context of testing social theory by field observations, it is not the case when such principle is precisely formulated and put under rigorous behavioural experiments. In this chapter I will illustrate how the rationality assumption has been tested and, indeed, falsified by experimental data.

Although I do not endorse Popper's methodological defence of the rationality principle, I side with him against some common enemies. They are the critics and sceptics who argue that behavioural and social science fails to be a genuine science because something like the rationality principle is conceptually, or *a priori*, presupposed. As a concrete target, I shall choose Donald Davidson, an enormously influential philosopher who has discussed this issue persistently and consistently in his writings. As noted in the previous chapter, Davidson in the 1950s was involved in the Stanford Value Theory Project, one of the first sustained empirical investigations of EUT. Although he made substantial contributions to the Project, Davidson turned later into a critic of behavioural science, for a number of reasons that we shall examine presently.

Before starting, some preliminary remarks are due. First, I will not provide a comprehensive interpretation of Davidson's philosophy (for that see, e.g., Evnine (1991)). Nor shall I attempt to rebut every point that he made in his (many) writings on this topic.[1] In the following, I will focus mainly on Davidson's mature position (in Davidson [1995] 2004), where he provides an extensive discussion on decision theory. Second, Davidson's ([1995] 2004) argument is based on a thought experiment: he first envisions a complete theory of human behaviour, and then evaluates it against his own criteria of respectable science. The complete theory, what Davidson calls 'the Unified Theory of Action and Speech', consists of decision theory and a theory of language interpretation (a Tarski-type theory of meaning). Although Davidson seems to hold that this combination is crucial (see also Davidson 1985), his main argument is not contingent on this combination, and thus I will discuss each component separately, mainly focusing on decision theory. Third, I will extensively discuss the problem of holism, which Davidson himself does not see as central to the problem. This is because another prominent critic of rational choice theory, Alex Rosenberg (1992), argues against the testability of EUT, based on the problem of holism.

The chapter proceeds as follows: section 2.2 makes the explicit connection between so called 'folk psychology' and decision theory to facilitate the discussion in

---

[1] See Bermùdez (2005: 153-163), who provides a critique of Davidson's ([1974] 2001) disillusionment with psychological experiments; Davidson's colleague in the project, Pat Suppes (1985), also criticizes Davidson's ideas about physical science, to which Davidson (1985) replies.

section 2.3, where the issue of the holism of the mental is analyzed into the problems of circularity and indeterminacy, and it is shown that both problems are solvable and solved. Section 2.4 briefly discusses externalism and its relation to the concept of causation. Section 2.5 discusses Davidson's main argument against behavioural science, i.e., the argument from normativity. I will illustrate the discovery of preference reversals and the subsequent responses from both economists and psychologists, in order to show that normativity is not a fundamental problem in testing decision theory. Section 2.6 concludes.

2.2 From Folk Psychology to Decision Theory

One of the goals of empirical decision theory is to yield accurate predictions of intentional or purposeful actions. To this end, it is not a reliable method to ask people direct questions about what they believe and what they want. People have various motivations, including motivations to deceive the experimenter, and sometimes even to deceive themselves. Any empirical theory of decision making thus must build upon the observation of not only what people say but also what people do. This distrust of people's motivations, however, does not usually go so far as a general scepticism about the fact that people act according to their motivations.[2] An ideal theory would be therefore one that relies on behavioural evidence (including verbal behaviour), while maintaining certain psychologically acceptable assumptions regarding the way in which people's behaviour is motivated.

The standard theory of decision making under uncertainty, Expected Utility Theory (EUT), is often said to presuppose belief/desire psychology, or 'folk psychology' (e.g., Rosenberg 1992; 1995). This is true for the subjective version of EUT, as manifested in Frank P. Ramsey's paper ([1926] 1988) which anticipated the axiomatization of EUT by von Neumann and Morgenstern in 1947 and Savage (1954).[3] Ramsey ([1926] 1988: 30) explicitly adopted folk psychological theory, according to which 'we act in the way we think most likely to realize the objects of our desires, so that a person's actions are completely determined by his desires and opinions'. Schematically put:

1. We *believe* that action A is most likely to realize object O.

---

[2] Of course, it is possible to go thus far, questioning the very idea that people's actions are goal-oriented. I confine my discussion in this chapter to the study of goal-oriented actions.

[3] Savage (1954) acknowledges Bruno de Finetti (1937) as well as Ramsey.

2. We *desire* O.

3. We *act* in the way we think most likely to realize the objects of our desires [folk psychological law].

4. Therefore, we do A.

Ramsey, while admitting its falsity, sponsored this folk psychological scheme as a good approximation to the truth in the domain of purposeful actions. Although implicit, it is thus possible to say that EUT amounts to *quantified folk psychology*. In the following, I will sketch how EUT can be used to quantitatively measure people's desires experimentally.

The experimenter offers subject S a choice of betting or not betting £5 against a certain amount of money (say £25) at various odds. By adjusting the odds (p), the experimenter can discover the offer which S would accept 50% of the time. This can be interpreted as meaning that she found the alternative of keeping £5 (outcome b) equal in preference to the prospect consisting of a certain chance (p) of winning £25 (outcome a) and a certain chance ($1-p$) of losing £5 (outcome c) (this prospect is denoted as [a if p; c if $(1-p)$]). By finding the odds (p) which results in equality of preference, the relative values (cardinal utilities) of the outcomes to S can thus be inferred. If we conventionally assign 0 to the worst outcome (EU(c)=0) and 1 to the best outcome (EU(a)=1), then we can compute the cardinal utility of the outcome b by finding the odds which result in equality (i.e., EU(b) $= p$). In a similar fashion one can measure the Expected Utilities of any material demands lying between the best option (a) and the worst (c).

Formally, the axiomatization of EUT postulates the following set of axioms regarding the weak binary preference relation over prospects, denoted as '$\geq$': in English 'is at least as preferred as':[4]

1. Completeness: for any two prospects q and r,

    either $q \geq r$ or $r \geq q$ (or both).

2. Transitivity: if $q \geq r$ and $r \geq s$ then $q \geq s$.

3. Continuity: if $q \geq r$ and $r \geq s$, there exists some probability p such that

    $r \sim [q$ if p; s if $1-p]$ ('$\sim$' denotes the indifference).

4. Independence: if $q \geq r$ then $[q$ if p; s if $1-p] \geq [r$ if p; s if $1-p]$

---

[4] 1 and 2 are sometimes combined and referred to as 'the ordering axiom'. I omitted the other axiom called 'reduction of compound prospects', which states that any complex prospects can be reduced to a simple one according to the ordinary probability calculus. See Luce and Raiffa (1957: 23-31) for a detailed discussion of these axioms.

5. Monotonicity: $[q$ if p; s if $1{-}p] \geq [q$ if p'; s if $1{-}p']$ if and only if

$$p \geq p'$$

From these axioms two important theorems are deduced: the *representation theorem* states that numbers can be assigned to beliefs and desires; and the *uniqueness theorem* states that numbers assigned to measure beliefs (subjective probabilities) constitute a ratio scale and that the numbers that track desires (utilities) constitute an interval scale.[5] In terms of measurement, it is crucial that the axiomatization is achieved. The merit of the first theorem is evident: if we want to accurately measure the agent's beliefs and desires, it is useful to assign numbers to them. The merit of the second theorem is to guarantee that we can do so as uniquely or non-arbitrarily as possible. In order to appreciate this point, consider different degrees of uniqueness in assigning numbers in measurement in general. Table 2.1 shows four different degrees of measurement, in order of descending strength:[6]

Table 2.1: Types of measurement (based on Davidson et al. 1955: 151)

Type	Uniqueness Characteristics	Example
1. absolute scale	absolutely unique	cardinality of classes
2. ratio scale	arbitrary unit	mass, length
3. interval scale	arbitrary zero and unit	longitude, time
4. ordinal scale	order preserving	university ranking

Which scale to use depends on at least two kinds of considerations, first, the purpose of a particular measurement, and second, theoretical feasibility. For example, if all we want is to rank the world's top 100 universities, an ordinal scale (4) should suffice, and there is no need to worry about whether we can say that the difference between e.g., Duke University (13th) and the University of Edinburgh (23rd) is the same as that between LSE (66th) and the University of Sheffield (76th).[7] On the other hand, it is essential for our everyday life that the time difference between 2pm and 4pm is the

---

[5] These two theorems are just one way of decomposing the point made in section 1.2 that preferences can be *represented* by a vNM utility function that is *unique* up to positive affine transformation.

[6] The table is not exhaustive, but it is sufficient for the present purposes. See Krantz et al. ([1971] 2007: volume 3).

[7] Times Higher Education, World University Rankings 2008. Although the rankings are based on numerical 'overall scores', these are used mainly to make ordinal rankings, not to compare universities on the interval scale.

same as that between 6pm and 8pm (scale type 3), although it is difficult and unnecessary to determine an absolute zero in this time scale (When did time begin?). The EUT uniqueness theorem enables us to measure degrees of beliefs on a ratio scale (2), and degrees of desires on an interval scale (3).

This is, intuitively, theoretical progress. First, instead of casually making numerical assignments to subjective probabilities and utilies based on the stipulation that these attributes are quantitative, EUT specified the structure of empirical systems under investigation, making explicit what was being measured. Second, it was mathematically proved that empirical structures were numerically representable with certain uniqueness properties.[8] The sense of progress implicit in this achievement can be appreciated by noticing the fact that medieval scientists had struggled for centuries just to conceptualize physical quantities such as 'distance' and 'velocity', on which the later achievements of Galileo and Newton are based (Michell 1999: 200, fn. 10). EUT made similar conceptual progress in psychological measurement.[9] Appropriately, von Neumann and Morgenstern ([1944] 2004: 1.2.2) note that '[t]he precise measurements of the quantity and quality of heat (energy and temperature) were the outcome and not the antecedents of the mathematical theory'.

Despite this progress in measurement, some philosophers criticize EUT for its dependence on folk psychology. In the following, I shall discuss three main arguments in turn.

2.3 Holism of the Mental, Circularity, and Indeterminacy

Davidson ([1995] 2004: 130) rightly points out that decision theory is based on the so called 'holism of the mental': the theory is 'designed to assign contents of beliefs, utterances, and values simultaneously because these basic attitudes are so interdependent that it would not be possible to determine them one at a time, or even two at a time'.[10] In the measurement of vNM utilities illustrated in the previous section, it was implicitly assumed that we could use the odds (p) as corresponding to the agent's

---

[8] Michell (1999: 198-199) makes these two points in relation to the measurement theory developed by Suppes and Zinnes (1963). Although EUT is a substantial hypothesis about particular empirical systems, rather than a pure theory of measurement, these points equally apply to EUT.

[9] As described in chapter 1, preference theory was equally axiomatized for decision making under certainty. But it wasn't meant for psychological measurement; quite to the contrary, it was meant for doing economics without such measurement.

[10] Actually, Davidson is talking about the Unified Theory of Action and Speech, the combination of decision theory and a Tarski-type theory of meaning. Since the core of his argument is not contingent on this combination, in the following I will simply regard him as talking about decision theory.

subjective beliefs. This is an example of holism: we cannot measure utilities without presupposing degrees of beliefs.[11]

2.3.1 Circularity

The holism of the mental[12] is often thought to be a big obstacle for the possibility of empirical decision theory. For example, Alex Rosenberg (1992), referring to EUT, says:

> [T]he Von Neumann-Morgenstern approach does not provide independent methods of 'holding constant' preferences or beliefs. In order to infer beliefs from choices, we must use the theory of expected utility to calculate preferences beforehand. In order to determine preferences from choices, we need to use the theory of expected utility to calculate the strength of beliefs beforehand. So there is no way to test the hypothesis that individuals are expectations-constrained, expected-utility maximizers, because we need the hypothesis to determine the expected utilities the hypothesis predicts they will maximize and to determine the expectations that constrain their maximization (1992: 123).

The argument seems to be this:[13]

(1) Since beliefs (B) and preferences (P) are not directly observable mental states, we must, in testing EUT, infer these variables from an agent's action or choice behaviour (C), which is directly observable.

(2) For this inference, we must depend on EUT, which has the following form:

$$C = f(B, P).$$

(3) In order to measure the value of either B or P from C, we need to fix that of the other variable in advance.

(4) For that, we need to use the form $C = f(B, P)$, the very theory we are trying to test.

(5) Therefore, EUT is empirically untestable.

What is wrong with this argument? To put it simply, the problem is that it is based on a hidden but false assumption, making in effect the argument a *non sequitur*. The implicit assumption concerns the so-called thesis of 'theory-ladenness of observation' which has been much discussed by philosophers of science (e.g. Hanson 1958; Kuhn 1962). This

---

[11] However, Howson (2001) argues that it is possible to disentangle a theory of rational beliefs under uncertainty from a rational theory of preferences.

[12] A similar but different aspect of holism is that items of each domain (belief, desire, meaning) cannot be isolated from other items in the same domain; e.g., the identification of one belief depends on that of other beliefs.

[13] This is in effect a two-valued version of the 'problem of nomic measurement' presented in Chang (2004: 59).

thesis states that theory-neutral observation is impossible in science. In one formulation, theory-ladenness suggests *infinite regress*: we need to test a theoretical hypothesis by empirical observation, but any observation is dependent on some theoretical assumptions. Those assumptions need be tested empirically, but observation for these is also dependent on some other assumptions, which cannot be tested by direct observation. Rosenberg's argument presupposes a different formulation of the problem, namely, *circularity*: the hypothesis in question cannot be tested by an observation that is itself interpreted by using that hypothesis. At first sight this assumption appears plausible; the test of a theory by observations which rely on the same theory seems to vacuously confirm that theory, hence not constituting a genuine test. Although intuitively appealing, this assumption is false. In fact, in empirical science it is not uncommon that theory-laden observations disconfirm the very theory presupposed. For example, in physical geometry, even if Euclidean geometry is stipulated in the physical laws used to compute the correctness for distortions in measuring rods, this does not guarantee that the geometry obtained by the corrected rods will be Euclidean (Grünbaum 1960: 82). Another example comes from astronomy. Although superluminal velocities (i.e. objects moving faster than light) are impossible in Einstein's relativistic physics, it has been observed that the relative velocity between two celestial bodies are superluminal in some cases, despite the fact that their relativity-based recession velocity is used to calculate the relative velocity (Brown 1993: 555-557). These examples show that a theory-laden observation can disconfirm the theory, or that the theory is 'F-B disconfirmable' by a F-B test.[14] In turn, if a particular hypothesis is F-B disconfirmable, it seems reasonable to think that that hypothesis could be confirmed should it pass a F-B test by yielding accurate predictions. For if the observation of O makes the probability of a hypothesis H being true given the background knowledge B lower than the probability of H given B only, then the observation of ¬O should make the probability of H given B higher than the probability of H given B only.[15] One may call such hypothesis testing 'circular' but not viciously so.[16]

---

[14] This is Shogenji's (2000: 291) terminology. F stands for Friedman (1979) and B for Brown (1993), who both discuss the problem of circular justification.

[15] Shogenji (2000: fn. 10) gives a formal Bayesian presentation. Brown (1994: 409) calls this idea of confirmation 'quasi-Popperian' since 'it requires the possibility of disconfirmation for a fair test, but allows for genuine confirmation as well'. My point remains the same whether one adopts subjective Bayesianism or some objective view about theory confirmation.

[16] I follow Brown (1994) in using 'circular' to refer to a class of tests that use the theory in question in observation (i.e., F-B tests), while 'viciously circular' to refer to a sub-class of circular tests that are not F-B disconfirmable. Shogenji (2000) prefers 'self-dependent', claiming no empirical test is genuinely 'circular'. I leave this semantic disagreement to the reader's linguistic intuition.

Once this point is appreciated, circularity can be seen even as a virtue in terms of experimental design. That is, if a theory is disconfirmed by observation despite the fact that the observation procedure is dependent on that theory, the accusation goes directly towards that theory, especially when there is no other auxiliary hypothesis involved in the experimental design. Hasok Chang (2004: 94-5) calls this experimental strategy 'minimalism', in discussing the 19th century French Physician Victor Regnault's experimental ingenuity to avoid all contentious assumptions that had been thought inevitable in the measurement of temperature. The strategy is minimalistic because it reduces to a minimum the number of auxiliary hypotheses that can be logically blamed when the theory in question is disconfirmed: Chang's motto is 'tighten the circle, to not break out of it'. To use Mayo's (1996) terminology, the strategy guarantees a 'severe' test.[17] Even if a theory is confirmed by observation that is independent of the theory, the degree of confirmation comes not from the fact of independence per se, but from the reliability of the independent theories used, which ultimately has to be tested, and which may also depend on other reliable theories. This means that the core of the theory-ladenness thesis is not circularity but infinite regress, which must be solved by ensuring the *reliability* of the background hypotheses. Independence is not essential, because independence in the ultimate sense—neutrality from all theoretical assumptions—is not attainable.

Having seen that the implicit assumption that theory-laden observations cannot test the theory does not generally hold, the next question is whether our case of interest, EUT, is F-B (dis)confirmable. In the following I will show that it is, by giving an example of an anomalous phenomenon called 'preference reversals' (PR). PR was first observed by Lichtenstein and Slovic (1971) and Lindman (1971), and came to be widely known (and believed to be a genuine phenomenon) among economists after Grether and Plott's (1979) paper in the *American Economic Review*. The phenomenon emerges in trying to infer people's preferences over a pair of gambles of comparable expected value by using two kinds of tasks.[18] One gamble (the H bet) offers a high probability of winning a modest sum of money; the other gamble (the L bet) offers a low probability of winning a relatively large amount of money. So for example:

---

[17] As an example of severe test, Mayo (1996) mentions the case of testing a hypothesis about the average SAT score of a group of students by checking all the students' scores. This is minimalistic in Chang's sense, but a little misleading as a good example of severe test, because the measurement of SAT score, unlike the measurement of subjective probabilities and utilities by EUT, is based on the arbitrary stipulation that what is being measured is quantitative.

[18] The following summary is taken from Tversky et al. (1990).

H bet: 28/36 chance to win \$10

L bet: 3/36 chance to win \$100

When offered a choice between the two options H and L, most subjects choose the H bet over the L bet. However, when asked to state their minimum selling price, the majority state a higher price for the L bet than for the H bet. That is:

(1) $H > L$ and

(2) $C_L > C_H$

where '$>$' denotes a strict preference relation, '$>$' a strict ordering of cash amounts, and C_L and C_H are the minimum selling prices (cash equivalents) of the L bet and H bet, respectively. According to EUT, (1) and (2) together (assuming more money is better than less) imply:

(3) $C_H \sim H > L \sim C_L > C_H$

where '$\sim$' denotes an indifference relation. Since (3) apparently violates the transitivity of preference orderings (i.e. it manifests '$C_H > C_L$' and its reverse at the same time), PR constitutes a serious anomaly to EUT, which, like most formal theories of rational choice, presupposes that preference orderings are 'well-behaved' and stable. The observation of PR is theory-laden in the sense that these presuppositions are stipulated in eliciting preference ordering from behaviour (choice and pricing). And yet the circularity involved does not vacuously confirm the theory under test, as the observation is anomalous and therefore can potentially disconfirm the theory. This non-vicious circularity derives from the fact that, in experimental contexts, the concept of preference—a theoretical construct of EUT—is not purely theoretical, but partly empirical because in order to be measured it needs to be given some interpretation through the use of at least one elicitation procedure. Once bridged to the world in this way, even such a theory-laden construct as preference can be measured, and tested with different elicitation procedures (more on this point in the next section).

It is a non-trivial question whether PR or some other anomaly, or a conjunction of various anomalies—there are many—has definitively disconfirmed EUT, just like whether the above-mentioned counter-example has definitively refuted Einstein's relativistic theory. But the important point here is that EUT is disconfirm*able*: the EUT-based observation creates an anomaly for EUT. The upshot is that although the premises (1-4) in the argument from circularity are true, its conclusion (5) does not follow because its hidden assumption is false in general, and in particular in the case of EUT.

2.3.2 Indeterminacy

The considerations above suggest that the real difficulty involved in the holism of the mental lies somewhere else. The problem is to measure the intentional attitudes 'one at a time', to use the Davidson's expression. Again, Rosenberg puts the point as follows:

> In order to determine strength of belief, we must observe behavior, holding strength of belief constant. In order to calculate strength of preference, we must observe behavior, holding strength of belief constant. In both cases, we may read some of the agent's psychological states from behavior, but only if we already know the agent's other psychological states' (1992: 123).

This quotation is immediately followed by Rosenberg's comment on circularity quoted above, suggesting that Rosenberg thinks that circularity is the problem. But as we saw, the difficulty of EUT lies not in the fact that it does not provide an *independent* method of 'holding constant' preferences or beliefs: the real problem rather is that it does not provide *any* methods of doing so, thus creating a problem of *indeterminacy*.

How does EUT manage to measure beliefs and preferences 'one at a time', holding constant the other variable? Consider the vNM utility measurement illustrated in the previous section. The problem of indeterminacy arises when implementing this measurement experimentally: it leaves room for some alternative interpretations of the data.[19] First, it may be the case that the subject evaluated the alternatives solely on the basis of their values, but it may equally be possible that she evaluated the alternatives based on some non-neutral attitude toward the risks or the uncertainties involved: if she is risk averse, a high probability of losing £5 will discourage her to choose that alternative, just like a lower utility score discourages the choice; if she is risk taking, the same odds will encourage her to choose that alternative, just like a higher utility score encourages that choice.[20] As long as the experimenter cannot separate these two effects, he cannot measure vNM utilities of the alternative outcomes a, b and c to the subject.

---

[19] The example is based on an illustration of Mosteller and Nogee's (1951) experiment in Davidson et al. (1955).

[20] Of course, an Expected Utility curve is interpreted as manifesting the subject's 'attitude towards risk' (risk-neutral if the curve is linear, etc.). However, this presupposes that the subject has a linear 'decision weight' function which mirrors the objective probability—an untested empirical assumption.

The measurement of subjective probability also suffers from the problem of multiple interpretations. In the above case we presupposed that the adjustment of the odds would be directly reflected in S's subjective probabilities. That is, if the odds are 1/3, for instance, this is supposed to invoke the same subjective probability 1/3 to her mind. Doubting this may seem unsoundly sceptical, but not necessarily so. Suppose the experimenter has changed the odds (p) from 1/13 to 1/12, and S moved from preferring £5 (b) to the prospect [£25, 1/13; –£5, 12/13], toward being indifferent between b and the new prospect [£25, 1/12; –£5, 11/12]. The chance of winning £25 (a) has increased by about 0.0064%, so it is possible to interpret that S became indifferent between the two options, increasing the confidence in obtaining £25 by 0.0064%. However, it may well be that she took the change of the denominator of the odds as a good omen (because she superstitiously dislikes number 13, for example), and overestimated the increase of the chance of winning £25 as, say, 1%. This may sound apparently 'irrational', but it is a possibility and cannot be excluded prior to empirical investigation. Thus we cannot simply identify the subjective probabilities with the mathematical (i.e. objective) probabilities; subjective probabilities need to be measured experimentally. But to do this, we need to measure vNM utilities, whose measurement also faces the problem of indeterminacy described in the previous paragraph.

A solution to the problem of indeterminacy can be found in Ramsey's ([1926] 1988) seminal paper, which was written more than 20 years before vNM's axiomatization.[21] According to Ramsey, an agent i is said to be 'ethically neutral' toward a proposition e if and only if (i) i believes that e is true with probability 1/2; and (ii) i is indifferent between two states of affairs that differ only in whether e is true or false. (In what follows I will talk about an ethically neutral *state E* in which e is true, instead of e.) A plausible example of an ethically neutral state is one in which a toss of a fair coin yields heads. With this assumption in hand, we can *first* measure i's subjective expected utilities of prospects, and *then* measure i's subjective probabilities for events in the following way:

(1) First, find out an ethically neutral state E^* which makes i indifferent between the two prospects [a if E^*; c if $\neg E^*$] and [c if E^*; a if $\neg E^*$], where a and c are the best and the worst outcomes for i, respectively (as in section 2.2). The utility of prospect [a if E^*; c if $\neg E^*$] is given by weighing the utilities of a and c by the probabilities of E^* and $\neg E^*$, that is, 1/2×1 + 1/2×0 = 1/2. Next, find out a sure option m such that i is indifferent between m and prospect [a if E^*; c if $\neg E^*$]. m can be assigned utility 1/2 because it is as

---

[21] The following exposition draws on Anand (1993: 7-10) and Pettit ([1991] 2002: 218-220).

desirable as the prospect with that utility. Using m as the midpoint of the utility scale, construct further prospects [a if E^*; m if $\neg E^*$] and [m if E^*; c if $\neg E^*$], whose utilities ought to be 3/4 and 1/4, respectively. Find options d and f such that i is indifferent between d and [a if E^*; m if $\neg E^*$], f and [m if E^*; c if $\neg E^*$]. Then d and f can be assigned the utilities of 3/4 and 1/4, respectively. Repeat this procedure until you fill in the scale with as many options as you want.

(2) In order to know the utility value of a new option, simply compare it against the options whose utilities are already known on the scale.[22]

(3) Once any option can be assigned a utility, you can measure i's subjective probabilities for states other than E^*. If you want to know i's belief about the likelihood of some state S, for instance, first obtain the utilities of the prospect $K = [x$ if S; y if $\neg S]$ and its component options x and y, and denote these as u_3, u_1, and u_2, respectively. The utility of K is given by $u_3 = pu_1 + (1-p)\,u_2$, where p is i's degree of belief that S will occur. Rearranging this equation, you get i's subjective probability $p = (u_3-u_2)/(u_1-u_2)$, the ratio of two utility differences.

Notice how much is achieved merely by relying on the relatively austere assumption that i has a preference ordering over options. This preference ordering makes it possible to identify an ethically neutral state, which in turn serves to determine in principle the entire expected utilities and subjective probabilities for i. Since the ethically neutral state is fixed throughout the procedure, it is possible to measure *first* expected utilities, and *then* subjective probabilities.[23] The Ramsey method was re-discovered by Davidson when he was working as a member of Stanford Value Theory Project in the mid 1950's, leading to a separate experimental measurement of expected utilities and subjective probabilities 'one at a time'.[24] More recently, Tversky and Kahneman (1992) have followed a similar procedure, measuring subjective attitudes toward risk ('decision-weighting functions') while holding the utility measurement constant.

Although the problem of indeterminacy was solved, Rosenberg is apparently unaware of this fact: '[i]t is ironical that the impetus of [the holism] thesis is to be found

---

[22] The utility for an item aa which is beyond the scale between a and c can also be calculated by finding an item (l) in the scale such that i is indifferent between prospect [aa if E^*; l if $\neg E^*$] and a. Similarly for an item which is below the scale. See Pettit ([1991] 2002: 219).

[23] 'Since the chance event E^* is fixed throughout [the experiment], it does not play any formal role in [the experiment] and *enters only via one particular empirical interpretation of the notion of utility differences*' (Suppes and Winet 1955: 259-60; my italics). In effect, the measurement of vNM utilities is 'completely divorced from any probability questions' (*ibid.*).

[24] Davidson ([1974] 2001) provides an incomplete sketch of his version of this method. See Suppes and Winet (1955) and the references therein for more detail.

in the same work of Frank Ramsey to which so much of the economic theory of choice under uncertainty is beholden' (Rosenberg 1992: 157-8). Not ironical at all: for not only did Ramsey base his theory on the holism of the mental, but also he provided a method to measure expected utilities and subjective probabilities separately. Both the circularity and indeterminacy arising from the holism of the mental are not obstacles peculiar to the study of the mental, but just an example of difficulties that any experimental scientists must face. Behavioural economists seem to have handled these problems rather well.

2.4 Incompleteness, Externalism, and Causation

Before moving on to Davidson's main argument, I will briefly discuss another common critique of formal decision theory, namely that the theory is *incomplete*: since the objects of choice are subjectively perceived, the identification of the relevant decision problem for an agent requires the identification of her subjective framing (how she divides the world into parts), a piece of information which is not provided by formal decision theory (Pettit [1991] 2002). For example, Anne's subjective framing about available drinks may be [caffeine; caffeine-free] in the morning, [hot; cold] in the summer, [cheap; expensive] when she has little money, [high-calorie; low-calorie] when she's on diet, [alcohol; non-alcohol] in the evening, or combinations of any such framings, rather than [drink 1; drink 2; ...] on the menu. In principle, her framing is as rich as her semantics.

Davidson ([1995] 2004) formulates it as a problem of *externalism* involved in the theory of meaning, the other component of Davidson's Unified Theory of Action and Speech. The idea is relatively simple: externalism in semantics is the thesis that the meaning of a sentence cannot be uniquely determined by checking up the brain states of the speaker. What one means by reference to, e.g., proper names like Socrates or natural kinds like H_2O, partly depends on the causal histories of the situations in which the references were learned and used, which are 'external' to the speaker's brain or mind; in order to know the meanings (referents in these cases) fully, we must consult historical documents on the man called Socrates, the definition of the substance called H_2O in the relevant scientific community, etc.[25] Davidson connects externalism to the question of the scientific status of the Unified Theory as follows: '[s]ince perceptual externalism of

---

[25] Since this characterization is enough for our purposes, I won't go into a detailed discussion as to whether externalism is a general characteristic of semantics, rather than just of reference. See Ross (2005: 47-8) for a discussion and a positive answer.

this sort introduces an irreducibly causal element into the interpretation of the theory, the theory cannot hope to emulate physics, which has striven successfully to extrude all causal concepts from its laws' ([1995] 2004: 130). This inference, however, cannot be justified.

Let us suppose for the sake of argument that, as Davidson says, physics has succeeded in extruding all causal concepts from its laws, whatever that means. Does this mean that physics as a whole discipline has become free from all causal concepts? The answer is *no*: even if the laws of physics themselves are causal-concept-free, physics as a whole is not. First, physicists must agree upon the meanings of concepts or constructs involved in these laws, such as mass, energy, electric field, etc. Since they must interpret what other physicists mean by these concepts, physics as a *scientific practice* cannot be free from externalism, and thus from causal concepts. Second, physics as a *scientific theory* cannot be free from causal concepts either. Since the laws of physics are meant to be about the world no matter how abstract they may be, the meanings of the constructs involved should be given in empirical contexts. Measurement is one of those important contexts in which these constructs are operationalized and thus given meanings through particular methods.[26] Now, there are two classes of constructs: 'those to which no physical operations correspond other than those which enter the definition of the construct, and those which admit of other operations, or which could be defined in several alternative ways in terms of physically distinct operations' (Bridgman 1927 quoted in Chang 2004: 151). An example of the former is the concept of electric field, whose meaning is exhausted by the definition of force and electric charge. Such constructs are not causal precisely because they have no physical reality: a definition is valid as a matter of tautology, not of reality. However, physics is full of other constructs which belong to the latter category, i.e., those which have broader meanings than their single operational definitions (temperature is one obvious example). In these cases, physicists perceive the multiplicity of operational meaning as 'the reality of things not given directly by experience' (*ibid.*), and thus they perform experiments to identify *the* meaning of a construct by empirically comparing different operational definitions. These experiments involve at least one empirical interpretation of the constructs, and therefore cannot dispense with considerations of causal dispositions of (some empirically interpreted aspects of) the constructs. Therefore physics as scientific theory cannot be free from considerations about causality.

---

[26] Although possessing a measurement operation is not a necessary condition for a construct to have a meaning (as Chang notes), this point does not affect my following argument, since a more general notion of 'meaning as use' cannot be free from causality, either.

So what Davidson means by 'causal concepts' must be *causal histories* that should be referred to in order to explain certain phenomena. That is, he means that the laws of physics describe universal regularities between its fundamental constructs, whereas the Unified Theory necessarily resort to some irreducible contingent causal histories about referents (how a speaker acquired particular words by the education provided by the community of the speakers of that language, for instance), whose meanings cannot be exhausted within the theory. In other words, the Unified Theory is not complete in the sense that it needs other theories that explain its explanans.[27] As Davidson recognizes, however, this feature 'in itself makes psychological theory no less scientific than volcanology, biology, meteorology, or the theory of evolution' (Davidson [1995] 2004: 131). But his presumption that these sciences (including behavioural science) are less scientific than physics is not uncontroversial. Davidson thinks that the causal-history-free laws of physics describe universal regularities between physical constructs. If one emphasizes 'universal', like Davidson does, then it seems that there is no competition against the laws of physics. But if one emphasizes 'regularities', like an empiricist does, then it becomes less obvious why dependence on causal histories should decrease the degree of scientific respectability of particular disciplines. For example:

> [T]he remarkable regularities in the geographical distribution of placental and marsupial mammals were explained only when continental drift was understood. That marsupials are found in Australia and South America but not Europe is a consequence of the historical fact that, relatively recently, Australia and South America were parts of a single continent (Sugden 2001:124).

Sugden (2001:125) also mentions a linguistic explanation of why Finnish is much more similar to Hungarian than it is to Swedish. In these cases, 'historical contingencies are not being used to explain one-off events, in the way that historians explain one event in terms of another: they are essential components of explanations of very general empirical regularities' (*ibid.*). By contrast, physics is silent about why such-and-such regularities hold between such-and-such constructs. In this sense, theories which refer to causal histories can sometimes explain *more* than those without causal histories do. Therefore, Davidson's presupposition—the more causal histories, the less scientific—is not guaranteed.

---

[27] Pettit's ([1991] 2002) claim is similar to this, but Davidson is even more radical in claiming that decision theory is incomplete *even if it is combined with a theory of meaning.*

2.5 The Argument from Normativity

Now let us turn to Davidson's ([1995] 2004) central argument against the science of human behaviour. The argument, which I call the *argument from normativity*, is this:

(1) In order to measure people's beliefs and desires experimentally, we must use a formal theory, such as Ramsey-type decision theory.

(2) But the use of a formal theory commits us to interpreting experimental evidence in such a way that the patterns of behaviour, belief and desire are to a large extent rational and consistent with the norms presupposed in the theory.

(3) There is no empirical way to check whether such norms are objectively correct.

(4) Therefore, belief-desire psychology, however exactly it is formulated, cannot provide a bona fide empirical explanation of human behaviour.

I shall argue that Conclusion 4 does not follow because Premise 3 is false. I will substantiate my argument by using the same example (preference reversals) from the history of experimental economics. Although one might suspect that Davidson is a straw man, his position is in fact sophisticated enough to be seriously discussed in the methodology of experimental psychology and economics. In order to convince the reader of this point, I shall comment on each premise in turn.

Premise 1 is unproblematic; the formalization of decision theory constitutes theoretical progress, which is necessary to improve the accuracy of the measurement of beliefs and desires, as I have argued in 2.2. A key claim is Premise 2.

2.5.1 The Principle of Charity as a Heuristic

Premise 2 concerns the so-called *principle of charity* that we must use in interpreting a speaker's meanings in a 'radical' situation where we have no background knowledge regarding the speaker's language (except that it is a language). In other words, our interpretation must be based solely on the speaker's 'verbal behaviour'. Quine (1960: ch. 2) claimed that radical interpretation is possible only on the presumption that the speaker shares most of our linguistic meanings, such as those of logical connectives ('and','or', 'if', etc.), i.e., that he is to a large extent rational in the same way as we are. Davidson is arguing that the situation is analogous in a behavioural experiment, where we must use decision theory in order to measure an individual's beliefs and desires based on the evidence regarding her choice behaviour:

> [T]he formal theory (as opposed to features of its empirical application) says nothing at all about inconsistencies. It not only postulates perfect logic and a consistent and rational pattern of beliefs and desires, but it assumes rationality in the treatment of what we take to be evidence. Inconsistencies and failures of reasoning power must be accommodated by injecting large doses of what has been called charity in the fitting of the theory to actual agents. [...] The formal theory leaves no room for irrationality, and therefore is powerless to explain it (Davidson [1995] 2004: 133).

Notice first that Davidson is not suggesting that we are never able to find inconsistencies.[28] Just like the interpreter can sometimes reasonably conclude that a speaker is mistaken in his speech,[29] the experimenter can sometimes reasonably attribute inconsistencies to his subjects. What Davidson is suggesting is rather that the formal theory is committed to explaining such inconsistencies within the framework of the theory, and that such explanations will be dictated by the norms implicit in the theory. Note, secondly, that this claim is surprisingly consistent with what has actually happened in the experimental studies of EUT. Experimental economists, facing the anomalous phenomenon of preference reversals (PR; see section 2.3.1), tried to modify EUT in such a way that the fundamental norm of formal rational choice theory is retained. Economists have proposed many ways to modify EUT in order to accommodate PR and other anomalies; most of the alternative theories proposed by economists modify or weaken one (or more) of the axioms of EUT, but in such a way that the formal achievements of EUT (the representation theorem and the uniqueness theorem) could be maintained. In other words, economists insist that the subjects' choice behaviour be seen as a maximization of some sort of utility functions, if not of the vNM utility function. Two major attempts along this line illustrate my point:[30]

(1) Modified EUT: Some economists questioned the elicitation procedure of minimal selling prices. One way of measuring the minimal selling price of a bet is just to ask the subject, 'If you were selling the bet, how much would your minimum price be?' Economists, however, prefer another method called the BDM method, named after its

---

[28] If he were, he would be arguing for circularity.

[29] Grandy (1973) notices this point, and accordingly modifies the principle of charity as the *principle of humanity*. See also Stich (1990: ch. 2).

[30] Arguably, prospect theory by Kahneman and Tversky (1979) is the most ambitious and successful attempt to modify EUT, but for two reasons I shall not discuss it in this context; first, its features are rather heterogeneous, mixing the conventional and nonconventional approaches (see below). Second, and more importantly, it has not been proposed as an explanation of PR, my main example. Kahneman and Tversky propose another theory to account for PR, as we will see below.

inventors Becker, DeGroot, and Marschack (1964).[31] This elicitation scheme begins by asking a subject the minimal selling price of a bet; then an offer (of buying) is generated by a random process: if the offer is higher than her selling price, the subject gets the price; if it is lower, then she has to play the bet. This is called an 'incentive compatible' scheme because an incentive to tell a price that reflects one's true preference is built in by forcing the subject to act upon the stated price when the chance to do so arrives. It has been pointed out that this procedure presupposes the independence axiom of EUT, and that if it is dropped then the stated price of a bet is no longer equal to its cash equivalent (Holt 1986; Karni and Safra 1987).[32] A few years earlier, Mark Machina (1982) had proposed a generalized expected utility model which weakens the independence axiom. However, Tversky, Slovic, and Kahneman (1990) demonstrated that the frequency of PR was not lower in the experiments without an incentive-compatible scheme like BDM (see e.g. Lichtenstein and Slovic 1971) than in those with the BDM. Thus they concluded that PR cannot be explained by the violation of the independence axiom. In order to make this point more strongly, Tversky et al. designed explicitly an incentive-compatible elicitation method without the elicitation of actual selling prices at all: the idea is that, in order to demonstrate PR, it is sufficient to know the subjects' ordering of the bets, without knowing how they actually price the bets. In this way one can explicitly avoid using methods that presuppose the independence axiom. With this design, they observed again systematic reversals, which establishes that PR cannot be explained as the violation of the independence axiom.[33]

(2) Regret Theory: A second attempt to account for PR while maintaining the formal structure of the theory is so-called *regret theory* proposed by Loomes and Sugden (1982). Essentially, regret theory redefines the outcomes that are the objects of choice. Giving up the consequentialist framework, according to which only the actual outcomes should matter to people, Loomes and Sugden proposed to explicitly incorporate into the theory the psychological intuition that people may evaluate consequences in comparison with a counterfactual scenario. For example, consider a simple case of choice between two bets B1 and B2 (see Table 2.2).

---

[31] See Guala (2000a) for a detailed discussion of the BDM mechanism and its relation to preference reversals.

[32] Segal (1988) pointed out the possibility of the violation of the reduction axiom, according to which it is possible to reduce a two-stage lottery to the equivalent one-stage lottery. Ironically, however, if subjects violate both the independence axiom and the reduction axiom, then the BDM procedure ensures that the result properly reveals the subjects' preferences (see Camerer 1995: 657, 659). Since the antecedent seems to hold, PR cannot be explained by the use of BDM.

[33] Since the irrelevance of the BDM procedure had been known as early as 1971, Camerer (1995:659) notes that this line of explanation 'may have received too much attention from talented researchers with better things to do'.

Table 2.2: Bets on the roulette

action\state	Roulette with 36 slots		
	State 1: 1-3 (p=3/36)	State 2: 4-30 (p=27/36)	State 3: 31-36 (p=6/36)
Bet 1	£100	£0	£0
Bet 2	£10	£10	£0

If a subject chooses B1, and S2 obtains, she would experience a psychological displeasure ('regret'), because she knows that she would have got £10 had she chosen B2. Similarly, if the subject chooses B2 and S2 obtains, she would experience a psychological pleasure ('rejoicing'), because she knows that she would have got nothing had she chosen B1. By the same token, the psychological experiences will be rejoicing and regret for B1 and B2 respectively, if S1 obtains. (It is assumed that there is neither regret nor rejoicing if S3 obtains, because under this state choosing B1 or B2 gives the same outcome, £0.) So what matters for the subject is not just the consequence she ends up with, but both the consequence *and* the counterfactual ('what could have been had I chosen differently'). Formally, the individual chooses between actions so as to maximize the following *expected modified utility function* of action A_i, evaluated with respect to action A_k at the *j*-th state of the world (among *n* states):

$$E^k_i = \sum [j{=}1{\rightarrow}n]\, p_j \{c_{ij} + R\,(c_{ij} - c_{kj})\}$$

where c (the abbreviation of C(.)) is a *choiceless utility function* which assigns a real-valued index to every conceivable consequence, whether or not it is the result of one's choice, and R(.) is a *regret-rejoice function* which assigns a real-valued index to every possible increment or decrement of choiceless utility. Loomes and Sugden (1983) argued that Grether and Plott's (1979) observations of PR could be predicted by regret theory if C(.) was assumed to be linear, in addition to some other restrictions on E^k_i. Tversky et al. (1990) in contrast argue that regret is not the main cause of PR. Camerer (1995: 660), based on somewhat varying evidence indicating the relative importance of intransitivity (10% according to Tversky et al. (1990) and Cox and Grether (1996); 20-25% according to Loomes et al. (1991) and Loomes and Taylor (1992)), concludes that the violation of transitivity partly explains PR.

Notice that although regret theory explains PR as a failure of transitivity, it still maintains that people's choices are rational in the sense of the modified expected utility maximization. That is, since the value of choosing an action depends on the nature and combination of the actions simultaneously rejected (because of the regrets and rejoices associated with the comparison), giving up the transitivity axiom of EUT renders people's choice behaviour neither normatively questionable nor difficult to make sense of (Loomes and Sugden 1982). Such normative defence of regret theory seems to confirm Davidson's claim that any formal theory of rational choice 'assumes rationality in the treatment of what we take to be evidence'. Guala (2000b), in line with this interpretation, points out that the weaker (stronger) *normative* plausibility of an axiom of EUT encouraged (discouraged) economists to abandon that axiom in modifying EUT in the face of anomalous *empirical* evidence.[34]

Based on Premise 2, which by now should appear rather plausible, Davidson goes on to argue that, since there is no empirical way to check whether such a normative way of dodging counter-evidence leads us objectively to a better theory (Premise 3), a formal theory cannot give a genuine, naturalistic explanation of human behaviour (4). Having motivated my discussion of Davidson's argument, I shall now turn to the critical mode and try to give reasons to reject Premise 3 and accordingly the conclusion of the argument from normativity.

2.5.2 The Principle of Invariance and Measurement

Davidson does not precisely characterize the concept of normativity, but I propose, based on my reconstruction of his argument, that it boils down to the fact that certain notions (e.g., that people are rational in the sense of some formal theory) are *presupposed* in the testing of these very notions. This does not, however, imply that such notions are empirically untestable, as I have argued in 2.3. As Davidson admits, inconsistencies can be (and in fact have been) observed in testing EUT in empirical contexts, that is, EUT was F-B disconfirmed, despite the fact that some normative concepts were presupposed in the theory. And *empirical* evidence such as PR convinced economists to abandon some *normative* concepts (expressed as axioms). So while this does not guarantee that a modified theory is closer to the true theory, it does suggest that

---

[34] The independence axiom is normatively weaker than the transitivity axiom, hence the historical order of their abandonment. While Guala (2000b) rationally reconstructs the history of decision theory as a history of 'normative falsification', Starmer (2000) criticizes economists' tendency to be influenced by normative considerations, and argues that any empirically plausible theory should explicitly model the psychological processes that result in choice (nonconventional, or 'procedural' approaches, as opposed to conventional, or 'as if' approaches). Although Starmer categorizes regret theory as a nonconventional approach since it is based on some intuition about actual human psychology, Wilkinson (2008) for example categorizes it as a conventional approach since it retains a commitment to representing people's behaviour as utility maximization. Based on these considerations, it may be possible to characterize regret theory as a transitory approach between the two.

at least the modified theory is empirically more satisfactory than the original EUT. Since we have no general account of what guarantees the truth of a scientific theory (including what exactly it means for a theory to be true), the fact that normative considerations worked as a heuristic for modifying EUT is insufficient to refute its objectivity. Unfortunately, however, economists have continuously failed to find a (rational) theory to accommodate anomalies such as PR. Although this fact seems to confirm the conclusion (an inability of formal rational choice theory to explain human behaviour), this is *not* because of the analytic truth of Premise 3; it is simply because of the contingent fact that no formal theory of rational choice has accounted for all the evidence so far.[35]

More importantly, a plausible *non-rational* explanation of PR is available. Remember that PR is observed in inferring people's preferences over pairwise choices using a two-task method, e.g., asking the subjects to choose between H bets and L bets, and eliciting their minimal selling price for each. This method should yield the same preference orderings *if* preferences over prospects are independent of the method used to elicit them. It has long been pointed out that this principle, known as *procedure invariance*, does not hold empirically. In contrast to most economists who try to accommodate the data of PR by the normative adjustment of EUT, experimental psychologists have been claiming that PR can be explained by the violation of procedure invariance, more specifically, overpricing of L bets over H bets, relative to the choice task (Tversky et al. 1990). Their explanation is called the 'compatibility hypothesis', stating that different elicitation tasks evoke different responses from people *either* because some information stimuli are more compatible with certain response modes than with others due to the associated computational costs (e.g. the dollar-dimension is more compatible with pricing (in dollar) tasks than choice tasks), *or* because some tasks evoke certain decision strategies rather than others (e.g. choice tasks evoke qualitative decision strategies such as elimination by aspects, lexicographic orderings, while pricing tasks evoke quantitative strategies such as anchoring and adjustment), or because of both reasons (see chapter 3 for more detail).

It is crucial to notice that *procedure invariance is not a normative principle peculiar to the measurement of beliefs and desires, but a general empirical presumption found in any empirical measurement.* Consider as an example the assumption that a pan

---

[35] And of course, this situation (persistence of anomalies) is quite common in science, including physics. For example, under some conditions water can boil only at a certain temperature beyond 100 degrees Celsius even under standard atmospheric pressure, and we don't know exactly why. This is an anomaly known as 'superheating'. See Chang (2004: 241, fn. 3) for contemporary explanations.

balance and a spring would yield the same ordering of two objects' weights in measuring mass (cf. Tversky and Thaler 1990: 203). Although this is generally assumed in measuring mass, the assumption is not part of any formal theory but rather is established by its empirical reliability: suppose that the spring is so rigid that two objects yield the same result (some length of the spring) while the pan balance shows that the two objects are not equally balanced. Then even in the physical experiment procedure invariance is not guaranteed. For a more realistic example think of a case of cardinal rather than ordinal measurement, e.g., temperature: the expansion rates of mercury and alcohol cannot be assumed to be identical prior to empirical investigations. The fact that we nowadays use the two types of thermometer interchangeably is due to the tested reliability of both tools in a certain range of temperature values (Chang 2004: ch. 2). Therefore, psychologists' explanation of PR as the violation of procedure invariance is not analogous to economists' modification or abandonment of the axioms of EUT: psychologists' explanatory strategy is not dictated by normative considerations such as the principle of charity. Rather, it is a triangulation strategy led by the reliability of diverse measurement methods.[36] A quote from a methodological textbook of experimental psychology clearly states this point:

> [S]ingle measures of complex states such as motivation, neurosis, or learning will be so limited as to produce conclusions of doubtful generality. Another way of saying this is that a single measure of a complex state provides a poor sample. To the extent that it is possible, multiple measures should always be used and compared. Sometimes the inconsistencies of different measures create problems that eventually lead to new insights (Plutchik 1968: 84).

I would add 'preference' in the list of 'complex states'.[37] A classic textbook on measurement makes the same point:

> In contrast to fundamental physical measurement, which is typically one-dimensional [...], many of the theories of measurement that appear applicable to behavioral problems are inherently multidimensional, and so the measurement theories deal simultaneously with several measures and the laws connecting them. These theories suggest new qualitative laws to be tested, and even when they are found to be wrong, much may be learned if the violations are systematic. Moreover, these theories lead

---

[36] Hacking (1983: chs. 13,14 and 16) is the classic work on the reliability of measurement in physics. Trout (1998) develops 'measured realism' in the behavioural sciences. Borsboom (2005) provides a comprehensive philosophical analysis of psychometrics, while Michell (1999) gives it a historical perspective.

[37] In fact, Plutchik (1968: 45) cites Slovic's (1964) early study as a good illustration of his point.

to selection among the many factors that might be relevant by focusing attention on those variables that enter into simple qualitative laws (Krantz et al. [1971] 2007, volume I: 32).

The authors' presumption that mental states are complex and multidimensional is based on their experience that the reliable measurement of these properties is empirically very difficult to establish; it is not based on *a priori* considerations. So even if decision theory does not seem to give a complete explanation of human behaviour, this is because of the empirical features of human psychology, not because of the truth of an *a priori* claim such as Premise 3. How successful a science can be depends on contingent facts such as historical coincidences, researchers' ingenuity, resources spent on research, and ultimately, empirical features of the objects of study.

One might object that Davidson allows for the possibility that the empirical application of a formal theory tells us something about inconsistencies in human behaviour by noting (though within brackets) that a formal theory tells us nothing about inconsistencies 'as opposed to features of its empirical application'. But in Davidson's argument, this crucial point is glossed over by his emphasis that the interpretation of evidence by means of a formal theory is dictated by the principle of charity. As I have argued, however, normative considerations such as the principle of charity constitute one type of heuristics in theory development, and empirical considerations seem to offer some support for the compatibility hypothesis, which was not developed on the basis of normative heuristics. One might also defend Davidson by pointing out that in the step from Premise 3 to the conclusion there is an implicit but defensible premise (alluded to in Premise 1) that any genuine explanatory theory must be formalized as an axiomatic system. If this is true, then Davidson is arguing that behavioural science fails because it cannot give a formal theory that explains inconsistencies in behaviour. However, I do not think that formality is a necessary condition for an explanation to be genuine. Of course, as suggested in Premise 1, a formal theory is instrumental in attempting the precise measurement of unobservable properties. But if the reliable measurement of target properties (such as utilities or subjective probabilities) is not achieved empirically, then the experimentalist is justified to modify or abandon the theory, and to propose an explanation, formal or not, of why this failure in measurement obtains.[38] Thus this objection from formality does not save Davidson's argument from being unsound. The upshot is that the argument from normativity fails, because it is possible

---

[38] In fact, Gold and List (2004) offer a formal theory (based on first-order predicate logic) to explain the violation of procedure invariance (as well as description invariance). See chapter 3.

to explain why EUT fails without relying on normative heuristics of rationality. In order to evaluate how successful such a theory is, we need to engage in scientific (i.e., theoretical and empirical) analysis, rather than trying to find out *a priori* reasons to reject the whole enterprise.

2.6 Conclusion

In this chapter, I have taken seriously the sceptic's challenge against the progress of behavioural science and have argued against three prominent arguments, the arguments from holism, incompleteness, and normativity. The results are important for the general discussion on the nature of empirical testing, in particular the test of decision theory. I have started from accepting the holistic folk-psychological framework as a foundation of decision theory (section 2.2). But I have argued that this holistic framework can be tested in a non-viciously circular way, and that such a test can thus confirm or disconfirm the theory (section 2.3). Further, I have argued that the normative character of decision theory does not prevent experimentalists from developing an explanatory theory while being guided by *empirical* rather than *normative* heuristics (section 2.5). More specifically, my central claim has been that what guides experimental psychologists is their trust in the reliability of measurement. Contrast their careful attitude with Davidson's untested commitment to the effect that intentional attitudes such as beliefs, desires, aversions, etc. 'don't have objects in any psychological or epistemic sense. The attitudes are simply states, and no more require objects before the mind than sticks require numbers in order to have a certain length' ([1995] 2004: 129). Although we talk about and refer to beliefs and desires all the time, perhaps more often than we talk about sticks and stones, this fact alone does not guarantee their existence. Carefully defined and measured observations of people's behaviour, on the contrary, suggest that beliefs and desires cannot be attributed to decision makers in the precise way presupposed by decision theory. This fact allows one to be critical towards the theory for its limited empirical success, but *not* for its lack of *scientific status*. Decision theory can be empirical, and it can be evaluated and improved accordingly.

I will conclude this chapter with a remark in relation to Popper's principle of rationality and his defence of it as a sound methodological policy, mentioned in the introduction (2.1): Popper says: '[w]e do not learn much in learning that [the rationality principle] is not strictly true: we know this already' ([1967] 1995: 178). But what

Popper (and others) did not know at that time is how *exactly* it is not true. We do know this now, and we have learned a lot in learning this.

Chapter 3

Unification and Causal Analysis: Inconsistency Anomalies

3.1 Introduction

In the previous chapter, we have seen that Expected Utility Theory (EUT) is testable and has been tested. Instead of demonstrating its truth, however, the rigorous tests of EUT have created persistent anomalies such as preference reversals (PR). Researchers are still busy proposing different explanations of these anomalies,[1] but there is little agreement about how to appraise these explanations. This chapter will examine a debate on possible explanations of PR, and argue that this debate cannot be resolved by appealing to a methodological criterion of theory appraisal, *viz.*, unificationism. Specifically, I will critically examine Don Ross (2005), who, advocating unificationism, argues that psychologists' and behavioural economists' explanation of PR (e.g., Tversky and Thaler 1990) is *ad hoc*. I will argue that this is not the case, based on an analysis of the psychological hypothesis which Ross criticizes. Through this exercise, it will become clear that the real issue in the debate is not so much methodological as empirical. I will re-frame the debate as a competition between two models of cognitive processes of decision making, i.e., the multiple-self model and the procedural model, and speculate on how this debate may be resolved.

The chapter proceeds as follows: first, the unificationist account advanced by Ross (2005) in decision research is analyzed using a Lakatosian framework (section 3.2). In particular, I will introduce models of intertemporal choice and show that the appeal to the development of these models makes Ross (2005) a Lakatosian unificationist. Section 3.3 evaluates Ross's 'Ptolemaic' critique of behavioural economics. Section 3.4 substantiates the argument of section 3.3 by explicating and defending the compatibility hypothesis proposed by some behavioural economists. It is then argued in section 3.5 that behavioural economics has progressed without being crippled by a 'Ptolemaic' paradigm, and that a new theoretical unification is attempted based on this progress. Section 3.6 discusses the relevance of neurological evidence to the debate. Section 3.7 concludes the chapter.

---

[1] Some economists however think that PR is not important because there are certain experimental conditions under which it disappears. Chu and Chu (1990) is often cited by the sceptics.

3.2 The Unificationist Approach to Anomalies

Lakatos (1970) provides an explication of the concept of *progress*: a scientific hypothesis is progressive if it not only successfully predicts novel facts, but does so while maintaining certain 'core' theoretical features. Lakatos calls such continuous explanatory enterprise a *research programme* (more on this below). Kitcher (1981) explicates a similar intuition as *unification*. Roughly put, Kitcher's unificationism is the thesis that scientific explanation should provide a unified account of many different phenomena, where the degree of unification increases as a theory allows us to derive descriptions of more phenomena from less patterns of argument. For example, if theory A allows us to derive the description of people's choices of mates, as well as choices of real estates, then A is more unificatory than theory B that allows us to derive only the description of the former type of choices, or theory C that allows us to derive only the description of the latter type of choices. Both Lakatos and Kitcher capture the intuition that a hypothesis should not be *ad hoc*, but while Kitcher emphasizes the synchronic aspect of hypothesis evaluation, Lakatos looks at its diachronic aspect. Since it is more relevant in the present case, I will mainly draw on Lakatos's diachronic formulation, and use the word unification to refer to his position.

Preference theory states that a decision maker's preference orderings should not change over the identical set of options. Although we could say in general that the decision maker reversed her preferences when she violated this presupposition, the term *preference reversal* (PR) is used to refer to a special class of reversals, i.e., a preference reversal is a phenomenon where the decision maker's preference over a pair of two option is reversed, depending on how we elicit her preference. For example, if Anne says she would price one banana £1 and one apple £2, and yet chooses a banana when an apple is available, we say that her choice behaviour manifests a preference reversal: the decision maker reversed her preference, depending on which elicitation methods (pricing and choice) were used. In the research on individual decision making, PR has established its status as an 'anomaly' in relation to EUT in the past forty years. An 'anomaly' in a research programme is, according to Lakatos, 'a phenomenon which we regard as something to be explained in terms of the programme' (1970: 159, fn.1). In other words, being an anomaly is a relational status *vis-à-vis* particular research programmes. The status of an anomaly therefore may change as these programmes advance: generally, in relation to programme P_1, an anomaly turns into an 'example' when explained within the theoretical framework of P_1; it 'disappears' when independently explained by another programme, P*; or it becomes a 'counterexample' when explained by P_1's rival programme, P_2 (*ibid.*). To say that PR is an anomaly thus means that at least one research programme is involved in this process. In the present case, there are two programmes involved; one is the psychological 'heuristics and biases' approach advanced by Kahneman, Tversky and Slovic, among others. The other is the economic approach characterized by its insistence that human decision making be modelled as utility maximization.[2] PR is an anomaly in relation to the economic programme (P_1), while a rival programme, the psychological programme (P_2) purports to explain it. And yet there is no universal agreement among researchers that the psychological programme satisfactorily explains PR, thereby leaving PR (in some sense) an anomaly to both programmes. Rather than evaluating the competing hypotheses based on the available evidence, the focus of this chapter is to assess whether methodological considerations regarding unification alone can say something in favour of the economic programme. I shall argue that it cannot, contrary to what Don Ross (2005)—one of the main advocates of the unificationist approach in economics and cognitive science—argues. First, I will describe the contrast Ross makes between 'Ptolemaic' (*ad hoc*) and 'non-Ptolemaic' (unificatory) science, and then clarify how the debate concerning PR can be interpreted according to this contrast, by illustrating the Ross's favourite case, intertemporal decision making.

3.2.1 *'Ptolemaic' Science and Ad Hocness*

Ross (2005) uses the adjective 'Ptolemaic' to refer to a research programme which relies on an 'ad hoc' explanation in order to accommodate anomalies. But what exactly does 'ad hoc' mean? I shall rely on the only worked out theory of *ad hocness* proposed by Lakatos (1970: 175, fns. 2, 3), who distinguished three senses of *ad hocness*: an explanation is *ad hoc$_1$* if it does not predict any novel facts (no excess content); it is *ad hoc$_2$* if it predicts novel facts but fails; it is *ad hoc$_3$* if it predicts novel facts and is corroborated by evidence, but its progress is led not by a general outline of the programme regarding how to accommodate anomalies (*the positive heuristic*). It seems that Ross has in mind *ad hoc$_3$* when he says some programme is 'Ptolemaic': a 'Ptolemaic' programme 'must sooner or later reach a point of diminishing returns, where the effort required to further improve careful models can no longer be justified by

---

[2] The distinction between the 'psychological' and 'economic' is not sharp. In fact, Tversky and Kahneman's Prospect Theory is a model of utility maximization, and so in this specific sense it is 'economic'. See section 3.5 for a more nuanced distinction.

gains in representational parsimony' (Ross 2005:176).[3] Again, to use a Lakatosian term, 'Ptolemaic' programmes are *degenerating* rather than *progressive*. However, being a practicing scientist, Ross does not outright reject 'Ptolemaic' science in the way Lakatos (*qua* historian/philosopher of science) rejects degenerating programmes; Ross concedes that 'Ptolemaic' phases are unavoidable and can sometimes be productive, by systematically summarizing data and preparing for adequate theorization (ibid.).[4] This is unsurprising because *ad hoc₃* explanations are at least empirically corroborated. However, Ross, just like Lakatos, further requires that a promising programme ought to have some principled way of unifying existing data. In Ross's (2005: 175) own words, 'non-Ptolemaic' science ought to be motivated by 'wider theoretical considerations' independent of the data it seeks to parsimoniously summarize.

In explaining PR, however, what constitutes such a unifying principle is not quite clear. Ross might have in mind, as a 'non-Ptolemaic' strategy, what Lakatos calls a 'creative shift' (Lakatos 1970: 137) in the positive heuristic of a research programme. In Ross's construal, the *negative* heuristic of the economic programme—which defines the irrefutable 'hard core'—requires that an agent's behaviour be modelled as a *maximization of utility* defined as indices of consistent and stable preference orderings (preference theory);[5] in addition, the *positive* heuristic tells researchers how to accommodate evidence within the framework of the programme. In the economic programme, the content of preferences is totally unspecified, thereby enabling the programme to be applicable to a large set of behavioural patterns. However, PR is regarded as a serious anomaly to the economic programme because the phenomenon apparently challenges one of its hard core assumptions, i.e., the requirement that preferences be consistent in the sense that they conform to the axioms of EUT or its variants. Now, Ross's creative shift is to hypothesize that not only the *content* of preferences but also the *agents*, who act upon preferences, are unspecified. More specifically, he proposes an auxiliary hypothesis that the economic agents characterized with their utility maximizing behaviour are *not* individual human beings but *parts* of individuals. In other words, individuals can consist of more than one economic agent. With this shift, an individual's behaviour exhibiting PR can be interpreted as resulting

---

[3] If non-parsimonious theories are inferior to parsimonious ones in predictive power, then Ross's 'Ptolemaic' programme is *ad hoc₂* as well as *ad hoc₃*.

[4] Ross alludes to Kuhn's (1962) notion of 'normal science' in this context (Ross 2005: 404, fn. 5). Lakatos's reconstruction of the history of physics, however, suggests continuous competitions among rival programmes, rather than a normal science followed by a 'revolution'.

[5] Ross identifies this hardcore with Revealed Preference Theory (RPT) advocated by Paul Samuelson. While many economists would agree with this, the interpretation of RPT itself is contested.

from the combination of more than one preference ordering per agent. In this way, the hard core of the preference-based programme may be saved from the refutation and the anomaly turned into an example manifesting the fruitfulness of the programme.

In what follows, I will explain several models of *intertemporal* choice, including one that motivates Ross (2005) to advocate the multiple-self model in the domain of *intratemporal* choice, such as the case of PR.

3.2.2 The Standard Model of Discounted Utility and its Rivals

The idea that an individual consists of more than one 'self', each following competing principles, has been discussed by the modern Western intellectuals (e.g., Kant, Freud, Goethe, Stevenson, etc.) but the idea goes back at least to Plato. Plato, in *Republic* (436b-), proposes that the soul consists of rational, spirited, and appetitive parts. This triparted soul theory is partly motivated to resolve the tension between his presupposition that the soul is the unitary source of motivation and his introspection that people often experience conflicting motivations. A contemporary version of this idea has been developed by the American psychiatrist George Ainslie since the 1970s in the context of intertemporal choice. In the following, I will first introduce its rival, the received model, whose empirical inadequacy led Ainslie's and others' to propose alternative models of intertemporal choice.

The standard model, called the *discounted utility model* (DUM), was originally formulated by Paul Samuelson in 1937.[6] DUM represents people's choices between consumption bundles across different times by flattening all the psychological factors involved into the single parameter of a *discount rate*.[7] Mathematically, DUM represents the utility at the time t of the consumption profile $(c_t, c_{t+1}, c_{t+2}, \ldots, c_T)$ starting in period t and continuing until period T as an *intertemporal utility function* defined as follows:

$$U^t(c_t, \ldots, c_T) = \sum[k{=}0 \to T{-}t]D(k)\, u(c_{t+k})$$
$$\text{where } D(k) = (1/1 + \rho)^k$$

The function $u(c_{t+k})$ can be interpreted as an individual's *instantaneous utility function*, representing her perceived well being in period $t + k$. The other function appearing on

---

[6] The summary in this section is based on Wilkinson (2008: chs. 5, 6). Wilkinson emphasizes that Samuelson believed neither in the empirical nor in the normative validity of this model.
[7] This is comparable to PRT's flattening of all the psychological factors involved in choice into one-dimensional concept of *preference*.

the right hand side of the equation, $D(k)$, is her *discount function*, representing the relative weight she attaches in time period t to her well-being in period $t + k$. The parameter in this function, ρ, refers to her *discount rate*, representing the rate at which the individual discounts future utilities. For example, Anne's utility from receiving her annual salary of £32,000 for three continuous years may be calculated as follows, if the utility from each year's income is always x and if the discount rate is 10%:

$$U^t \,(£32{,}000,\, £32{,}000,\, £32{,}000) = x/(1{+}0.1) + x\,/(1{+}0.1)^2 + x\,/(1{+}0.1)^3 \doteqdot 2.45x$$

In the present context, it is essential to notice three features of DUM. First, DUM assumes that people use the same discount rate, ρ, over their lifespan (*stationary discounting*). This means, for example, that Anne discounts her £32,000 by 10% at any year t, regardless of whether she is a teenager, middle-aged, or retired. Second, DUM assumes that at any period of time the same discounting by the exponential k is applied to all future periods (*constant discounting*). Third, these two assumptions of stationary and constant discounting ensure that people's preferences do not change over time (*time-consistent preferences*).

Not only is DUM introspectively unrealistic and counter-intuitive, but also it has been shown to be inadequate as a model of actual people's choice behaviour both in the field and in laboratory experiments. For example, ρ is known to decrease as people enter middle age, but increase again as they get older (Read and Read 2004; Harrison, Lau and Williams 2002). The unavoidable implication of this and other observations is that people's preferences are not consistent over time. This, however, does not mean that modelling intertemporal choice is impossible; it is still possible to represent time-inconsistent choices by using some other discount function. In fact, various such models have been proposed. The most famous one is called the *hyperbolic* discount function, whose development Ainslie (e.g., 1991) contributed to. Let u_t be the instantaneous utility an agent gets at time t. In a discrete-time form, a hyperbolic, or 'quasi-hyperbolic' discount function is then represented as follows:[8]

---

[8] I gloss over the mathematical details and use the terms 'hyperbolic' and 'quasi-hyperbolic' interchangeably. Originally, this function was developed by Phelps and Pollak (1968) for modelling intergenerational altruism. Strotz (1955) is one of the first economists to discuss time-inconsistency. Rabin (2002: 669) notes that recently researchers use the discrete-time form instead of the continuous-time form '[i]n part because the continuous-time hyperbolic discounting function is difficult to deal with, and in part because the specific functional form of hyperbolic discounting is neither literally correct nor very important'. See also Laibson (1994).

$$U^t(u_t, u_{t+1}, \ldots, u_T) = (\delta)^t u_t + \beta \sum[\tau = t+1 \rightarrow T](\delta)^\tau u_\tau$$

where δ and β are parameters less than 1, with δ very close to 1. If $\beta = 1$, the hyperbolic utility function reduces to the exponential function. Figure 3.1 contrasts these two types of discounting.

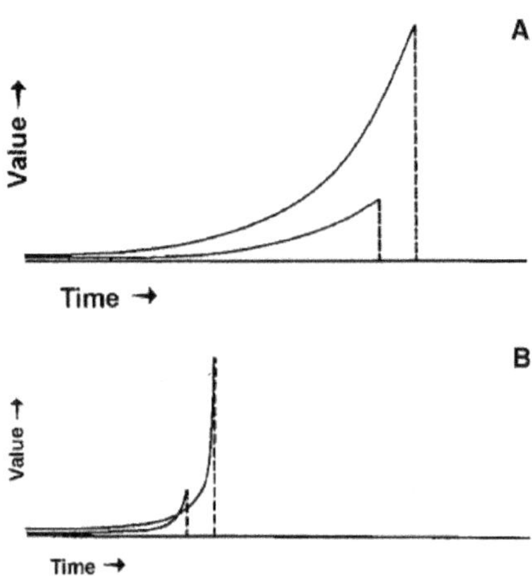

Figure 3.1: Exponential discount curves from a smaller-sooner (SS) and a larger-later (LL) reward (A) contrasted with hyperbolic discount curves from an SS and an LL reward (B) (from Ainslie 2005: 636).

In Figure 3.1.B, but not in 3.1.A, the smaller reward is temporarily preferred just before it's available, which is shown by the curve of the smaller reward crossing that of the larger one from below. Although hyperbolic discount functions may be seen as a mere technical adjustment to the exponential function, adopting such models inevitably raises a difficult question of *consciousness* or self-awareness about inconsistencies on the part of individual actors. In order to understand this point, imagine the following scenario: Anne purchased two packages of her favourite giant chocolate toffee cookies from Tesco because they were on a 'buy-one-get-one-free' discount. But she knows that eating too much of them can cause health problems that she would like to avoid. So at the time of purchase (t=1) she decided to eat one package per week, her usual quota. Now the first chance to eat the cookies (t=2) arrives. Quickly finishing one package, Anne glances at the second one on the shelf, reaches down and eats it all. One of her housemates, Alex, who happens to be a devoted follower of DUM himself, enters the room and screams 'Your preferences are inconsistent, Anne! At time 1 you preferred eating one package per week to two per week, because of your concern for health. But now, at time 2, you prefer to eat two! If I remember correctly, you bought two packages to get a discount, not to eat them all at once.' What would Anne's reply be? I predict that most people would feel uneasy with the following answer: 'Sure, Alex, my preferences are indeed time-inconsistent. But what's wrong with them? My discount function is *hyperbolic*, not *exponential* like yours!' The oddity of this answer comes from the fact that hyperbolic functions may describe your inconsistent behaviour but cannot capture the psychological fact that you are aware of your preference at $t = 1$ and that you still see that preference as reasonable at $t = 2$. People are in fact usually aware of their past preferences; in this imaginary case Anne would also see the reasonableness of her past preference. One might object that the individual's self-awareness is irrelevant for the empirical issue of how an observer best models and explains behaviour, but the fact that people often talk about their choices' inter-temporal consistencies in this kind of situations suggests the important empirical fact that people are capable of foreseeing changes in their preferences and act accordingly. For example, in an alternative scenario, Anne may, as a means of self-command, choose to buy only one package, forgoing the chance of discount.[9] Strotz (1955) labels a decision maker who accurately anticipates the future change in her preferences as 'sophisticated', as opposed to a 'naïve' hyperbolic decision maker, who erroneously believes that her future preferences will be identical to the current ones. It seems that most people lie somewhere in between these two extreme cases. Wherever exactly people are located, it seems necessary to rethink the rationale of the hyperbolic discount model, once such 'internal conflict' is recognized as underlying mechanisms of time-inconsistent choices. Wilkinson (2008: 236), for example, suggests that the hyperbolic discounting approach 'lacks a psychological foundation'. This is not necessarily the case, once one recognizes the possibility of interpreting the hyperbolic discounting *realistically*.[10] Specifically, the hyperbolic discount model may be interpreted realistically as representing distinctive mechanisms underlying individual intertemporal decision making, rather than a mere 'curve-fitting' adjustment to the exponential model.[11] Such a literal interpretation of a utility function is unusual not only for the exponential model, but for the economists'

---

[9] Actually, being well aware of this consumers' tendency, food companies sell 'naughty goods' in small packages. See Hoch and Loewenstein (1991).

[10] I thank Don Ross for suggesting this possibility.

[11] We will see how this is done in chapter 6.

general modelling strategy, which has minimal ontological commitment to the functional representation of utilities (see chapter 1). In this respect, the hyperbolic discounting model is a radical departure from traditional economics.

In order to explain why people have 'hyperbolicky' discount utility functions, Ainslie and others have developed so called the 'multiple-self model'. In this model, 'multiple-self' refers to the existence within each person of several agents defined by their own interests, or preference orderings. Typically, the short-term 'self' and the long-term 'self' are defined by their distinct preferences, e.g., indulging yourself with your favourite sweets vs. maintaining good health, respectively. There are at least three reasons that lend some support for this idea. First, conceptually this is a simple way to make sense of the common observation that we encounter self-control problems: if self-control is a real phenomenon, then there must be at least two 'selves', one controlling and the other being controlled. Singular utility models cannot even conceptually make sense that there is an issue of self-control (Wilkinson 2008: 232). Second, functional magnetic resonance imaging (fMRI) studies on brain activities of decision makers suggest that choices between two delayed rewards and those between immediate and delayed rewards are associated with the activity of distinct brain areas, namely, the lateral pre-frontal cortex and the limbic system, respectively (McClure et al. 2004).[12] This suggests that models of conflicting 'selves' are not mere metaphors but may have some physical correspondence at the neuro-physiological level. Finally, some models of multiple-selves provide accurate predictions of time-inconsistent choices. Specifically, Ainslie (2001) models interactions of short- and long-term interests as repeated Prisoner's Dilemma games (cf. chapter 4), accurately predicting a set of various addictive behaviours. Fudenberg and Levine (2006) also apply a dual-self model to predict not failure (addiction) but success of self-control, i.e., non-pathological behaviour such as people's strategic limiting of pocket cash to prevent overspending later at a nightclub where their preferences may change under the influence of alcohol and drugs (they also discuss cognitive costs involved in self-control). Ross (2005: 341) takes Ainslie's results as 'the principal source of [Ainslie's model's] empirical persuasiveness'; further Ross suggests that a wider range of game models (assurance, coordination, inspection games etc.) should be able to explain a wider range of behavioural patterns resulting from interactions of different selves within the 'subpersonal marketplace' (see also Ross (forthcoming)). Here, it is evident that Ross's methodological justification of the 'non-Ptolemaic' model comes not only from its

---

[12] See chapter 6 for a more careful discussion of this result.

empirical success—which even *ad hoc₃* models may achieve—but also from its potential unifying power: with the creative shift of seeing whole individuals as communities of distinct economic agents, it becomes possible to unify models of (both inter- and intra-temporal) individual decision making using the theory of games.

3.3 The 'Ptolemaic' Critique and its Problems

Does the success of the multiple-self model in the domain of intertemporal decision lend some support to adopting this model in the domain of intratemporal decision making? Ross (2005) seems to suggest that it does. In the following I will argue that such considerations of unificatory power needs to be counter-balanced by empirical considerations regarding causal mechanisms behind phenomena. In this section, I will highlight some problems in Ross's critique of 'Ptolemaic' models of individual decision making. I will further argue that this critique misses the point of experimental research.

Ross (2005) characterizes various attempts to model individual decision making under uncertainty using formal maximization principles (EUT, Prospect Theory, etc.) as 'Ptolemaic', or *ad hoc₃* in our Lakatosian terminology. That is, these models are presumed to be unable to unify various phenomena under the umbrella of a single powerful research programme. More specifically, in discussing the preference reversal phenomenon, Ross criticizes *the compatibility hypothesis* proposed by psychologists and some behavioural economists as 'Ptolemaic'. One version of this hypothesis states that people attach greater weight to input stimuli (or information) that are more compatible with output selection tasks (see section 3.4 for a more detailed analysis). Tversky and Thaler (1990) employ this hypothesis to explain PR. The main pattern of PR is such that people *price* low-probability high-payoff bets (L bets) higher than high-probability low-payoff (H bets) bets, while *choosing* the H bets, making the apparent 'reversals' of preferences in the two kinds of tasks. This pattern can be explained in terms of the compatibility bias because the information regarding price seems to be weighted more in the pricing task, while in the choosing task there is no such bias. Ross criticizes this interpretation for two reasons, one empirical and the other conceptual. The empirical reason is simply that other experimental data (by Loomes, Starmer and Sugden 1991; Loomes and Taylor 1992) suggest that reversals occur regardless of compatibility biases. Since Ross does not regard this as decisive evidence, here I focus on the conceptual reasons. Ross (2005: 179) disregards the compatibility hypothesis because he thinks that it depends on a classical computational model of the mind which presupposes that there are 'facts of the matter about whether and how data are matched, as a distinct processing step during computation' of information in the brain of the decision maker. Second, Ross thinks that the compatibility hypothesis is inadequate as an economic theory because he interprets this hypothesis as an explanation by reference to evolutionarily formed heuristics that minimize cognitive efforts.

Regarding the second reason, it surely would be a problem for 'a defender of a separate economic science' (Ross 2005: 180) like Ross, but I see no reason why an explanation is conceptually problematic just because it is evolutionary and/or psychological rather than economic. Here he seems to require that genuine explanations be unifications *by economics*, which is far more controversial than the mere requirement of unification. Ross provides no argument for this claim. If the heuristics causing compatibility effects developed under some evolutionary pressure, then that fact will be at least relevant for the explanation of compatibility effects; in such cases it will be very difficult to methodologically justify a rejection of the compatibility hypothesis simply based on the fact that it is not an economic explanation.

Before analysing the first reason, it must be noted that Ross's interpretation of the compatibility hypothesis is not accurate. Ross interprets the compatibility hypothesis as concerning one mechanism related to mental computational processing. This is understandable because Ross refers to Tversky and Thaler (1990), a review article which was written for economists at the time the compatibility hypothesis was further elaborated by cognitive psychologists. I will here point out some problems of Ross's interpretation. First of all, the hypothesis is not simply that compatibility biases result from minimizing computational burdens. Although psychologists themselves talk about heuristics in terms of reducing cognitive burdens, such comments need not be taken as the only explanation of why heuristics exist at all. For example, in discussing 'neglect defaults', a type of evolved heuristics, Margolis (2007: 88-9) suggests that what defines such heuristics 'is not the economy of using them on particular occasions (which is usually slight), but that the occasions for the default responses are so very common. Without neglecting almost all such occasions by default, a person would be overwhelmed by hesitations'. This passage clarifies a distinct evolutionary character of the explanations by reference to various heuristics, as opposed to a simple economizing-type explanation. Second, and more importantly, the compatibility hypothesis turns out to consist of two distinct causal hypotheses. I will therefore give a detailed and more accurate account of the compatibility hypothesis in the next section, before continuing the critique of the unificationist approach in section 3.5.

3.4 Decomposing the Compatibility Hypothesis

In this section, I will review the literature on the compatibility hypothesis in some detail, in order to show that Ross's criticism is largely misguided. In particular, the compatibility hypothesis is decomposed into two distinct models, namely, *the scale compatibility hypothesis* and *the strategy compatibility hypothesis*.

3.4.1 History

In one of the first studies of preference reversals, Lichtenstein and Slovic ([1973] 2006: 75-6)[13] proposed the hypothesis that 'the compatibility or commensurability between a cue dimension and the required response will affect the importance of the cue in determining the response'. The idea is based on the input-output model of human perception, information processing and cognition. According to this model, when a subject receives some stimuli, these stimuli (input) are processed within the subject's brain in order to produce appropriate responses (output). Schematically put, this approach thus focuses on the mechanisms of either the selection of stimuli or the process of stimuli, or both.[14] We will shortly see that Slovic et al.'s studies concern both phases. 'Compatibility' or 'commensurability' is meant to capture the comparability or similarity *for the subject* between the initial stimuli and the information used to make decisions, although input (stimuli) and output (responses) are not necessarily comparable in the objective sense (hence 'compatibility'). In other words, compatibility refers to the subjective perception of a relationship between options and tasks.

In the 1970s, parallel to his early work on preference reversals, Slovic was engaged in a separate line of research investigating the difference between choice and matching responses through the use of two-dimensional stimuli, such as batting averages vs. number of home runs (where tasks are to choose between baseball players), speed vs. accuracy (where subjects choose between typists), and so on. In four experiments, Slovic (1975) asked his subjects first to match different pairs of options (making each pair equal in subjective value), and then to choose between the matched options. He found that the subjects did *not* choose randomly (as was predicted by the

---

[13] Page references of the psychologists' articles are, whenever available, to the reprinted versions in the anthologies, *Choices, Values, and Frames* (Kahneman and Tversky 2000), *Heuristics and Biases* (Gilovich, Griffin and Kahneman 2002) or *The Construction of Preference* (Lichtenstein and Slovic 2006).

[14] The final stage, namely, the production of responses does not seem to be an explicit subject matter of this model. Goldstein and Einhorn's (1987) *expression theory* explicitly models the production phase. See chapter 6.

equality in subjective value) but tended to select the option that was superior on the more important dimension (e.g., batting average and typing accuracy). Slovic's (1975) judgement that a particular dimension is 'more important' than the other is not solely based on the observation of which dimension weighted more heavily in responses, which would make the meaning of 'more important' somewhat tautological. Rather, he hypothesized in advance which dimension would be more important, based on the estimation of how easily one could apply and justify the response; he also confirmed this hypothesis by interviewing the subjects *ex post*, asking for an explanation of their choices.

Later, Tversky saw in this finding 'the seeds of a general theory of response-mode effects that had the potential to explain a wide variety of empirical findings, including preference reversals',[15] and jointly elaborated and tested this theory in Tversky, Sattath and Slovic ([1988] 2000) and in Slovic, Griffin and Tversky ([1990] 2002). In the former, the authors generalized Slovic's (1975) hypothesis as the *prominence hypothesis*[16], which states that the more prominent (important) attribute will loom larger in choice than in matching. They further suggested that the prominence hypothesis might be interpreted as an instance of a more general hypothesis, the *principle of compatibility*,[17] which states that the weight of a stimulus attribute (input) is enhanced by its compatibility with the response mode (output). The rationale of this suggestion is that the prominence hypothesis indicates that qualitative considerations loom larger in the ordinal procedure of choice than in the cardinal procedure of matching, which may be explained by the principle of compatibility.

The principle of compatibility as such, however, tells us little unless substantiated by auxiliary hypotheses regarding what is (and what isn't) compatible with what, so here a homely example may be helpful:[18] a kitchen stove usually has a square array of four burners, with the knobs being linearly arrayed in front of the stove. People often make mistakes regarding which knob to use in order to control, say, the burner in the upper right corner of the square array. This type of mistake can be reduced if the knobs are also squarely arrayed so that each knob is visually matched to the

---

[15] See Slovic (1995) for his account of this interaction.

[16] Originally, the hypothesis was somewhat clumsily labelled the "more important dimension hypothesis" (Slovic 1975: 281).

[17] Decision research psychologists tend to use 'hypothesis' and 'principle' interchangeably, sometimes referring to the latter as 'explanatory principle'. See e.g., Tversky et al. (1990). Moreover, whenever their 'hypothesis' or 'principle' seems confirmed, those terms are substituted with 'effect' or 'bias', indicating that their hypothesis or principle is a causal one.

[18] This example is from Slovic et al. ([1990] 2002: 217-8). The authors are aware of the lack of an independent procedure for assessing the compatibility between stimulus elements and response modes (218; 228), and resort to an unproblematic example similar to the one I'm using here.

corresponding burner (the upper right knob for the upper right stove, and so on). In the latter arrangement, input stimuli (visual perceptions of the burners) and output responses (controlling of the knobs) are compatible, while in the former they are not, which explains the difference in performance in the two arrangements. This is an example of compatibility in display. Extending from this simple and unproblematic example, one can talk about incompatibility in scale, semantic correspondence, and so on. In each case, the hypothesized mechanism is twofold: at the first stage of the input-output scheme, the compatibility between the stimulus attribute and the response mode increases the availability of stimuli by priming or focusing attention on the compatible features of the stimulus; then in the second phase, the compatibility increases (or the lack thereof decreases) the computational ease of processing the stimuli, both phases resulting in the enhanced weight of the compatible stimuli in responses.

In order to elaborate on the compatibility hypothesis, Slovic et al. ([1990] 2002) designed five experiments, two of which concerned the role of compatibility in prediction (of market value [study 1] and academic performance [study 2]), and three concerned compatibility in preference (over monetary vs. nonmonetary outcomes [study 3], immediate vs. delayed payoffs [study 4] and by matching vs. pricing [study 5]). In particular they were interested in ways in which the compatibility effect creates preference reversals in the latter set of experiments. The study was partly motivated by their discovery of an asymmetry in the PR data: PR was due mainly to the overpricing of low probability, high payoff bets (so-called $-bets or L-bets) (more than 65% of all PRs. See Tversky et al. (1990: 210). From the compatibility principle, they inferred that the payoffs (which are expressed in dollars) would be weighted more heavily in pricing (which is expressed also in dollars) than in choice. Since the payoffs are much larger in the L bets than in the H bets (high probability, low payoff bets), the compatibility effect seemed to explain the overpricing of L bets, and thus the main cause of PR. Although the results of study 3 and 4 of Slovic et al. ([1990] 2002) were encouraging for this interpretation, they encountered some surprise in study 5, in which they used a *matching* procedure to elicit preferences: that is, they first required subjects to fill in a missing value so as to equate a pair of options, and then inferred their preference from the value they used. This made it possible to compare percentages of particular preferences across four different elicitation procedures as shown in Table 3.1 for $H > L$.

Table 3.1: Percentage of responses favouring the H bet over the L bet for four different elicitation procedures (from Slovic et al. [1990] 2002: 225).[19]

(Task) (Bets)	Choice	Probability Matching	Payoff Matching	Pricing
Small bets (H, L)				
(35/36, \$4), (11/36, \$16)	80	79	54	29
(29/36, \$2), (7/36, \$9)	75	62	44	26
(34/36, \$3), (18/36, \$6.50)	73	76	70	39
(32/36, \$4), (4/36, \$40)	69	70	26	42
(34/36, \$2.50), (14/36, \$8.50)	71	80	43	22
(33/36, \$2), (18/36, \$5)	56	66	69	18
Mean	71	72	50	29
Large bets (H, L)				
(35/36, \$100), (11/36, \$400)	88	76	69	65
(29/36, \$50), (7/36, \$225)	83	64	31	55
(34/36, \$75), (18/36, \$160)	77	79	65	55
(32/36, \$100), (4/36, \$1,000)	84	68	28	61
(34/36, \$65), (14/36, \$210)	78	80	36	57
(33/36, \$50), (18/36, \$125)	68	75	58	46
Mean	80	74	48	56
Overall Mean	76	73	49	37

In Table 3.1, the comparison between the results of choice and pricing shows the familiar PR pattern: the subjects choose L bets but priced H bets higher (76 vs. 37% by overall mean). In addition, the comparison between probability matching and payoff matching reveals what seems to be the result of the compatibility effect: probability matching favours the H bets, whereas payoff matching favours the L bets (73 vs. 49%). But what surprised the experimenters most was the comparison between choice and matching. They reasoned that, if only the compatibility effect was involved, the probability matching would bias the responses in favour of the H bets and payoff matching would bias the responses in favour of the L bets, relative to choice. For the choice procedure was neutral with respect to the compatibility effect. They thus predicted that the percentage of responses favouring the H bets would be ordered as:

% (probability matching) > % (choice) > % (payoff matching).

---

[19] Note that apart from the direct choice task, these percentages are inferred from the probability and payoff matches and stated prices.

In fact, however, they observed:

$$\% \text{ (choice)} \fallingdotseq \% \text{ (probability matching)} > \% \text{ (payoff matching)}.[20]$$

Slovic et al. ([1990] 2002) explained this with the prominence hypothesis, according to which the more prominent (important) attribute will loom larger in choice than in matching. Tversky et al. ([1988] 2000), who extensively investigated the prominence hypothesis, interpreted PR as caused by the compatibility effect rather than the prominence effect, because they 'saw no *a priori* reason to hypothesize that probability is more important than money' (Slovic et al. [1990] 2002: 226). But given the new result that the subjects favoured the H bets in choice as much as (or sometimes even more than) in probability matching, they reconsidered the possibility that PR may be caused by the prominence effect rather than (or in addition to) the compatibility effect. Their interpretation that probability is the prominent dimension in risky choice is also supported by the finding that the rating of bets is dominated by probability (see Slovic and Lichtenstein ([1968] 2006; Goldstein and Einhorn 1987). From this perspective, the result in Table 3.1 can be understood as the combination of two effects: 'a compatibility effect that is responsible for the difference between probability matching and payoff matching (including pricing), and a prominence effect that contributes to the relative attractiveness of *H* bets in choice' (Slovic et al. [1990] 2002: 226).

3.4.2 Separating Causes

The interpretation by Slovic et al. ([1990] 2002) might appear a little confusing, since Tversky et al. ([1988] 2000: 513) suggested that the prominence hypothesis 'may be constructed as an example of a more general principle of compatibility'. But how can a special case (the prominence effect) occur in choice tasks separately and independently from its general manifestation (the compatibility effect)? Fischer and Hawkins (1993) clarify this confusion by explicitly distinguishing *scale compatibility* from *strategy compatibility*. The former says that the 'weight of any input component is enhanced by its compatibility with the output' (Tversky et al. [1988] 2000: 513), the mechanism behind this being that scale compatibility makes particular stimuli more accessible and reduces the burden of computation. The latter states that '[q]ualitative preference tasks are more likely than quantitative tasks to evoke a preference for the alternative that is superior with respect to the most important attribute' (Fischer and Hawkins 1993: 583).

---

[20] $76 \fallingdotseq 73 > 49.$

This is presumably caused by the compatibility between the nature[21] of the response task and the nature of the decision strategy it invokes, *not* by the compatibility between the units of payoff dimension of the stimuli and the units of the response scale. The logical structure of the strategy compatibility hypothesis is as follows (ibid.):

> (St. 1) Quantitative response tasks evoke quantitative strategies in which the decision maker makes trade-offs between value attributes.
>
> (St. 2) Qualitative response tasks evoke multi-stage decision processes that involve a mix of quantitative and qualitative strategies, with the latter being used to resolve close decisions.
>
> (St. 3) Qualitative strategies give primary consideration to differences with respect to the prominent attribute.[22]
>
> ---
>
> (St. 4) Qualitative tasks are more likely than quantitative tasks to lead to a preference for the alternative that is superior with respect to the prominent attribute (*strategy compatibility hypothesis*).

Thus stated, the strategy compatibility hypothesis turns out to be a generalized version of the prominence hypothesis; it generalizes choice-matching comparison to include any comparison of a qualitative and quantitative preference task. Compare this with the logical structure of the scale compatibility hypothesis:

> (Sc. 1) A response mode primes or focuses attention on the compatible features of the stimulus.
>
> (Sc. 2) Compatibility (noncompatibility) between the input and the output scale requires less (more) mental operations, often decreasing (increasing) effort and error.

---

[21] Fischer and Hawkins use the word 'metaproperty' instead of 'nature' presumably in order to indicate that the two properties in question are not obvious to the experimenter: regarding the property of a response task, what distinguishes quantitative from qualitative response tasks is unknown prior to empirical investigation (in Experiment 2 they address this question; see p. 587); regarding the property of a decision strategy, it is even less obvious which task evokes which strategy.

[22] Fischer and Hawkins note that (St. 3) holds only if we assume the use of particular qualitative strategies, such as lexicographic ordering or elimination by aspects. For example, if a qualitative strategy involved is a conjunctive rule (in which one eliminates any option that falls below one's aspiration level on any attribute), (St. 3) (and thus (St. 4)) does not necessarily hold.

(Sc. 3) The weight of a stimulus attribute is enhanced by its compatibility with the response mode (*scale compatibility hypothesis*).

This input-output compatibility can be applied not only to scale (e.g., dollar => pricing in dollar), but also to other dimensions, that is, the notion of compatibility can be extended to the nature of the information and the nature of the task (e.g., ordinal info => ordering, common features => similarity judgement) in general. Now it should be clear, however, that strategy compatibility is not generalizable to this hypothesis, since the compatibility of the former concerns different things, i.e., response tasks and decision strategies. The two are thus distinct hypotheses. It is therefore conceivable that they imply opposite predictions. For instance, in choice and matching tasks involving jobs with two dimensions (salary and vacation time), the strategy compatibility hypothesis predicts that the prominent dimension (i.e., salary in this case) looms larger in choice than in matching tasks. On the contrary, the scale compatibility hypothesis predicts that salary will be weighted more heavily in dollar-matching tasks than in choice. Based on this insight Fischer and Hawkins (1993) designed four experiments to detect the strategy compatibility effect and the scale compatibility effect separately (in riskless choice), and observed that the strategy compatibility effect is much larger than the scale compatibility effect.

This is not the end of the story: some anomalies persist, as is often the case in experimental science. For example, Fischer and Hawkins (1993) note a further puzzle, namely that in a study of risky choice by Goldstein and Einhorn (1987) attractiveness rating tasks evoked stronger preference for H (high-probability, low-payoff) bets than choice did, a phenomenon that neither the scale-compatibility hypothesis nor the strategy-compatibility hypothesis (nor a combination of the two) predict. But the point should be clear by now: the compatibility hypothesis is a causal hypothesis, and two distinct causal mechanisms have been found.

3.5 The Procedural Approach

The discussion in the previous section makes it clear that the strategy compatibility hypothesis, distinguished from the scale compatibility hypothesis, does *not* presuppose any specific computational model of the human mind. While scale compatibility biases presumably take place in order to minimize computational cost (Sc. 2), strategy compatibility biases are neutral with regard to the presumption of such mechanism.

Although the first premise of strategic compatibility hypothesis (St. 1) says that quantitative response tasks evoke quantitative strategies, the use of quantitative strategies is not necessarily minimizing computational costs; in fact, quantitative strategies (e.g., maximizing profit) can sometimes require more mental efforts than qualitative ones. The fact that quantitative tasks evoke quantitative strategies may be explained by some other causes such as *framing*. Regarding this point, there is a highly suggestive study by Rubinstein (2006), who conducted a set of questionnaire-based experiments to investigate the effects of economic education on people's decision making. In the experiments the subjects were asked to make a decision, as a CEO of a company, on how many employees they were willing to maintain in order to increase profit. The subjects were presented a table which showed seven combinations of numbers of workers who would continue to be employed and the resulting profits of the company, and asked to decide upon the number of employees they were willing to continue to employ. The table was constructed in such a way that there was a trade-off between employee protection (reducing a number of layoffs) and profit maximization, as is typically the case in recession phases. Rubinstein found that the group of economic students tended to prioritize profit maximization (45-49% choosing the profit-maximizing number, 100), while other groups sacrificed profit maximization to a various extent in order to reduce the number of employees who would be fired (only 13-16% of philosophy and mathematics students choosing the profit-maximizing 100). Interestingly, this variation among different groups disappeared once the table showing various results was replaced by a formula (profit function) which yields similar values to those presented in the table: in this condition, a similar proportion of subjects (73-77%) regardless of their educational backgrounds chose the profit maximizing value, 100. This result can be interpreted as an example of strategy compatibility biases, where, although the response task is identical (i.e., deciding how many workers to keep), different ways of framing the similar information (table vs. formula) induce different response strategies (choosing from multiple alternatives vs. solving an equation), resulting in different decisions. It seems that the prominent attribute for economics students in this choice is profit, while for non-economics students employee protection also matters. But the majority of non-economics students, who balanced between conflicting goals (employee protection vs. profit-maximization) in the 'table' condition, seemed to have paid less attention to this conflict in the 'formula' condition. Instead, they simply solved the equation to yield the profit-maximizing number of employees. Computational economy does not explain this shift of response strategy because solving the equation is not computationally easier than choosing a value from the table. In the 'table' condition, the subjects only had to identify the maximum profit on the table, and then see the corresponding number of employees. In the 'formula' condition, by contrast, subjects had to compute the profit-maximizing number of employees (x) based on the function '$2\sqrt{x} - 0.1x - 8$'. Note that in both conditions it was explicitly stated that profits would still be positive even if no workers were laid off.

Nor can the shift be explained by the differences in training, since there was no significant variation among different groups of students. Although economics education seems to influence what dimension one sees as prominent in choice options, this effect ceases to be significant once the quantitative strategy (i.e. solving the equation) is primed by manipulating the presentation of the relevant information. These findings suggest that strategy compatibility effects can be quite powerful, regardless of considerations of computational costs.

A second thing to note is that the scale compatibility and the strategy compatibility hypotheses are not presumed to be mutually exclusive rival hypotheses, but are expected to capture different but both causally relevant mechanisms underlying preference reversals. As in this case, psychological models typically presuppose that a particular phenomenon results from compound causes of heterogeneous natures. This fact refutes Ross's allegation that the compatibility hypothesis is based on the old-fashioned computational model of human minds. On the contrary, it may be argued that psychological models are relatively 'liberal' in allowing for diverse theoretical presuppositions, making a sharp contrast with the standard economic models committed to some form of utility maximization. Criticizing psychological models because of their presumed rigid theoretical commitments is not well grounded.

Contrary to Ross's suggestion, the strategy compatibility hypothesis in fact reflects two different traditions in research on decision making, namely, the reason-based and value-based approaches (see Shafir, Simonson and Tversky [1993] 2000). Value-based models (such as EUT and Prospect Theory) model individual choice as a maximization of utility which an individual assigns to different objects of choice based on her intrinsic preference. By contrast, reason-based models model individual choice as a result of certain inferential processes. Choosing an option that is more valued with respect to a prominent attribute (e.g., salary as opposed to the number of holidays when choosing a job) from two equally valued options is an example of reason-based decisions. In the strategy compatibility hypothesis, quantitative strategies correspond to value-based models, while qualitative strategies are better captured by reason-based models. These two approaches are not mutually exclusive, but are meant to capture two different types of mechanisms involved in decision-making processes.

Should such a 'liberal' approach be condemned because it lacks a unifying theoretical framework? Not necessarily: first, the strategy compatibility hypothesis is not a mere conjunction of two types of decision process models, but rather it concerns perceptual or cognitive mechanisms through which different processes (i.e., reason-based and value-based decision strategies) are evoked depending on the nature of tasks. In other words, the hypothesis not only identifies two types of mechanisms, but purports to identify the conditions under which these mechanisms are triggered. Second, although the value-based approach is theoretically much more sophisticated, some theorists have started to provide a formal and unifying framework for the reason-based approach. Gold and List (2004) have recently proposed a formal framework that unifies the strategy compatibility effects and framing effects. According to this framework, the violations of both types of invariance—procedure invariance associated with compatibility effects and description invariance associated with framing effects—take place because the agent considers a set of implicitly inconsistent propositions (*the logical condition*) along different decision paths that lead to mutually inconsistent decisions (*the empirical condition*). Although several interpretations of the empirical conditions are possible (e.g., Does an agent consider different propositions in different temporal orders? Or does she weigh those propositions differently? Or are some propositions more focal than others for the agent?), I shall refer to this model as the *procedural* model in order to remain neutral with respect to these interpretations.[23] Rubinstein (2003) proposes a similar procedural model in the domain of intertemporal decision making, claiming that the procedural model is empirically superior to and more intuitive than the hyperbolic discount model that is popular among behavioural economists (see section 3.2.2). Although relatively new in economics, the procedural approach has the potential to explain both inter-and intra-temporal inconsistencies of choice. The compatibility hypothesis laid the basis of this line of research, by providing detailed psychological mechanisms. One cannot therefore criticize the compatibility hypothesis as *ad hoc* or 'Ptolemaic' as Ross (2005) does: the hypothesis was more than 'systematically summarizing data', and if taken seriously as an explanation, it points to a rather different theoretical possibility (the procedural model) from the one Ross envisages (the multiple-self model).

---

[23] Starmer's (2000: 35) defines 'procedural theories' as the theories that try to model the psychological processes that lead to choice. Note that how such 'processes' are interpreted is left open under this definition.

3.6 Can 'Wider Theoretical Considerations' Help?

I have defended the compatibility hypothesis against the criticisms that it is based on a misguided theoretical framework and that it is based on no theoretical framework at all. Now I turn to Ross's claim that the latest neuroscientific research and the model of the mind supported by it favour the multiple-agent model. I will show that this is not so, and why.

In criticizing Slovic et al.'s compatibility hypothesis, Ross (2005: 233, 235) explains neither what the 'classical model of the mind' is, nor why the model is invalid, although in several places he suggests that human brains are 'parallel information processors'. The idea seems to be that no centralized process takes place in the brain when the decision maker is considering some choice problem; instead, various parts of the brain process information in various ways without having the 'central processer'. This idea seems congenial to Ross's hypothesis that a decision maker consists of several economic agents, each doing its own maximization based on different preferences (see the fMRI study by McClure et al. 2004 cited in section 3.2.2). The contrast seems to be that while in the classical model a computer-like algorithm is performed by the unitary decision maker, in the model informed by the latest cognitive science the decision-making processes are 'decentralized'.

Now, assume for the sake of argument that such 'decentralized' model of the mind is supported by neuroscientific or some other wider evidence. This would not favour Ross's multiple-self model relative to the procedural model. Note first that the strategy compatibility hypothesis is also consistent with this new picture of the mind. As I suggested above, it is an open question how a 'decision path' should be interpreted; Gold and List (2004: 260) define a decision path as 'the order in which the agent considers the propositions in a sequential decision process', but suggest that several empirical interpretations are possible: if we interpret a decision path actually taken by the agent as a set of the propositions which are considered heavier or more focal than other propositions, then the hypothesis will be consistent with the fact that different parts of the brain process information in a parallel way. But even if a decision path is literally interpreted as a temporal order, the hypothesis may be consistent with the decentralized processing model, which is compatible with the idea that different parts of the brain are 'taking turn', as in a sequential game between different selves. These considerations suggest that the procedural model and the multiple-agent model are both compatible with the decentralized model of the mind.

It is also possible to point out that the multiple-agent model and the procedural model may be mutually compatible. Recall that the procedural model consists of two conditions, logical and empirical. The former is a requirement that different decision paths lead to different final decisions on the target proposition. Gold and List (2004) explicate that an agent's initial dispositions must be *implicitly inconsistent* for this 'path dependence' to happen. An agent's initial dispositions are implicitly inconsistent with respect to a proposition φ in a set X if there exist two logically consistent sets of propositions Ψ_1 and Ψ_2 such that the agent has dispositions to accept all propositions in Ψ_1 and all propositions in Ψ_2, but Ψ_1 entails φ and Ψ_2 entails $\neg\varphi$. Implicit inconsistencies can happen in two ways. First, when the agent violates *deductive closure*, i.e., when there exists a logically consistent set of propositions Ψ such that the agent has dispositions to accept all propositions in Ψ, Ψ entails φ, and yet the agent has no disposition to accept φ. For example, suppose that the agent has initial dispositions to accept P and (P =>Q), but for some reason she also has a disposition to accept $\neg$Q. The set {P, (P=>Q)} entails Q but the set {$\neg$Q} (trivially) entails $\neg$Q, meaning that the agent's initial dispositions are implicitly inconsistent. Also, an implicit inconsistency occurs whenever the agent's disposition is *explicitly inconsistent*, i.e., when the agent has dispositions to accept both φ and $\neg\varphi$ simultaneously. Although Gold and List suggest that path dependence occurs mainly because deductive closure is violated, they do not exclude the possibility that the agent is explicitly inconsistent with regard to the decision on the target proposition. In this case, a natural way to interpret the underlying psychology is to suppose that the individual has mutually contradicting dispositions, one accepting and the other rejecting the target proposition. This interpretation is consistent with the idea that the individual really consists of more than one agent, each characterized by its own distinct set of preferences. Therefore the multiple-agent model may be compatible with the procedural model. Because both are compatible with the decentralized model of the mind which Ross advocates, and because both may be interpreted as compatible with each other in the sense explicated above, the decentralized model of the mind, nor neuroscientific studies purported to support such model, can lend any support in favour of one over the other model.

However, there is a respect in which the procedural model is superior to the multiple-agent model. On the one hand, the multiple-agent model presupposes a game-like interaction among different agents in determining the final decision as an equilibrium (or equilibria). On the other, the procedural model presupposes certain cognitive or perceptual mechanisms through which one decision path rather than others is taken depending on how problems are described or how decisions are elicited (one of the empirical conditions is explicated by the strategy compatibility hypothesis). These mechanisms are presumed to capture ways in which individuals change their responses to extensionally equivalent decision problems depending on descriptions of the problem and procedures of preference elicitation. By contrast, the multiple-agent model alone cannot explain these framing and elicitation effects (this, of course, is not the case if a multiple-agent model is coupled with some model of framing at the whole-person level). If the decision at the whole-person level derives from games among the agents within an individual, why does framing at the whole-person level matter? In sum, although the multiple-agent model has some intuitive appeal in the domain of intertemporal decision making, the procedural approach, in particular the strategy compatibility hypothesis, explains anomalies in the domain of intratemporal decision making, whereas the multiple-agent model does not.

3.7 Conclusion

In this chapter, I have examined a debate on possible explanations of PR (the multiple-agent model vs. the procedural model), and suggested that this particular debate cannot be resolved by appealing to a methodological criterion of theory appraisal such as unification. Specifically, I have criticized Ross's (2005) claim that the compatibility hypothesis proposed by psychologists and behavioural economists are *ad hoc*. I have first explicated *ad hocness*, based on Lakatos's (1970) framework of research programme. Second, I have motivated Ross's critique by illustrating how the Lakatosian framework works in the domain of intertemporal choice, and potentially also in the domain of intratemporal choice. Third, I have argued that Ross's critique of the compatibility hypothesis as 'Ptolemaic' is unjustified, by showing that the hypothesis consists of two distinct causal hypotheses regarding decision making processes. I also suggested that the compatibility hypothesis is based on a well-motivated theoretical framework, i.e., the reason-based, procedural approach, as opposed to the value-based, multiple-self approach. These considerations suggest that the real issue of the debate is not so methodological as empirical. Further, I have shown that this empirical debate is not easily resolved by appeal to wider theoretical considerations such as what the true model of the mind is.

It must be noted that, although I have been more sympathetic towards the procedural model than towards the multiple-self model, the scope of my examination is rather limited: it does not exclude the possibility of a better formulation of a multiple-self model that explains the data better than any procedural models do. This is an entirely empirical issue. Also, my exercise does not deny the usefulness of unification as a criterion of theory appraisal in general: it just shows its limited applicability in this specific debate. Still I think this exercise to be useful. After all, a general, abstract rule must be evaluated against specific, concrete cases, and my attempt has been to do exactly that.

Although the multiple-self model is radical in the sense of abandoning individualism, in a sense it is 'ready-made for adoption by economists interested in improving the behavioural realism of [their] models', because economists are already familiar with the tool for doing this—dynamic game theory (Rabin 1998: 40). In this sense, intertemporal decision making is a fortunate case, where economic theory happens to be useful for modelling psychological mechanisms under study. The real challenge for economists, however, is to resist the temptation to let their familiar modelling tools dictate the direction of empirical research regardless of the evidence at hand. The extensive study of preference reversals and the elaboration of the compatibility hypothesis suggest the possibility that preferences are 'constructed' rather than simply 'revealed' in behaviour. I have suggested the procedural approach as an alternative that emphasizes an oft neglected cognitive process in decision making, namely, *reasoning*. In general, people are reason-giving beings, so much so that they sometimes create one even if there was no particular reason for doing one thing rather than other (Nisbett and Wilson 1977). Although this makes the empirical study of reasoning processes rather difficult, it does not mean that theorists can safely assume that there is no such thing. What we need to do is to come up with a better theory, while taking the evidence at hand seriously.

Chapter 4

Testing Game Theory with Repetition: Cooperation Anomalies

In the previous chapters, we have examined some serious anomalies in individual decision making and different research strategies to explain these anomalies. This chapter and the next examine anomalies in *strategic* decision making, where the outcome of an individual's decision depends not only on chance events, but also on decisions by the others with whom she is interacting (and *vice versa*). In particular, I shall focus on the existence of cooperation in certain classes of strategic interactions among human subjects in the laboratory (*cooperation anomalies*). Cooperation anomalies are anomalous *in relation to game theory*. So in order to respond to these anomalies, it is important to be explicit about what exactly game theory consists of. In behavioural experiments, the crucial point is that game theory is always tested together with some hypotheses about subjects' preferences, i.e., what they care about (Do people care only about money, or something else?). Another important point is that preferences (whatever they are about) are measured using preference theory *and* game theory. This chapter examines some methodological issues arising from these complications. I will selectively review how the methodology of experimental game theory has evolved over the last half century. My narrative is pitted against two conceptual and methodological arguments that challenge what I see as innovative experimental designs. The first argument, which is found in the writings of the prominent game theorist Ken Binmore (e.g., 1994), states that game theory is a tautology. The second argument, which is put forward by the methodologist/philosopher of science Jim Woodward (2008), states that people's real preferences cannot be measured by letting subjects play a game just once in the lab. I will argue that both arguments are confused and harmful to the progress of empirical game theory, and that therefore they must be abandoned.

The chapter proceeds as follows: section 4.1 provides necessary concepts to the following discussion drawing on the Prisoner's Dilemma game and its multiple-person variant, the public goods game. Section 4.2 reviews the main findings from public goods experiments conducted by economists, sociologists, and psychologists. Section 4.3 analyzes in detail several recent attempts to measure subjects' preferences using public goods games. The two arguments that potentially threaten these attempts will be then presented, and criticized. Section 4.4 concludes.

4.1 The Prisoner's Dilemma

I start my discussion from the Prisoner's Dilemma,[1] which is a special class of mixed-motive games (i.e., games in which players' preferences over outcomes are partly aligned and partly opposed). The original illustration of the game attributed to Alfred Tucker goes like this: two suspects who jointly committed some major crime are detained separately by the Chicago District Attorney, who does not have enough evidence to convict them for the main crime, and therefore needs a confession from one of the suspects. The District Attorney offers the following deal separately to each suspect: if you confess while your partner refuses, you will be set free and your partner gets the longest sentence; if both you and your partner remain silent then both will get the minimum sentence; and if both agree to confess, both will receive a moderate sentence. Each prisoner, knowing the other is facing the same problem, has to make a decision separately. A matrix, or a *normal-form* representation of this game is shown in Table 4.1.

Table 4.1: The Prisoner's Dilemma

Prisoner 2

		silence	*confess*
Prisoner 1	*silence*	2, 2	−1, 3
	confess	3, −1	0, 0

In each box, 'payoffs' of Players 1 and 2 are represented by the number on the left and right, respectively. Payoffs represent players' preference orderings for outcomes, everything considered. Unlike a typical decision-theoretic situation in which a decision maker does not have any influence on which state of the world she is in ('Nature' decides it), this is a strategic situation in which what Prisoner 1 (P1) will end up with depends (partly) on Prisoner 2 (P2)'s decision, *and vice versa*. What will and should each prisoner do to minimize her sentence? Standard game theory gives a clear answer: choose *confess* whatever the other chooses. First, each player is assumed to choose a strategy with the aim of maximizing her payoff. In this example, maximizing a payoff means minimizing a sentence. Now, imagine you are P1, and suppose P2 chooses

---

[1] Melvin Dresher and Merrill Flood at Rand Cooperation are credited as the inventors of this game (Binmore 1994: 102, fn. 12).

confess. You will be better off by choosing *confess*, as it gives you only the moderate sentence rather than the major one (payoff 0 vs. −1). Suppose P2 chooses *silence*. You will be still better off by choosing *confess*, as it lets you walk free rather than serve the minor sentence (payoff 3 vs. 2). The upshot is that, *regardless of P2's choice*, you will be better off by choosing *confess*. In this case, we say that *confess* strictly dominates *silence*, because the payoff from choosing *confess* is higher than the payoff from *silence*, for *any* strategy choice by the other player's strategy (strategy A *weakly* dominates B if A's payoffs are higher for some choices by others, and never lower). The 'reasoning by dominance' tells you to choose *confess*, because it gives you better payoffs no matter what you think P2 will do. P2 reasons exactly the same way and reaches the same conclusion. Thus both choose *confess*, ending up with the moderate sentence (payoff 0).

In general, any rule for specifying predictions as to how players are expected to behave in any given game is called a 'solution concept'. A solution concept gives the prediction(s), or 'solution' to a given game as a 'strategy profile' (or strategy profiles), a combination of each player's strategy (or a set of combinations). The dominance reasoning is an example of a solution concept, and its prediction in the example above is a unique strategy profile (*confess, confess*). A strategy profile reached by the dominance reasoning is sometimes called a 'dominant strategy equilibrium'. Another important solution concept is the 'principle of best-reply strategies', which says that each player will maximize her own payoff, given the supposed actions of the others. When each player follows this principle, any predicted strategy profile is a 'Nash equilibrium': a Nash equilibrium is a strategy profile in which each player's strategy is a best response to the other players' strategies. That is, no player has an incentive (in terms of improving her own payoff) to deviate from her part of the profile, if no other player will deviate.

Although the strategy profile (*confess, confess*) is a Nash equilibrium as well as a dominant strategy equilibrium, in choosing *confess* you need not think of what is best for the other player. In this sense, it seems that there is no complicated strategic interdependence in the Prisoner's Dilemma. However, there is a sense in which this game has a character of interdependence: (*confess, confess*) is *Pareto dominated* by (*silence, silence*), meaning that by moving from the former to the latter at least one of the players is better off while no other player is worse off. In fact, in (*silence, silence*) *both* players are better off than in (*confess, confess*). Therefore, both players should be happier in (*silence, silence*) than in (*confess, confess*). Yet reasoning by dominance tells each player to choose *confess*. It is worth emphasizing that this unfortunate result does not necessarily follow from the players' selfishness; rather it is a consequence of the game's payoff structure. What is formally required is the players' particular preference orderings over the outcomes—(*confess, silent*) > (*silent, silent*) > (*confess, confess*) > (*silent, confess*), which is represented by the payoff inequalities 3 > 2 > 0 > –1 in Table 4.1; how each strategy is labelled and why a particular outcome is preferred over another is thus irrelevant. Even if players have altruistic motives, the Pareto dominating outcome is not chosen as long as the payoff structure is that of the Prisoner's Dilemma.

Standard game theory gives the same prediction and prescription when there are more than two players in the Prisoner's Dilemma (a Multiple-person Prisoner's Dilemma, or MPD), which shares essentially the same structure as the two-person version of the game.[2] Figure 4.1, one version of what Margolis (2007) calls 'Schelling diagram', illustrates MPD.

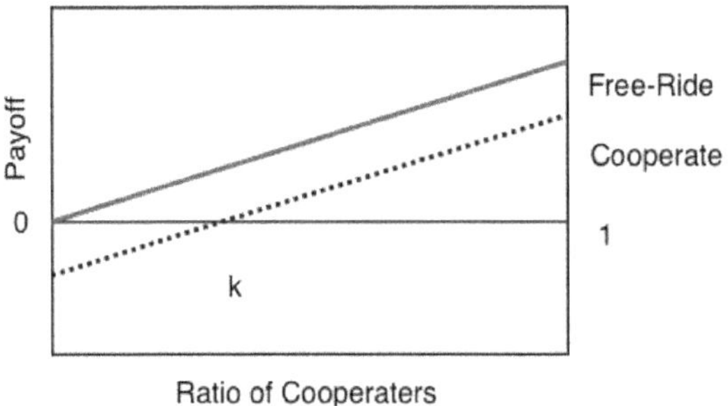

Figure 4.1: A Schelling diagram (from Margolis 2007: 51)

The horizontal axis measures the ratio of those who choose cooperate from 0 (no one is choosing *cooperate*) to 1 (everyone is), and the vertical axis measures the payoff of an individual chooser given a certain cooperation rate (divided by the zero-payoff line).[3] The solid line ('Free-Ride') plots payoffs to individuals when they choose free-ride (equivalent to *confess* in the original PD), while the dotted line ('Cooperate') plots individuals' payoffs when they choose *cooperate*. Each individual chooses a strategy which gives a higher payoff, given the others' strategies (the principle of best-reply

---

[2] Economists are familiar with the problem as undersupply of a public good. See Samuelson (1954).
[3] While Schelling's (1978) original version interprets the chooser everywhere as an average chooser, Margolis's (2007: 50) version hypothesizes the 'marginal' chooser at each point in the horizontal axis. This difference is not essential for the present discussion.

strategies). So the fact that the line FR is above C anywhere in the graph means that an individual will not choose *cooperate* regardless of the cooperation rate. Although *cooperate* yields a positive payoff if the cooperation rate exceeds a certain threshold (k in the graph), this fact does not make a difference, for *free-ride* always pays off more. Here again, reasoning by dominance implies the dominant equilibrium *(free-ride, free-ride, ...)*, where no one cooperates, yielding zero payoff to everyone.[4]

The MPD captures the structure of a market for a 'public good', in economists' jargon. A public good is a good (i) whose consumption by an individual does not inhibit another's benefit from it *(non-rivalry)*; and (ii) whose consumption cannot be restricted to those who have paid for it *(non-excludability)*.[5] These characteristics make consuming a public good (or producing a public bad) without paying an appropriate price always beneficial to individuals; as a result, no one has an incentive to pay for consuming the good (or for producing the bad). Standard game theory thus predicts that there will be little or no voluntary provision of such goods (or restraint from producing such bads). The claim that particular goods are public goods is often used as both explanation and justification of the fact that such goods as national defence and public broadcasting—classical examples of public goods—are usually financed by coercive or quasi-coercive means (such as tax and TV licence fee).[6] The economist/political scientist Mancur Olson (1965) extended the notion of public goods to analyze *collective actions* by various economic and political groups,[7] arguing that the pursuit of common interests by a large group (as opposed to a small one) is difficult because actions that promote the large group's cause is essentially a public good. The ecologist/microbiologist Garrett Hardin (1968) applied the same logic to population problems, arguing that an ever increasing population would ruin commons—free but limited resources such as pastures for cattlemen, oceans for fishermen, airs to pollute for enterprisers, etc.—because the benefits from exploitation is always larger than its costs for each individual, while the overall costs are such that the commons is exploited beyond its sustainable level (the 'tragedy of the commons').[8] Although without

---

[4] To indicate the status quo, the payoff from zero cooperation is defined as 0, as in the two-person version.

[5] A related economic notion is 'externality', which refers to an economic action's impact on a third party that is not involved in the decision making process. A public good has external benefits, and a public bad external costs.

[6] Sugden (1982: 341) lists examples where economists use the MPD structure as a justification for their policies, including compulsory transfers of income through the tax system, public policy to stimulate saving and investment and the subsidisation or public provision of health care.

[7] The book is subtitled as 'Public Goods and the Theory of Groups'.

[8] Concerned with population problems, Hardin's (1968) recommendation is more radical than that usually provided by economists: to legally restrict the freedom to breed, rather than the freedom to consume the commons.

formalism, the core part of the argument of these classical studies is essentially an *a priori*, game-theoretic analysis of MPD. (Hardin explicitly uses the word 'tragedy' as having a connotation of necessity; Olson uses the word 'logic' in the same sense.) At the same time, however, these studies showed how such an *a priori* analysis can be applied to problems of great practical interest, contributing to the general acceptance of game theory by social scientists: specifically, it explained or 'rationalized' (i.e., made it less puzzling) why actions by instrumentally rational individuals can result in outcomes preferred by none of them.

The game-theoretic analysis of PD (which 'proves' an impossibility theorem of cooperation), however, immediately raises other questions: first, why do we sometimes observe individual behaviour that seems equivalent to *silence* or *cooperate* in PD? The majority of people vote despite each individual's infinitesimal influence on the result and the relatively high costs associated with turnout; in many civilized cities littering is not so common as to make cities unacceptably dirty even though there is no fine. It seems that the clear prediction of standard game theory is not confirmed so unambiguously by the behavioural evidence of actual human choice (call this the PD 'anomaly'). Second, is *confess* or *free-ride* really a rational choice in PD? Some people—including some philosophers, who are supposed to be experts of rationality—dispute this intuition and argue that *cooperate* is the rational choice in the game (call this the PD 'puzzle'). Although this chapter mainly concerns empirical applications of game theory, people's intuitions about what ought to be done in a situation like PD is relevant to explaining the PD anomaly, for people's normative intuition may be a cause of such anomaly (Bacharach 2006). In the next section, I will review how experimental evidence regarding PD can illuminate these questions. I confine my discussion to MPD in part because that version is more relevant for large-scale cooperation, and in part because experimental economists have mainly conducted MPD.

4.2 Public Goods Experiments: Testing Game Theory?

Although the Prisoner's Dilemma had been played experimentally in a casual manner among the small circle of game theorists in the 1950s, it is only in the '70s and '80s that social scientists started to systematically test its implications to multiple-person interactions in the controlled laboratory.[9] The history is strikingly similar to that of

---

[9] Ledyard (1995), on which this section is heavily based, mentions Bohm (1972) as one of the first public goods experiments. For a social psychologist's review of two-person and multiple-person PD experiments

preference reversal experiments reviewed in chapter 2: non-economists—this time not only psychologists (Dawes, McTavish and Shaklee 1977) but also sociologists (Marwell and Armes 1979, 1980)—argued that they observed relatively high contribution rates in public goods experiments despite game theory's contrary prediction (hence the appearance of an anomaly); economists (Kim and Walker 1984; Isaac, McCue and Plott 1985) reacted by designing 'tighter' experiments in order to eliminate such anomaly (the strategy of 'explaining away'), only to find that it persists (Isaac, Walker and Thomas 1994). Ledyard (1995: 121) summarizes this and other anomalies as the following 'stylized facts':

1. In one-shot trials[10] and in the initial stages of finitely repeated trials, subjects generally provide contributions halfway between the Pareto-efficient level and the free riding level.
2. Contributions decline with repetition, and
3. Face to face communication improves the rate of cooperation.

These stylized facts are robust. For example, in a casual classroom experiment following the Holt and Laury (1997) design with two groups of $N = 15$, I have replicated all of these stylized facts (except the finding in one-shot trials), although many confounds were not carefully controlled for (see Appendix, also Guala: 2008). However, implications of these findings are far from obvious, and thus careful interpretations are needed. In what sense are these findings anomalous to game theory? In order to answer this question, we need to ask another question: What exactly is the status of game theory in these experiments? It is helpful to look at public goods experiments within the framework of experimental economics, since it will give a clear sense of the role of game theory in economic experiments.

4.2.1 Environment

First, in the modern language of experimental economics, public goods experiments have a particular class of environment, which specifies a range of exogenous variables such as the number of players, their preferences, endowments, etc. In general, a public-goods environment has N (>2) players ($i = 1, \ldots, N$) each with endowment z_i which is divided into x_i (the 'private' good) and t_i (the 'public' good), the latter of which is increased according to the 'production function' $y = g(t)$. The experiment's outcome is interpreted customarily as a distribution of payoffs ($y, x_1, \ldots, x_N$). The crucial element

---

see Colman (1995: chs. 7 and 9). Dawes and Thaler (1988) is not neutral but a short and crisp review by a behavioural economist and a psychologist.

[10] According to Sally's (1995) meta-analysis of one-shot PD games anonymously played with real money, typically 40-50% of the subjects choose *cooperate*.

of this environment is that these variables are controlled so that the game's payoff structure becomes that of MPD.[11] As an example consider an environment with 10 players and a production function $y = 1/4(t)$. Each receives two tokens (that are convertible to real money after experiment), which are to be divided into the private good and the public good. Tokens kept as private goods remain unchanged, while tokens contributed to public goods are pooled, and each player receives the total amount divided by 4. So if everyone puts two tokens as the public good, the payoff is 5 tokens ($2 \times 10/4$); if everyone puts one token as the public good, the payoff is 3.5 tokens ($1 + 1 \times 10/4$). More generally, if the total of contributed tokens by others is n ($0 \leq n \leq 18$), player i's payoff is either $2 + n/4$ (when she keeps all tokens as the private good); $1 + (n + 1)/4$ (when she keeps one privately and contributes one as the public good); or $(n + 2)/4$ (when she contributes all tokens). Since

$$2 + n/4 > 1 + (n + 1)/4 > (n + 2)/4$$

for all n, to keep all tokens in her private account maximizes her payoff, which is the dominant strategy for i. Since everyone else is in the same situation as i, the only equilibrium strategy of the game is no contribution, and the equilibrium outcome is two tokens per player.

The fact that subjects do contribute in one-shot trials (stylized fact 1) is an anomaly because *prima facie* it contradicts standard game theory's prediction of unanimous free-riding. Economists initially modified environments in two ways to make the anomaly disappear. Since the environment of Marwell and Armes (1979) used a threshold production function, their experiment was formally turned into a coordination game with multiple Nash equilibria rather than MPD (see footnote 12 above). In order to avoid this, Kim and Walker (1984) and Isaac, McCue and Plott (1985) used linear production functions to make *free-riding* strictly dominant. Next, they introduced production functions with a declining marginal payoff, so that the incentives not to contribute would increase as the contribution rate increased.[12] With

---

[11] Strictly speaking, if the production function is of a 'threshold' type (i.e., $g(t) = 1$ if $t \geq t^*$ and $g(t) = 0$ otherwise), then the preference structure is not that of PD but of games of 'chicken', in which there are multiple Nash equilibria (Ledyard 1995: 144-146). Although Ledyard (1995: 174, Appendix) classifies a range of environments including some with threshold production functions as public goods environments, I use 'public goods' and MPD interchangeably.

[12] See Ledyard (1995: 136) for detail. Graphically this means that the 'Free-Ride' payoff line in Figure 4.1 gets steeper than the 'Cooperation' payoff line, making the payoff difference larger as the chooser moves towards the right.

these changes in environment, they still observed substantial contribution rates (68% and 50%, respectively) at the initial rounds.

4.2.2 Institution

Another important element in experimental economics is an institution (or mechanism), which mediates between behaviour and environment to yield an outcome. An institution aggregates information and coordinates actions by specifying who can communicate with whom, which actions are permitted at which timing and how often, etc. In a typical public goods experiment players make decisions simultaneously and privately (voluntary contribution mechanism without communication) in multiple rounds. Two important institutional factors in public goods experiments are *communication* and *repetition*, on which I will comment in turn.

Social psychologists Dawes, McTavish and Shaklee (1977) were, independently of economists and sociologists, interested in MPD, or what they called 'social dilemma' situations. In the 1970s they conducted experiments to investigate effects of communication upon cooperation rates in social dilemma situations. They designed a public goods environment with four communication conditions crossed with two payoff functions, one with a possibility to monetary loss and the other without.[13] The four communication conditions were distinguished as follows: (N) no communication was allowed and subjects worked silently for 10 minutes on an irrelevant task (e.g., estimating a percentage of people within a certain income range in Oregon); (I) subjects discussed the same irrelevant topic for 10 minutes before making their contribution; (C) subjects discussed the social dilemma decision for 10 minutes before making their decisions; and finally (C+V) subjects made a non-binding declaration of intended decision after the relevant discussion. The proportions of free-riders were 73% (67% in the no-loss condition) for (N), 65% (70%) for (I), 26% (30%) for (C), and 16% (42%) for (C+V). Since the effect of the loss/no-loss condition manipulation was insignificant and did not account for variations, Dawes and colleagues averaged the results and found (i) that the effect of relevant, but not irrelevant, communication is 'extremely significant' (stylized fact 3) and (ii) that the structured communication with the vote did not change the cooperation rate. Economists' studies with repetition (Isaac et al. 1985; Isaac and Walker 1988; 1991, see below) also confirmed (i), and observed that the

---

[13] In the terminology of this chapter (which follows Ledyard 1995), their environment was: $N = 8 \times 40$ (284 in total because some people didn't show up). $z_i = 0$, $g(t) = [(12/9.5)t]$ (where $t_i \in \{0, 9.50\}$, i.e., the choice was binary). Each individual's payoff is then $-t_i + 1/8\sum g(t)$. In the no-loss condition, individuals received 0 if $-t_i + g(t) < 0$. Note that the payoff structure is that of MPD in both cases.

cooperation-inducing effect of communication was even *enhanced* in repeated conditions, although repetition alone decreases cooperation. According to standard game theory, preplay communication is just 'cheap talk', which shouldn't make any difference to the contribution rate. Clearly this is not the case. I will discuss the role of communication in the next chapter.

If communication is the feature specific to psychologists' experimental design, *repetition* is an institutional factor that distinguishes economic experiments from the others:[14] while the design of both Marwell and Armes (1979) and Dawes et al. (1977) was one-shot, Kim and Walker (1984) and Isaac et al. (1985) introduced multiple-round design.[15] With this, both studies observed substantial cooperation rates at the first round, which however sharply declined toward the last round (8% and 9% respectively) (stylized fact 2). Before interpreting these results, some explanation as to why repetition was introduced by economists is needed. The first question is: *Why reduce contribution?* A chief goal of mechanism design—the modern paradigm of experimental economics—is to design institutions that will achieve a desirable outcome according to a performance criterion (a ranking of feasible outcomes) such as Pareto-efficiency. Since less contribution in the public goods environment means less Pareto-efficiency, it appears as though experimenters were trying to find an institution that performs poorly. Trying to decrease cooperation rate appears *prima facie* perverse on experimenters' part. One explanation is that experimental economists did this because they were looking for institutions that perform not only well but also reliably. From a mechanism designer's perspective, an outcome must be robust against relevant environmental and institutional variations. Because repetitive interaction is a prevalent feature of modern organizational life, it is understandable then that these experimenters introduced repetition in their public goods experiments.[16]

This reconstruction becomes more plausible by noticing that introducing repetition does not necessarily test game theory in a clearer manner than in one-shot games. First, since the subjects did not know the number of repetitions in Kim and Walker (1984) and Isaac et al. (1985), it is unclear whether the sharp decline of the

---

[14] Although Ledyard (1995) categorizes repetition as an environmental variable, it seems to be a natural extension of his characterization of institution to include repetition in institutional or design variables: An institution 'aggregates information and coordinate activities'; it 'specifies who should communicate with whom and how, as well as who should take various actions and when' (p.116). Repetition concerns 'how many times'. See footnote 23 below.

[15] In psychology, Kramer and Brewer (1984) introduced repetition.

[16] Although Ledyard (1995) is an excellent review of public goods experiments up to the time of his writing, he does not ask why repetition was introduced, presumably because he shares the mechanism designer's perspective (cf. Ledyard 1995: 173).

cooperation rates is confirming the theory. Standard game theory predicts that an infinitely or indefinitely repeated PD (i.e., a multiple-round game with a certain probability of ending at each round) has many Nash equilibria,[17] so the observed contribution patterns might be some of such equilibria.[18] On the other hand, if the subjects inferred (rather reasonably, one might think) that the experiment must end after a certain number of rounds (since, say, they were told that the experiment would last for one hour), then the experiment may have been interpreted as finitely repeated games.

Second, the test is not necessarily sharper in finitely repeated games. In order to let the subjects know that games are finite, Isaac, Walker and Thomas (1984) explicitly informed that there would be only 10 rounds, and observed 51% contribution at the initial round, which slowly declined to 19% at the last round. Game theory predicts that a finitely repeated PD game has only one unique equilibrium, namely, *defect* from the beginning until the end by everyone. In order to see this, let us represent a repeated two-person PD game using an *extensive form*, or a *game tree* (see Figure 4.2).

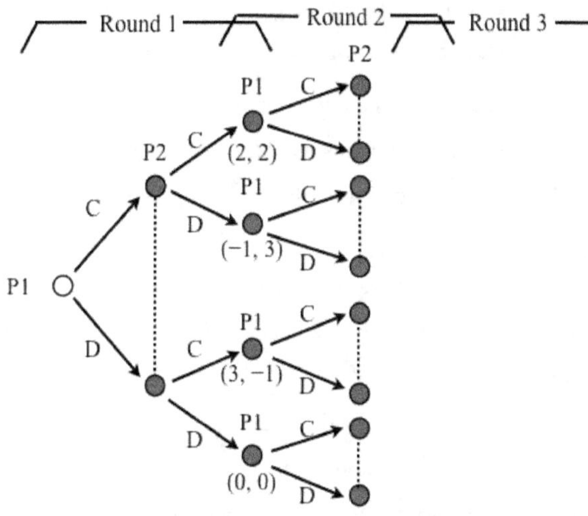

Figure 4.2: Extensive-form representation of the repeated PD (partial).

<hr>

[17] This is the result of the so-called *folk theorem*, or *general feasibility theorem*. See Hargreaves Heap and Varoufakis (2004:196-202) for discussion; for a formal proof see e.g., Myerson (1991: 331-337).

[18] Among many equilibrium strategies, the most famous and successful one in a two-person PD is called 'tit-for-tat' (Axerlod 1984), i.e., to cooperate initially, and after that simply replicate the other player's strategy in the previous round. While being a plausible strategy in a two-person PD in particular when you can build your reputation, tit-for-tat is not applicable to public goods games (MPDs) because a player has to respond to the total contributions from all the other players. If many players play tit-for-tat on the assumption that any non-full contributions are a defection by 'the others', then the contributions will quickly converge to zero.

Dots in Figure 4.2 are called decision *nodes*, where one player (specified by the label 'P1' or 'P2') makes choice. The first position of the game is represented as an open dot. Choices are represented with arrows with labels ('C' for *cooperate*, 'D' for *defect*). Payoffs for P1 and P2 are shown in brackets at the left and the right, respectively. This game has a mixed feature of *static* and *dynamic* games: it is static in the sense that at each round each player moves simultaneously, or without knowing the other player's move;[19] it is dynamic in the sense that at the second round (and onwards) each player moves after observing the other player's move(s) at the previous round(s). Game theory states that rational players follow the principle of *backward induction* in extensive-form games: any predictions that can be made about the strategies of players at the end of a game must be anticipated by the players earlier in the game. For instance, in the ten-round two-person PD game, the prediction about the outcome at the tenth round is (*defect, defect*) by dominance, whatever the history of the game is. So now let's consider what should players do in the ninth round. Again, (*defect, defect*) is the dominant strategy equilibrium, whatever the path taken previously is. And so on backwards, until the very first round, where (*defect, defect*) is the dominant strategy equilibrium. It is not rational to cooperate at the early rounds to establish the reputation as a cooperator, because decisions in the future are not path-dependent according to backward induction. The equilibrium thus reached is called a *subgame perfect Nash equilibrium*.[20] Defection by everyone from the beginning until the end is the subgame perfect Nash equilibrium of any finitely repeated (M)PD game. This is not confirmed by Isaac et al. (1984). In one sense, the result disconfirms game theory more clearly than in the case of infinitely or indefinitely repeated games, because the prediction is made narrower. However, repetition itself introduces additional factors, making it difficult to see what exactly is being tested. Is it the dominant strategy, backward induction, subgame perfection, or some combination of these, that are not followed by actual human players? Furthermore, Kreps, Milgrom, Roberts and Wilson (1982) showed that if there is incomplete information in the sense that the players are unsure about each other's rationality, then cooperation until near the final round is predicted. Data seem to be consistent with this possibility, but we need to find a way to assess the degree of completeness of information before concluding that incomplete information is the main

---

[19] The fact that P2 does not know P1's actual move is represented by the dashed line ('information-set') which joins nodes.

[20] Selten (1965) formally defined this equilibrium concept for extensive-form games. A *subgame* is the continuation game from a singleton node (i.e., a node which has no other nodes in its information set) to the end nodes which follow from that node. *Subgame perfection* is the idea that players will actually play their equilibrium strategy if a subgame is reached.

cause of the cooperative pattern we observe. The one-shot design is superior in avoiding these complication. The upshot is that experimental economists' use of repetition is not motivated by their willingness to test game theory; rather, the point of their experiments seem to be finding conditions under which game theoretic predictions are good approximations.

This brings us to the second question regarding experimental economists' design strategy: *Why do they think that repetition works?* There is nothing in game theory that tells experimenters that repetition would *reduce* contribution, because game theory predicts zero contribution in *both* one-shot *and* finitely repeated MPD. Although experimental economists believed that repetition would make the outcome closer to the prediction of game theory (i.e., zero), this belief therefore must have come from some non-theoretical hunch that repeating games would reduce contribution by some mechanisms, e.g., by giving subjects a chance to get used to the condition, correct errors, or learn what the rational strategy to choose is.[21]

4.2.3 Game Theory as a Model of Behaviour

The two points above make clear the role of game theory in economic experiments: first, game theory is used as a predictive model of individual behaviour for designing institutions that work in different environments;[22] since a behavioural model with formal properties is a precious source of tractability and predictability, and game theory is quite unique in this respect in social science, experimenters try to find out the 'right' environmental and institutional conditions under which game theory works. Isaac et al. (1985) note that their experiment's purpose is 'to explore the behavior of groups within a set of conditions where [they] expected the traditional model would work with reasonable accuracy' (cited in Ledyard 1995, 134): but their interest seems to be in exploring 'a set of conditions' rather than in exploring the behaviour of people itself. Perhaps experimental economists had personal motivations to prove the truth of game theory which is so dear to them, but their design suggests that such parochial motivation could be only part of the whole story. Second, game theory is not the only resource available in mechanism design, and experimenters modify both environments and institutions based on their informal hunches, experimental data, computer simulations,

---

[21] Plott (1996) and Binmore (1999) explicitly argue for the idea that players learn through trial-and-error. Cubitt, Starmer and Sugden (2001) criticize the argument from learning in the context of EUT.

[22] The distinction between environment and institution in this sentence is conceptual rather than practical; some environmental factors (such as the number of participants and monetary rewards) can be part of design in artificial contexts such as auction design, while some institutional factors (such as how often interactions can be made) may have to be taken as given in less artificial contexts such as designing organizational structures.

etc.[23] The mechanism design perspective of experimental economists makes it difficult to compare their results with those from the experiments designed by other social scientists with different backgrounds, and to draw clear-cut conclusions relevant to game theory from the public goods experiments conducted in the 70s and 80s. That said, at least one thing is clear: the standard prediction of game theory in public goods experiments (zero contribution) has never been confirmed: 'Even the most fervent economic experimentalist cannot force rates of contribution much below 10 percent' (Ledyard (1995: 172) referring to Isaac et al. 1985).[24] In the next section, I will review possible explanations of this and other anomalies from a preference measurement point of view.

4.3 Measuring Preferences with Game Theory

Instead of attempting to make an exhaustive list of the hypotheses that have been devised to explain the cooperation anomalies, I will focus on one prominent type of explanatory strategy, namely, 'payoff respecification'. There are several related methodological concerns regarding this strategy. I will evaluate two arguments, one about tautology and the other about dilemma.

4.3.1 Is Game Theory a Tautology?

The 'payoff respecification' approach tries to respecify or refine the 'true' payoff structure of a game so that the observed anomalies will be the equilibrium (or one of the equilibria) of the game thus re-defined. The intuition behind this strategy is that the prediction of game theory appears falsified only because the analyst is using the wrong game to represent a given situation. In the literature of experimental economics, an individual i's preference ordering is represented as a utility function such as $U_i(x_i, y) = px_i + y$, that is, a linear function of i's personal payoff in money (private good plus public good).[25] This implies that what the individual cares about is only her monetary reward. This is however often presupposed, rather than argued for based on sound evidence. It is not only possible, but also intuitively more plausible to think that i cares

---

[23] Roth (2002) illustrates this point clearly with his own experience of labour market design. He made sure that an employer-employee matching mechanism works by using both experimentation and computation, when *none* of the theorems concerning simple matching market is guaranteed because of the existence of complementarity.

[24] Of course, this is the same as to say that the prediction of game theory is guaranteed almost 90% in the most favourable conditions, as Ledyard points out.

[25] Although y refers to the whole production of a public good, this matters only in so far as increasing i's own income.

about non-monetary rewards such as psychological pain and pleasure. For concreteness, consider the two-person PD represented in Table 4.1. In outcomes where she confessed, Prisoner 1 may feel some psychological distress from not trusting her partner. Table 4.2 represents a game with a PD-type material payoff structure (call it a *PD-material game*) played by two such 'conscience-sensitive' players.[26]

Table 4.2: A payoff respecification of the Prisoner's Dilemma

Player 2

		cooperate	*defect*
Player 1	*cooperate*	2, 2	−1, 3−x
	defect	3−x, −1	0−x, 0−x

If $x > 1$, *cooperate* dominates *defect*, making (*cooperate, cooperate*) as the unique Nash equilibrium. In a multiple-person version, players may feel some such psychological distress when playing *free-ride* if more than a certain number of other players are playing *cooperate*. Then the FR curve in Figure 4.1 may become less steep and intersect with the C curve at some point, beyond which *cooperate* dominates *free-ride*. In what follows I will discuss some preliminary issues concerning the nature and legitimacy of the 'respecification' approach.

One immediate worry is whether this explanatory strategy makes game theory irrefutable, thus empirically empty. This is not the case, but Binmore (1994: 102-115) contends that game theory is indeed a tautology, and that there is nothing to worry about it. Although it is less controversial to say that the theoretical 'core' of game theory is tautological (after all, all theorems must be derived from relevant axioms), Binmore claims that game theory applied in studies of strategic interactions among rational people (as well as evolutionary biology) is a tautology. His argument for this claim is this:

(1) When applying game theory to real situations, the theorist first needs to identify players' preferences over outcomes.

(2) Players' preferences are inferred solely from their choice behaviour using the principle of revealed preference.

---

[26] This modification is from Binmore (1994: 113, Figure 2.3 (b)). Many other variations with different solutions are possible with appropriate psychological assumptions.

(3) Preference theory does not make any psychological assumptions regarding players' motives; its primitive concept is choice behaviour, not preference (or utility as its mathematical expression).

(4) Therefore, game theory's predictions (such as (*defect, defect*) in PD) are nothing but a derivation from (or tautology of) prior information regarding players choice behaviour.[27]

Let us examine each premise in turn. Premise 1 is unproblematically true. I will first discuss Premise 3 and then Premise 2.

Premise 3 is false: first compare preference theory with EUT. In chapter 2, we have seen that EUT has subjective probabilities (beliefs) and vNM utilities (desires) as its primitives. Although it is possible to insist that EUT is a pure behavioural theory (as some economists do), this is inconsistent with practitioners' use of EUT as a *subjective* theory of decision making. The specific ways in which EUT's axioms have been modified suggest that its requirement of choice consistency is not merely formal but has some implicit assumptions regarding how people reason and feel. The independence axiom was abandoned based on the former consideration (that people's reasoning is valid without it), while regret theory abandoned the transitivity axiom based on the latter (that people's feeling of regret/rejoice is realistic enough to make the transitivity axiom of EUT inapplicable). Essentially the same thing can be said concerning preference theory. Although preference theory as a formal theory does not presuppose that subjective probabilities and preferences are operationalized in terms of choice, *when applied to human behaviour*, it presupposes *both* agent's subjective beliefs *and* ordinal preferences (Hausman 2000). First, just like decision theory is incomplete without subjective individuation of options, preference theory also cannot get started without some assumptions about an agent's subjective framing of the choice situation she faces (what are the available and feasible options, etc.). Second, preferences are defined over options thus specified. In other words, preference theory, when applied to human behaviour, implicitly assumes the functional relevance of theoretical constructs such as beliefs (subjective framing of options) and desires (ordinal preferences over these options). Thus the concept of 'choice behaviour' is not primitive. It cannot be a purely behavioural concept.

---

[27] Although Binmore uses 'Revealed Preference Theory' to mean both the principle of revealed preference and preference theory as a whole, I distinguished these to avoid ambiguity. See my discussion of preference theory in chapter 1.

Now let us look at Premise 2, which states that specifications of people's preferences over outcomes are done solely via the principle of revealed preference. In game theory this is not true. In experimental games, players' choices over different outcomes do not simply 'reveal' the players' preferences over outcomes; the choices are the result of their preferences *plus* their strategic reasoning, which is specified by the principles of rational play such as best-reply strategies, backward induction, etc. That is, in experimental games the concept of preference is usually operationalized using both preference theory *and* game theory.

In sum, Premises 2 and 3 are both false, and therefore Conclusion 4 does not follow. Game theory applied to people's strategic interactions is not a tautology. As in the case of EUT, game theorists and experimentalists do not treat the principles of rational play as mere formalism; as we will see below, these principles are sometimes regarded as psychological hypotheses concerning the way people reason strategically. Of course, it is neither unusual nor illegitimate to use a rational principle just to model some aspect of players' behaviour without assuming the corresponding mental operation. In an extreme case, for example, one can use the principle of dominance reasoning in order to behaviourally model a player's 'irrationality' in the sense of taking a particular course of action regardless of what other players do where she should change her action strategically (see Kreps 1990: 480-482). This modelling practice suggests one important aspect of game theory, i.e., convenient mathematics to model people's behaviour, but at the same time, it also shows game theory's fundamental commitment to the idea that people (sufficiently or not) respond strategically to others' perceived action. Although how psychologically 'realistic' a particular game-theoretic model is intended to be must be judged case by case (some are surely psychologically unrealistic in hypothesizing demanding computational processes), it seems thus undeniable that game theory commits itself to the reality of strategic thinking as a psychological process.[28] Binmore (1994: 106-107) tries to gloss over the difference between game theory and preference theory by pointing out that dominance reasoning is just a 'pale shadow' of Savage's (1954) sure thing principle (i.e., the independence axiom of EUT). This is misleading because dominance reasoning is the least strategic principle in game theory (you do not have to take the others' perspectives); there are other important principles that are distinctly game theoretic. In particular, the role of beliefs in game theory is not reducible to that in EUT. Even if it were, EUT in itself

---

[28] An alternative interpretation of game theory is that Nash play emerged as a result of repeated interactions in the course of our evolution. Evidence does not seem to support such interpretation. See section 4.3.3 below.

does not reduce beliefs to choice behaviour. The argument from tautology is just rhetoric appealing to formalism of game theory. Its appeal disappears once we carefully look at how the theory is used in practice.[29]

The fact that game theory is always coupled with preference theory in application does not make game theory a tautology, but instead makes its test rather difficult, because logically speaking anomalies imply that either game theory or preference theory (or both) is wrong. Perhaps what Binmore (1994) means by the tautology argument is that game theory is immune from empirical refutation because preference theory takes care of anomalies. This is too optimistic considering the fact that preference theory itself is full of anomalies when tested alone (as EUT or its variants), as we have seen in the previous chapters. Furthermore, Binmore does not provide any well-motivated reason why we shouldn't blame game theory in the face of anomalies. Even though it is difficult to test game theory and preference theory 'one at a time', this is no excuse to insulate game theory from severe tests.

Should we, then, conclude from Binmore's reluctance to put game theory under severe test that the 'payoff respecification' approach is *ad hoc*? More specifically, is the approach not in line with the rational choice research programme? The respecification approach is not necessarily *ad hoc* in this sense, because preference theory leaves agents' goals completely open. So incorporating non-monetary rewards into payoffs is not only permissible but a natural move to make preference theory more generally applicable to many situations where money is not (the only thing) at stake. Moreover, the assumption that people care only about their own material gains all the time (the selfish axiom) is intuitively implausible to most of the people. Since first modifying empirically implausible assumptions is a normal strategy in science, the payoff respecification approach is legitimate within the rational choice programme. In other words, the real challenge to this approach does not come from Lakatosian methodological criteria of appraisal. Rather, the challenge is to come up with precise and accurate measurement methods of preferences. First, experimentalists have to measure people's preferences (what they really care about, and how much) relying on both game theory and preference theory. This requires experimentalists to make sure

---

[29] A related point is made by Grüne-Yanoff and Schweinzer (2008), who suggest that informal stories (such as the one about the two prisoners illustrated in section 4.1) are necessary in applying game theory to model real-life strategic situations. That is, formal theory is just part of the entire practice of applying game theory to analyze real humans' interactions. At a more general level, some philosophers (e.g. Machamer, Darden and Craver 2000) have argued that in practice biologists and neuroscientists rely on hypotheses about 'causal mechanisms', which may not necessarily be represented as formal theory (I will examine this idea in chapter 6). My point is that game theory also has such hypotheses about how people reason.

that the assumptions of game theory used are not too cognitively demanding (dominance reasoning appears to be a good assumption in this sense). Second, an individual may have different and conflicting preferences. The multiple-self model examined in chapter 3 suggests that final 'revealed' preferences of an individual may be constructed with multiple sets of preferences within the individual. If this is the case, experimentalists need to explicitly model such underlying compositions of preferences. Third, different individuals may have different preferences. That is, individuals may be categorized into different types according to their preferences. Finally, subjects in experiments may make mistakes, failing to 'reveal' their true preferences. We will see these problems in concrete contexts below. I will start from a simple model.

4.3.2 Altruism and its Refutation

Altruism is a relatively simple type of non-monetary preference, but it is important to distinguish two types of altruism. Let us first consider so called 'pure' altruism. Table 4.3 illustrates this idea in a PD-material game.[30]

Table 4.3: PD-material game played by pure altruists

Player 2

		cooperate	defect
Player 1	cooperate	$2+2y,\ 2+2y$	$-1+3y,\ 3-1y$
	defect	$3-1y,\ -1+3y$	$0,\ 0$

The payoffs in the matrix show that each player cares about not only her money but the other's as well (with some parameter y) because each sympathizes with the other.[31] When altruism is sufficiently large, (*cooperate, cooperate*) can be a Nash equilibrium (when $1/3 < y < 1/3$ the game becomes a coordination game with mixed motives, i.e., Stag Hunt where (*cooperate, cooperate*) is one Nash equilibrium and (*defect, defect*) the other; when $y > 1/3$, (*cooperate, cooperate*) is the dominant equilibrium).

A distinct type of altruism, sometimes called 'impure' altruism, is a preference for the *act* of cooperating, not necessarily the *result* of that act (i.e., others becoming

---

[30] This is also taken from Binmore (1994: 113), with a slight modification to make it consistent with the game of Figure 1.
[31] This payoff respecification is possible without sympathy if, for example, P1 and P2 are a couple who try to maximize their common household income. In such case $y = 1$, unless one cares about who earned the money.

better off) (Andreoni 1990). Table 4.4 illustrates a PD-material game played by impure altruists with a preference for a 'warm glow'.

Table 4.4: PD-material game played by warm-glow altruists

Player 2

		cooperate	defect
Player 1	cooperate	$2+z, 2+z$	$-1+z, 3$
	defect	$3, -1+z$	$0, 0$

If the 'warm glow' each player takes from the act of cooperation is sufficiently large (in this example if $z > 1$), then (*cooperate*, *cooperate*) can be a dominant equilibrium.

Although these are both models of altruism and therefore make similar predictions (e.g., that people will choose *cooperate* in PD material games), the two models can make distinct predictions. An important point is that a 'warm glow' is supposed to be felt from an act of giving, cooperation, contribution, etc., in itself. So others' payoffs or behaviours should not directly affect an impure altruist's behaviour. That is, her contributions should be *unconditional* on others' contributions. By contrast, pure altruism is *conditional*. This is for two reasons. First, a pure altruist cares about others' material gains, rather than taking pleasure from the act of contributing to others' material gains. Second, however, she also cares about her own material gains.[32] The standard assumption about a pure altruist is that her utility be modelled as a convex combination of the group money and her own money, meaning that her own monetary gains become more important as others' money increase, and vice versa (in consumer theory this is assumed for preferences for ordinary consumption bundles such as coffee and cake: see Figure 4.1). Because of these reasons, the pure altruist should *reduce* her contributions if others contribute a lot (Sugden 1982; see also Margolis 1982).[33]

It is difficult to test these hypotheses in standard public goods experiments. A first challenge is to differentiate altruistic predictions from the prediction of the 'error' hypothesis, which states that non-zero contributions are due to decision errors, mistakes, or confusions. This hypothesis implies that people will learn to play rationally from

---

[32] One might object to calling her a 'pure' altruist for this reason. Although it is possible to model a truly pure altruist who does not care at all about her own material gains with adjusting parameters, social scientists agree that such a model is empirically very implausible. I keep using the term 'pure' altruism to distinguish it from a preference for a warm glow.

[33] Some field data are inconsistent with this implication of pure altruism models. Abrams and Schmitz (1978; 1984) and Clotfelter (1985), for instance, suggest that the government's funding of public goods doesn't change the rate of voluntary provisions very much (5-28%). Sugden (1982) makes the same point referring to the data on the British Lifeboat Service, which is entirely funded through public donations. Since these data are to a large extent consistent with the main findings from laboratory experiments which will be discussed below, I shall not mention field data any further.

experience, which appears to be consistent with stylized fact 2, i.e., that the contributions decrease towards the end of a repeated MPD game. The predictions of altruistic models are difficult to differentiate from that made by the error hypothesis. Since (i) the standard prediction is zero contribution and (ii) all deviations from this prediction is in the same direction (positive contributions), the data that can be explained by altruistic preference models can be explained by the error hypothesis as well. Saijo and Nakamura (1995) tried to differentiate these hypotheses with a unique modification to the standard repeated public goods experiment.[34] In one condition, they changed the production function of the public good such that the strategy 'contributing all tokens to the public good' strictly dominates, i.e., this maximizes own payoffs regardless how much others contribute. Specifically, this was done by increasing the return from one token of investment in the public account ('marginal per capita return', or MPCR) above 1. They used MPCR = 1/0.7 (>1) for this condition, and MPCR = 0.7 (<1) for a control condition.[35] Notice that when MPCR >1, according to the standard game theory, the 'mistake' is not to deviate from zero contribution, but to deviate from *full* contributions. Somewhat surprisingly, in this 'inverted' public goods condition, Saijo and Nakamura observed stable contributions throughout the whole game but far from the 100% equilibrium level (47-85%). An even more surprising finding was that the mean non-contribution level in this condition was significantly *higher* than that in the control condition (MPCR = 0.7). That is, the difference between the observed strategy profile and the dominant equilibrium profile in the 'inverted' condition was bigger than the difference between them in the standard condition.

Saijo and Nakamura inferred that this data pattern refuted altruism. Their inference seems to be this: in the normal condition, there is a cost or risk to contribute even to an altruist (own money might decrease). Since the 'inverted' condition removes this cost or risk completely, the altruist should contribute more. However, the data suggests the opposite pattern. Hence, there are few altruists among the subjects, if at all. This inference, however, is not valid. First, an impure altruist may *reduce* her contributions in the inverted condition because she is unable to feel a warm glow any more when contribution is simply profitable to everyone. The change in the payoff

---

[34] The subjects are Japanese students (mixture of economics major and others) ($N=7\times16$). The basic design was the same as Isaac and Walker's (1988). I won't discuss another condition pair they introduced in order to see the effect of information (i.e. rough table vs. detailed table of payoffs) since it is less relevant for our purposes.

[35] Regarding the choice of these particular values, the authors note that the high marginal return (0.7) was chosen 'to be the reciprocal of the low marginal return for symmetry' but that there is no 'theoretical basis' for the fact that the high return is about double the low return (Saijo and Nakamura 1995: 539, fn. 6).

structure may change the meaning of an action. Second, while the two conditions may cause different degrees of confusion or error, this is not controlled for. Saijo and Nakamura (1995) conducted *post hoc* surveys with the subjects (interviews and questionnaires), and concluded based on the analysis of these data that the subjects understood the payoff structures of the games with both conditions very well. Although this partially replies to the second criticism, the first point remains unanswered.[36]

Palfrey and Prisbrey (1997) devised a new design to explicitly test the hypotheses of pure altruism, warm glow, and error. Although I cannot describe their rather complicated experimental design and statistical models in full detail here, the main ideas underlying the experiment are relatively simple and worth a discussion. Their reasoning can be reconstructed as follows: the error hypothesis is always a possibility in the standard design because the prediction of game theory is too specific, making any deviations from the prediction interpretable as errors. Saijo and Nakamura's (1995) design reversed the prediction from zero to full contributions, but still this gives the same room for the error hypothesis. So first the design must narrow the range of data interpretable as 'errors'. Second, the predictions of two models of altruism (pure and impure) must be differentiated. For these purposes, manipulating only MPCR is inadequate: we need to manipulate more variables. So they specified an individual i's monetary payoff as follows:

$$r_i(z_i - t_i) + V \sum_j t_j$$

where r_i is the marginal value of the private good and V is the marginal value of the public good (z_i is i's endowment and t_i is i's contribution to the public good, as in section 4.2.1). Normally, $r_i = 1$ and $V < 1$, so that zero contribution becomes i's dominant strategy. Saijo and Nakamura made $V > 1$ to make full contributions as her dominant strategy. This is understandable because for testing the prediction of standard game theory, the only relevant variable is V/r_i (i.e., MPCR), which determines the dominant strategy (i.e., zero contribution if MPCR<1; full contribution if MPCR>1). However, Palfrey and Prisbrey (1997) reasoned that manipulating both r_i *and* V was the key to separate the predictions of pure and impure altruism. Specifically, they inferred as follows: (i) i has a pure altruistic motivation if her contributions increase with V,

---

[36] Although evidence was not unambiguous, Saijo and Nakamura (1995), based on the contents analysis of the interviews, propose a hypothesis that subjects are 'spiteful', i.e., that they primarily care about the *ranking* among subjects. They also speculate that Japanese may be more 'spiteful' than e.g. Americans are. See Brunton, Hasan and Mestelman (2001) for a similar experiment in Canada.

other factors held constant; and (ii) i has a warm-glow motivation if her contributions increase with an increase in $(r_i - V)$, other factors held constant.[37] The rationale for (i) is that a pure altruist primarily cares about the monetary gains to others, which increase with V. The rationale for (ii) is that an impure altruist gains a warm glow solely from the act of contribution (notice that these rationales are consistent with my characterization of each model above). Palfrey and Prisbrey then manipulated these variables, and estimated the significance of each variable to the contribution level.[38] Using different variations of the probit model (a standard way to measure the probability of contribution as a function of the different treatment variables), they reached the following conclusions: pure altruism is insignificant, while both errors and impure altruism are small but significant.

From a methodological point of view, two things need to be mentioned. First, the design by Palfrey and Prisbrey (1997) separated two types of altruism in an operationally meaningful way, which was not possible before. Second, however, their methodology has a limit. Notice that Palfrey and Prisbrey (1997) adopted a standard economic approach, i.e., (i) to make different models based on theory (game theory plus altruism), (ii) to compute comparative statistics predictions based on these models, and then (iii) to compare these predictions using standard hypothesis tests (such as the probit model). Ledyard (1995: 163) suggests that in many cases this methodology 'circumvents the need to measure utility functions [...] directly because the indirect predictions are independent of the precise details of those functions', referring to Palfrey and Rosenthal's (1991) study that employed the same economic approach to test EUT using public goods experiment. This may be a virtue in experiments such as Palfrey and Rosenthal's (1991), but the same point does not apply to Palfrey and Prisbrey (1997) because the latter are interested in the precise details of utility functions (whether they are altruistic or not, pure or impure). Therefore a more direct measurement of utility functions seems to be needed.[39]

Fischbacher, Gächter and Fehr (2001) recently designed a simpler but sharper experiment. Instead of manipulating variables such as r_i and V, they invented a more

---

[37] More specifically, their simple model assumes that an impure altruist has the following decision rule R: *contribute* if $(r_i - V) < g$; *keep* if $(r_i - V) > g$; *contribute* or *keep* if $(r_i - V) = g$, where g is a positive number called the *warm-glow effect*. The assumption of the standard model is $g = 0$.

[38] They varied r_i across subjects and across rounds for the same subject. The value of r_i was private information.

[39] Whether a measurement of utility functions is 'direct' or 'indirect' is a matter of degree, since neither subjective probabilities nor vNM is directly observable, as argued in chapter 2.

direct method to elicit preferences from subjects' choices.[40] First, Fischbacher et al. did not adopt a repeated experimental design, in contrast to most experimental economists performing public goods experiments (see section 4.2.2). This is an improvement in terms of the measurement of preferences, because the considerations of subjects' reasoning inevitable in a repetitive design (backward induction, reputation building, etc.) are controlled for, and only a relatively unproblematic principle (dominance) is presupposed. Second, in addition to normal decisions of how much to contribute to the public good, the subjects were asked to make *conditional* decisions concerning their own contribution level given various levels of contributions from other players. This was done by asking each subject to make her *decision schedule* for 21 different average contribution levels of the others (from 0/20 to 20/20) by filling in the 'Contribution Table'. Both types of decisions (standard and conditional) were made privately. In order to give the subjects monetary incentive to take both types of decisions seriously, the experimenters devised a random mechanism that picked up one decision per player, according to which the actual payment was made.[41] Fischbacher et al. were interested particularly in how subjects made conditional decisions. The standard assumptions of game theory (rational play plus selfish preference) predict that all subjects will choose zero contribution no matter what the average contribution levels of others are. This is the strictly dominant strategy (see the Schelling diagram in Figure 4.1). Instead of confirming this prediction, the data show that some subjects are *conditional* cooperators, that is, those subjects' contributions increased (weakly monotonistically) as the average contribution level of others increased. About 50% of the subjects were such conditional cooperators. At the same time, about 30% of the subjects behaved consistently with the standard prediction, i.e., they did not contribute anything regardless of the average contribution levels of others (free-riders). 14% of the subjects displayed 'hump-shaped' contributions, i.e., their contribution rate increased until the 50% contribution level by others (10 tokens), beyond which level their contributions steadily declined. Finally, a couple of subjects showed 'other patterns', i.e., these were difficult to interpret (see Figure 4.3 for the overall result). Fischbacher and Gächter (2006) replicated this experiment and obtained very similar data (55% conditional contributors; 23% free-riders; 12% hump-shaped contributors; 10% others).

---

[40] Their environment was: $N = 4 \times 11$ (11 groups of 4 university students: no economic majors). $z_i = 20$, $g(t) = 0.4\sum[j=1\rightarrow4]t_j$. Each individual's payoff in token is then $20 - t_i + 0.4 \sum[j=1\rightarrow4]t_j$. This is the standard public goods environment where zero contribution from all subjects is the dominant equilibrium.

[41] For each subject, the probability of the conditional decision being picked up was 1/4, which was common knowledge. The monetary incentive was relatively high: on average subjects earned 27.6 Swiss Franc (about $21 at the time of the experiment).

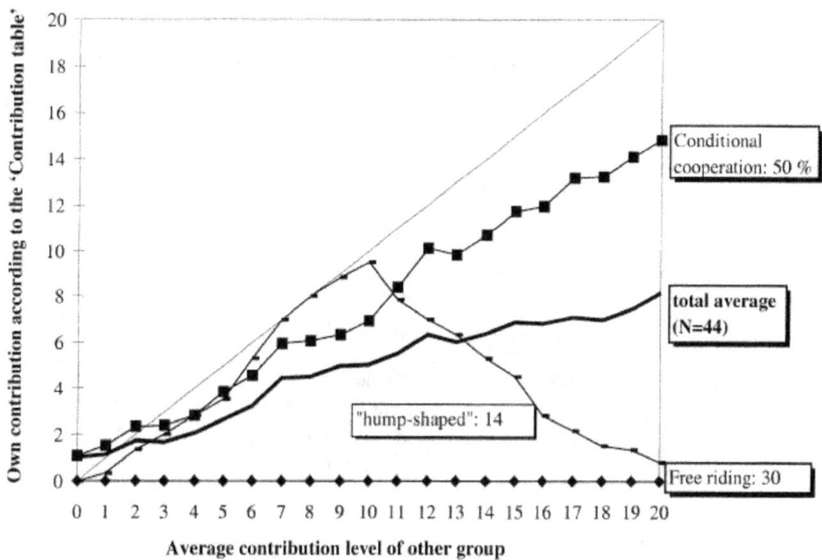

Figure 4.3: Subjective Heterogeneity in a Public Goods Game (from Fischbacher et al. 2001: 400).

Figure 4.3 shows the average own contribution level for each average contribution level of other members. The diagonal line indicates the level of perfectly conditional cooperation (see also Fischbacher and Gächter 2006: 12). The first finding of this experiment (and of Fischbacher and Gächter 2006) is that subjects are *heterogeneous*, which is clear from the data. This is one step forward from Palfrey and Prisbrey (1997), who assumed (in one model) but did not explicitly measure heterogeneity. Given this clear measurement of heterogeneity, our initial question—*Are people altruistic?*—needs to be qualified. Now the relevant question is: *How many are altruistic?* The second finding of Fischbacher et al. (2001) is that the answer to this qualified question seems to be: not so many. First, the data is inconsistent with impure altruism, or the warm-glow model, which implies that contributions be *unconditional*. About the half of the subjects are *conditional* cooperators, who give more if others give more. Second, while the 'hump-shaped' behaviour may be interpreted as motivated by pure altruism with convexity, they are at most 14% (Fischbacher et al. are apparently unaware of this possibility). In sum, altruism (pure or impure) does not explain most subjects' choices.

4.3.3 The Argument from Unnatural Habitat: Is There A Dilemma?

Before considering the implications of subjects' heterogeneity and the conditional nature of cooperation, we must answer one methodological question: Did Fischbacher et al.'s (2001) experiment control for the error hypothesis? Some proponents of the error hypothesis criticize a one-shot design such as Fischbacher et al.'s as not only failing to control for errors but introducing a further problem.[42] Before evaluating this critique, a clarification of the meaning of 'one-shot' is due (see also Woodward 2008: 652, fn. 4).

Table 4.5: (M)PD experiments with 2 by 2 designs.

| | | **Playing against:** | |
		the same player(s)	different players
Number	R = 1	'one-off' (*defect*)	n/a
of rounds	R > 1	'repeated' (*defect* if finite; indeterminate if infinite or indefinite)	'one-shot' (*defect*)
(R)			

Table 4.5 shows three (M)PD experimental designs. The standard predictions are shown in the brackets. The problem of the 'repeated' design I have already noted (in 4.2.2) is that the standard prediction is not clearly testable (i) because an infinitely or indefinitely repeated (M)PD game has many Nash equilibria, and (ii) because a finitely repeated (M)PD game has a unique prediction (zero cooperation) but brings into test a further assumption regarding strategic reasoning (backward induction). Playing a game only once ('one-off') eliminates these problems, but leaves room for the possibility that subjects make errors (deliberation errors such as clicking the wrong icon, or strategic errors such as not understanding dominance). Usually these errors are controlled for by familiarizing subjects with experimental facilities and game structures, running some exercise sessions. Another way of avoiding this is to perform a 'stationary replication' (i.e., repeating an experiment in the same condition). Camerer and Fehr (2004: 65) suggest that this can be achieved by repeating the game while changing the group composition (in MPD) or matching different players (in two-person PD) from round to round so that no player ever meets another player more than once. I shall call this design 'one-shot' and distinguish it from both the 'repeated' design and the 'one-off' design.[43]

---

[42] This debate over the one-shot design took place over the game-theoretic experimental/anthropological studies of the subjects from 15 small-scale societies (Henrich et al. 2004), which employed the one-shot design. Binmore (2005) and Larry Samuelson (2005) criticize the one-shot design in commenting on the book. Camerer and Fehr (2004) contained in Henrich et al. (2004) and Gintis (2006), another author of the book, defend the one-shot design against the Binmore-Samuelson critique. Since my focus is on methodology, I will mainly discuss Woodward (2008), without going into the details of the evolutionary aspects of the debate.

[43] Although the expressions 'one-off' and 'one-shot' do not have semantic differences as suggested here, I use these just as labels for notational convenience.

The following argument is a critique of both the 'one-shot' design and the 'one-off' design.

The argument, which I call 'the argument from the unnatural habitat' (following Camerer and Fehr 2004), is this:

(1) People inhabit in society where most real life interactions are of repeated-type (*the frequency of repetition claim*).

(2) Because of (1), when people play a one-shot or one-off game in the laboratory, either

    (i) they make mistakes, confused by the unnatural context (*the mistake hypothesis*); or

    (ii) they import cooperative behaviour, which is a rational strategy in the real life repeated interactions (*the importation hypothesis*).

(3) Therefore, the one-shot and one-off designs cannot exclude the possibility that subjects cooperate because of mistakes or importation.

I have already noted that the repetition claim (Premise 1) was implicit in experimental economists' use of repetition (section 4.2.2). Now this claim is employed explicitly as a reason why one-shot experiments increase the chance of mistakes or cause importation. Although it is possible to criticize Premise 1 by pointing out that one-shot type interactions are fairly common in our society (e.g. tipping behaviour at a city you would never visit again), this does not establish that repeated interactions are more frequent than one-shot ones. We interact with strangers whom we will never meet again quite often, but at the same time we interact with our family members, friends and business partners repeatedly. In any case, it seems possible to claim for Premise 2 without definitively solving the question of relative frequency, since the weaker and more plausible claim that repeated interactions with the same people are common in real life seems to be sufficient. So let us accept this weaker version of Premise 1 and examine Premise 2.

Premise 2 is essentially the claim that people are not good at adjusting their behaviour in response to structural changes of strategic situations. Specifically, it suggests two possibilities, (i) mistakes by confusion, and (ii) inflexible importation. I will examine them in turn. First, there is evidence which speaks strongly against the mistake hypothesis regardless of whether mistakes are due to deliberation errors or reasoning errors. Andreoni (1988) designed a repeated public goods experiment with two ten-round games. The first game was played as usual, but the second one was a 'surprise', meaning that the subjects were not told that there would be the second game after the last round of the first game. Andreoni observed the usual pattern in the first game (steady decline of contribution levels), but he also observed an increase of the contribution level at the first round of the second, 'surprise' game (similar to the initial levels in the first set). The mistake hypothesis implies that people will learn to play rationally (i.e., zero contribution) by repeating the game, but the observed increase of the initial cooperation level (so called the 'restart effect') is inconsistent with this implication. Therefore, the mistake hypothesis is false.

Some evidence casts doubt on the second possibility, the importation hypothesis, as well. In public goods experiments (MPD), contributions decline over time irrespective of whether subjects stay together in the same group or form a new group each time (see Camerer and Fehr 2004: 66), but in two-person PD experiments, subjects cooperate more in the 'repeated' condition (i.e., matched with the same player) than in the 'one-shot' condition (i.e., matched with a different player each time), suggesting that they understand the strategic differences between the two conditions and respond to such differences (Andreoni and Miller 1993). Evidence from different types of two-person games suggests also that people can differentiate 'one-off' and 'repeated' games (see Fehr and Fischbacher 2003 for Ultimatum Games; Camerer, Chong and Weigelt 2002 for Trust Games). In sum, even if the unproblematic version of Premise 1 is accepted, Premise 2 is unlikely to hold empirically. Therefore, Conclusion 4 does not follow. That is, the one-off and one-shot design may measure subjects' preferences while controlling for mistakes and importation.

With a little twist to the argument from unnatural habitat, Woodward (2008) challenges the possibility of measuring subjects' preferences with the one-off or one-shot design. His argument is put in the form of a dilemma, as follows:

(1) There are only two logical possibilities to explain the cooperation in one-off and one-shot PD games:
   (i) People *do* import rational cooperative behaviour from their real life to experiments in the lab.
   (ii) People *do not*.
(2) On the one hand, if (i) is the case, the preference measurement in one-off and one-shot experiments is confounded with importation. (Indeed, the cooperation in one-shot PD games we observe will be explained by selfish preference plus importation.)

(3) On the other hand, if (ii) is the case, this means that one-off and one-shot experiments cannot measure people's preferences outside the lab.

(4) Therefore, in either case, one-off and one-shot experiments cannot be used to measure people's true preferences.

Although Woodward (2008) agrees to the empirical critique against the unnatural habitat argument above, his point is that *to the extent that the empirical critique is successful*, i.e., to the extent that importation does not happen, one-off or one-shot laboratory experiments cannot measure people's preferences in real life interactions. Woodward paraphrases the same point as the lack of 'external validity'—i.e., inferences based upon experimental evidence from the lab cannot be exported to explain observations outside the lab because importation does not happen. Woodward also explains his point in terms of the lack of 'robustness'—i.e., phenomena constructed inside the lab are not stable across different conditions, in particular under naturally occurring conditions. Yet another way of making the same point is that if importation does not happen, then behavioural patterns in the lab are not representative samples of those outside the lab. This means that experiments cannot measure what they intend to measure, i.e., people's preferences game theory is interested in.

I submit that Woodward's (2008) argument fails because the dilemma is not genuine. He fails to recognize the possibility that importation happens but not in the way presupposed by the unnatural habitat argument: the possibility is that *people import their preferences in one-shot real life interactions into one-off or one-shot experiments*. To understand this point, consider first how an individual differentiate 'one-off' and 'one-shot' type interactions in real life. A 'one-shot' game is the 'same' game repeatedly played against different people. Since the identity of the opponent(s) or partner(s) is always different, the individual has to frame a given strategic interaction either as the 'same' as some other interaction or as 'different' from it, relying on various environmental cues other than the identity of the players. While it is a logical possibility that the individual frames every single case of such interaction as a unique, 'different' game, it is cognitively and perceptually implausible: in general, instead of seeing each and every instance as unique, people use induction or some sort of pattern recognition to make the 'sameness' judgment. This point has been made in different contexts by the authors like Goodman ([1954] 1979), Barnes (1983) and Sugden 1998. Cognitive psychology has accumulated evidence that seems to point to the same conclusion (see e.g., Holland et al.: 1986). If this is the case, then it is quite unlikely that the individual frames a certain interaction as 'one-off' in the strict sense, i.e., a game played only once with any one. Conclusion: the individual is unlikely to play 'one-off' games in real life. Second, the same conclusion equally applies to experimental games in the laboratory, since the individual needs *some* pattern recognition in the lab as well. That is, a game is framed, or interpreted as some strategic situations in the real world. Thus, the individual is unlikely to play 'one-off' games in the lab, either. This means that 'one-off' as well as 'one-shot' experiments are framed either as 'one-shot' or 'repeated' interactions, based on her real life experiences (the generalized importation thesis). Now, the real issue is whether the individual imports framing from 'repeated' or 'one-shot' interactions in real life (the unnatural habitat importation thesis vs. its empirical critique). Regarding this issue, we have already seen that some empirical evidence suggesting that people are able to import 'one-shot' frames into 'one-off' or 'one-shot' experiments. Woodward (2008) fails to see the distinction between the generalized importation thesis and its variants, and erroneously supposes that denying the unnatural habitat version automatically denies the general importation thesis, and poses a false experimenter's dilemma. If my argument is successful, there is no dilemma here: preferences can in principle be measured while controlling for mistakes and importation.

Having answered general methodological critiques of 'one-off' and 'one-shot' designs, let us now go back to Fischbacher et al.'s (2001) 'one-off' experiment and think more concretely. In their experiment, a general worry about errors were taken care of by conducting proper instructions and exercise sessions; and the majority of the behavioural data are easily categorized into types (i.e., they were not random), suggesting that deliberation errors were sufficiently controlled for. The control questions also made sure that the subjects correctly understand the payoff structure of the game, and dominance is not too demanding a reasoning principle. Regarding importation, since this is a 'one-off' game, subjects framed the game either as 'repeated' or 'one-shot'. The 'repeated' interpretation would explain the heterogeneous data by saying that 30% correctly understood the game (i.e., these subjects did not import 'repeated' frames and correctly chose 'free-ride'), while others imported the 'wrong' frame or were confused. This interpretation is conspicuously arbitrary because the majority of non free-rider's choices (either conditional cooperation or hump-shaped) are difficult to explain in terms of repeated frames. Thus it is more natural to interpret that the subjects framed the game as an instance of 'one-shot' MPD-type interactions. Given this interpretation, Fischbacher et al.'s (2001) explanation that the subjects are heterogeneous with respect to their preferences seems plausible.

I will end this section by briefly describing further development of the experimental study of heterogeneous preferences in public goods games (see Gächter 2007 for review). Fischbacher et al. (2001) conjecture that the existence and the composition of heterogeneous individuals (rather than mistakes and its correction by repetitive learning) can account for the decline of contribution levels in repeated public goods games (stylized fact 2). Their inference is that the behaviour of free-riders gradually convinces the conditional cooperators that their contributions are not rewarded by others' contributions (i.e., conditional cooperators realize that they are 'duped'), thereby reducing the overall contributions as the game is repeated.[44] Fischbacher and Gächter (2006) tested this hypothesis using a ten-round repeated public goods game with the same preference elicitation method, and concluded that the interaction of different types of individuals (in terms of preferences) largely explains the observed cooperation decay. Gächter and Thöni (2005) conducted a repeated public goods game in which subjects played the game in groups of 'like-minded' people (subjects' types were inferred from a preliminary one-off game and re-grouping was done according to its result). The authors observed that to be among like-minded people (and to know that) strongly affects cooperation behaviour of all types upwards (even free-riders cooperated more when grouped together). In sum, these findings suggest the existence of some dynamic mechanisms involved in the interactions of individuals with different types of preferences.

4.4 Conclusion

In this chapter, I have discussed the cooperation anomalies observed in experimental Prisoner's Dilemma games and its multiple-person variant, Public Goods games. Section 4.1 introduced the logic of game theory using these games. Section 4.2 reviewed the anomalies in public goods experiments. I have emphasized that typical experimental designs in 1970s and '80s by experimental economists, in particular its use of repetition, are difficult to rationalize from the perspective of testing game theory.

---

[44] Gächter (2007: 30) seems to think that a decrease can be explained by the fact that the *average* conditional cooperators do not fully match the others' contribution (see figure 4.3 above). It seems to me, however, that, in order to make this causal story convincing, we need to hypothesize that conditional cooperators have different levels of 'marginal willingness to cooperate', and that first the individual most sensitive to others' free-riding stops cooperating, then the second sensitive one stops cooperating, and so on, until the least sensitive conditional cooperator stops cooperating (see Margolis 2007). In principle, we should be able to test this by analyzing conditional cooperators' contribution schedules.

This is not because economists did not know how to test the theory clearly, since alternative designs by other social scientists at the same period were available to them. I suggested the hypothesis that experimental economists were not really interested in testing game theory with public goods experiments; rather, their main goal was to find out environmental and institutional conditions under which game theory reliably works. In recent years, however, experimental and behavioural economists have started to conduct experiments with new designs to test game theory clearly. The first challenge was to use public goods experiments in order to measure subjects' 'real' preferences. I have reviewed several attempts do this in section 4.3. First I have argued that game theory is not a tautology but a theory of how people reason coupled with hypotheses as to what people care about, and preference theory. Next, I have shown that, although this combination poses several challenges to a clear test of game-theoretic predictions, some of them have been managed by ingenious experimental designs. I have defended the use of one-off and one-shot games against two arguments. Against the argument from unnatural habitat, I have suggested some empirical evidence pointing to the falsity of the premises. Against Woodward's argument, I have argued that his dilemma is false, suggesting that truly one-off games are unlikely in the lab as well as in real life. Rebutting these methodological charges, we are left with evidence that suggests individual heterogeneity. The main methodological lesson of this chapter is that preferences can be measured in one-off and one-shot public goods games, and that the findings from these games can even tell us something about how people behave in repeated games. The main empirical lesson is that altruism has not been successfully measured. The next chapter critically examines whether some other preferences can be measured and used to explain people's behaviour across different games.

Appendix: Results of a 'Casual' Classroom Experiment

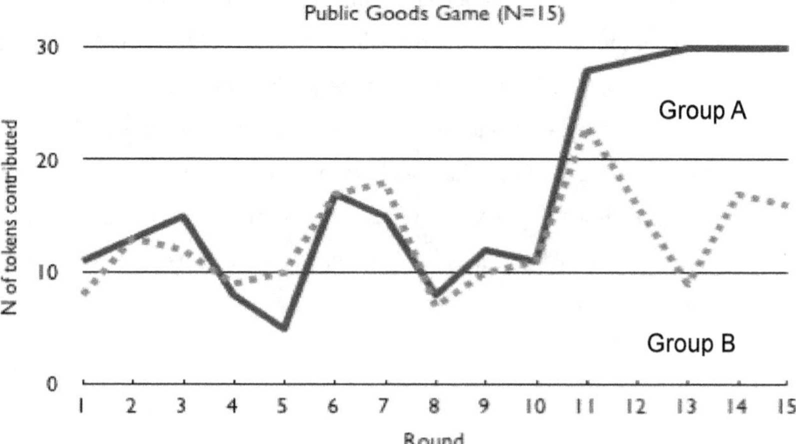

Figure 4.A: Results of a 'casual' classroom experiment (following Holt and Laury's (1997) design)

Thirty students (mainly philosophy students from both BA and MA courses) who showed up at the first lecture of an introductory course on game theory at the University of Tartu, Estonia, were divided into two groups (A and B) and played a repeated public-goods game. $N=15\times2$, $z_i = 2$ tokens. One token of x_i (private good) was hypothetically converted to 40 Estonian kroon [approximately 2.5 euro], while one token of t_i (public good) was hypothetically converted to 10 kroon (i.e., $g(t) = 1/4\times\sum[i=1\rightarrow N]t_i$). After round 5, it was announced that the hypothetical value of one token of x_i is reduced to 20 kroon (i.e., $g(t) = 1/2\times\sum[i=1\rightarrow N]t_i$). Further, after round 10, there was an open discussion on what was going on during the game (chaired by myself), followed by a separate group discussion by A and B (led by a volunteered 'leader' per group) on what to do in the next five rounds. The results are shown in Figure 4.A. Under the strong initiative of the leader, group A agreed upon adopting a strategy of unanimous contribution, whereas group B could not reach an agreement because there was a student who insisted that zero contribution is the only 'rational' strategy whatever others do. The average initial contribution level at round 1 was about 33%, which declined towards 25% by round 5. This increased to 60% at round 6, after the announcement of the private good's 'devaluation', followed by a fluctuating decline. The effect of the group discussion and the agreement (or lack thereof) was remarkable: Group A, apart from one or two token kept privately at the beginning, adhered to the strategy of unanimous contribution from round 13 till 15. Group B, by contrast, followed a similar declining course as in rounds 6-10, although there was a stark increase of contribution at round 11, the beginning of the new session.

Although the devaluation of the private good at rounds 6-10 does not change the dominant strategy of free-riding, subjects might have misunderstood that that changed their payoff structure: answering my question regarding this point, one student in the open discussion said (as I interpret him) that the game had changed from PD to a coordination game.

Chapter 5

From Social Preferences to Cognitive Rational Choice

In the previous chapter, I have examined how experimentalists have strived to identify the exact contents of preferences using public goods experiments. I have disputed with two arguments, Binmore's tautology argument that tries to trivialize such attempts, and Woodward's dilemma argument that tries to impose an unnatural constraint on them. Altruism has not been measured not because it is impossible to measure, but rather because there are few altruists. What do people really care about, then? 'Second wave' behavioural economics includes an attempt to measure people's *social preferences* that are subtler than altruism. This chapter reviews the strategy of modelling social preferences, and identifies two limits in this strategy. More generally, I will argue that an approach to accommodate all the anomalous experimental data by re-specifying subjects' payoff structures (the 'payoff respecification approach') faces serious problems. The first problem concerns the path dependency of outcome individuation, and the second one is related to the exogenous nature of social norms. These are genuine methodological problems arising from recent empirical research. These limits suggest the necessity of alternative approaches to explain anomalies in game theory. I will evaluate two distinct but not necessarily incompatible approaches, one incorporating cognition and the other extending rationality.

The chapter is organized as follows: Section 5.1 describes some stylized models of social preferences to convey the essence of this approach, and points out two problems. Section 5.2 introduces a model of *social norms*, as a prominent example of the cognition incorporation approach. Section 5.3 examines group identification, an important cognitive mechanism that is disputed by Bicchieri's (2006) social norm model. Section 5.4 looks at the theory of *team reasoning* as an example of the rationality extension approach. I will review recent attempts to test these models, with some suggestions to improve the tests. Section 5.5 concludes the chapter.

5.1 Limits of the Payoff Respecification Approach

In recent years, subtler motivations than (pure and impure) altruism have been proposed in an attempt to explain various anomalous results in public goods experiments and other types of experimental games. I will first introduce three simplified models using the PD-material game that we have been examining in the last chapter. I will then briefly describe three other important experimental games and explain how these games differ from Prisoner's Dilemma and public goods games as tools for measuring social preferences.

5.1.1 Models of Social Preference

Models of social preference try to capture motivations related to people's judgements about collective outcomes.[1] There are many criteria for outcome desirability, and so are the models of social preference. One prominent example is *inequality aversion* (Fehr and Schmidt 1999; Bolton and Ockenfels 2000), according to which an individual prefers more money to less, but also prefers less discrepancy between her own monetary gain and others' gains.[2] For concreteness think of a simplified distributive fairness utility function:

$$DFU_i \equiv \$_i - \beta|\$_i - \$_{-i}|$$

where $\$_i$ and $\$_{-i}$ represent i's own monetary reward and the others' mean monetary reward, respectively, and β is a positive parameter that determines the weight of the inequality aversion consideration relative to monetary gains to self. If played by individuals with this preference structure, our PD-material game will be something like this (Table 5.1), where (*cooperate, cooperate*) is one of the two Nash equilibria if $\beta > 1/4$.

Table 5.1: PD-material game played by inequality averse players

| | | **Player 2** | |
		cooperate	*defect*
Player 1	*cooperate*	2, 2	−1–4β, 3–4β
	defect	3–4β, −1–4β	0, 0

Another type of motivation is a preference for *social welfare*, which is defined by Pareto-efficiency of monetary outcomes. One simple social welfare utility function is:

---

[1] See Camerer (2003: 101-113) for a summary of these models with precise mathematical representations. My presentation in the following is simplified. I also follow Camerer's judgment regarding empirical performances of these models, unless otherwise stated.

[2] Fehr and Schmidt (1999) distinguish 'envy' (others get more money than you do) and 'guilt' (you get more money than others do), and use different parameters to each component. My representation is more similar to Bolton and Ockenfels's (2000), which has no such distinction. This difference has important implications to models' performance, just like the difference between pure and impure altruism does, as we have seen in chapter 4. Fehr and Schmidt's (1999) version fits with the data better.

$$SWU_i \equiv \$_i + \beta \sum[k{=}1{\rightarrow}N]\$_k$$

A PD-material game played by individuals with such utility functions will be something like Table 5.2, where (*cooperate*, *cooperate*) is the dominant equilibrium if $\beta > 1/2$.

Table 5.2: PD-material game played by social-welfare players

		Player 2	
		cooperate	*defect*
	cooperate	$2+4\beta$, $2+4\beta$	$-1+2\beta$, $3+2\beta$
Player 1	*defect*	$3+2\beta$, $-1+2\beta$	$0, 0$

Rabin (1993: 1258) proposes yet another model, claiming that incorporating a preference for *reciprocal fairness* is essential for 'incorporating psychology into economic research'. According to this model, an individual cares not only about distributional outcomes but also about others' *intentions* and tries to reciprocate others' 'nice' behaviour with a 'nice' response, and 'mean' behaviour with a 'mean' response. Rabin (1993) formalizes this idea, using *psychological game theory*, an approach that originates from Geanakoplos, Pearce and Stacchetti's (1989) work. While in standard game theory player i's subjective expected utility function consists of her strategies (or actions, a_i) and those of others, in psychological game theory two additional factors influence her overall utility. These are b_j: i's belief about what strategy j is choosing, and c_i: i's belief about what j believes i is choosing.[3] i's material payoff is defined as $\$_i$ (a_i, b_j). i's *kindness function*, representing how kind i is toward j is defined by using j's material payoff and its relation to some reference point.[4] For example, if we take the reference point as the counterfactual payoff which could have been available to j had i chosen the other of the two strategies available, a kindness function will be something like:

$$K_i\,(a_i,\, b_j) \equiv \$_j\,(b_j,\, a_i) - \$_j\,(b^*_j,\, a^*_i)$$

---

[3] These beliefs are subsets of the actual feasible strategy sets.

[4] In Rabin (1993), this reference point is given by the 'equitable payoff' which is defined as the halfway between the lowest possible payoff and the highest possible payoff to each player. How one defines the reference point is crucial in the model building but Rabin claims that in his (1992) paper he showed that 'most of the [formal] result of [Rabin 1993] hold if multiple kindness functions are allowed' (1993:1286).

where the strategies with * are the ones that were not played. Next, i's belief function, representing i's belief about how kind player j is being to her, is also defined using i's material payoff and its relation to her reference point (the counterfactual payoff i would have gotten had j played differently). i's belief function will be therefore;

$$B_j\,(b_j,\,c_i) \equiv \$_i\,(c_i,\,b_j) - \$_i\,(c^*_i,\,b^*_j)$$

Using these two functions plus the material function, it is possible to define the total utility function for a *reciprocally fair* player i as follows:

$$RFU_i\,(a_i,\,b_j,\,c_i) \equiv \$_i + \beta\,(K_i \times B_j)$$

where β is a positive parameter that weighs the reciprocal fairness consideration compared to i's material payoffs.[5] Rabin (1993) defines 'fairness equilibrium', a solution concept in psychological games analogous to Nash equilibrium in the standard games by adding a condition that all higher-order beliefs match actual strategies (i.e., $c_i = b_j = a_i$), in addition to the condition that players try to maximize reciprocal fairness utilities defined in the above way. The PD-material game is respecified as in Table 5.3:

Table 5.3: PD-material game played by reciprocally-fair players

		Player 2	
		cooperate	*defect*
Player 1	*cooperate*	$2+2\times2\beta,\ 2+2\times2\beta$	$-1-3\times3\beta,\ 3-3\times3\beta$
	defect	$3-3\times3\beta,\ -1-3\times3\beta$	$0+2\times2\beta,\ 0+2\times2\beta$

If $\beta > 1/13$, then (*cooperate, cooperate*) is a fairness equilibrium, where each player reciprocates the other's 'kind' action by one's own 'kind' action ('friendly' fairness equilibrium). However, (*defect, defect*) is also a fairness equilibrium, where each player reciprocates the other's 'mean' action by one's own 'mean' action ('hostile' fairness equilibrium). Rabin (1993) claims that this type of models can explain behaviour better

---

[5] Instead of adding such parameter, Rabin (1993) allows weighing between one's material payoffs and the reciprocal fairness consideration by imposing the lower and upper bounds to the kindness and belief function (normalization). Such mathematical details are not essential for our present purposes. Also I used Rabin's V rather than U for simplicity. See Rabin (1993:1287, in particular fn. 10).

than simple altruistic and other social preference models because it explicitly incorporates the 'role of intentionality in attitudes about fairness' (Rabin 1993: 1289).[6]

In order to examine whether and how these social preferences can be measured, I need to introduce three extensive-form games, which have been frequently used to test these models of social preference.

5.1.2 Sharpening the Tools: Ultimatum, Dictator and Trust Games

Camerer (2003: 46) points out that PD and MPD (public goods games) are 'blunt tools for guiding theories of social preference'. He notes two problems: first, (M)PD games cannot distinguish between altruistic players and players who match expected cooperation. As we have seen in the last chapter, however, this problem was solved by Fischbacher et al. (2001), who used the contribution schedule method to elicit preferences and rejected altruism in favour of conditional cooperation plus free riding. Since Camerer is not against this elicitation method itself, we can infer that this problem can be circumvented in (M)PD.[7] The second problem Camerer notes is that (M)PD cannot distinguish between players who are selfish and those who have reciprocal preferences but pessimistically think others will free ride. This problem too was handled by the contribution schedule method, which clearly differentiated unconditional free riders (i.e., 'selfish' players) and conditional cooperators. Moreover, Fischbacher and Gächter (2006) attempted to measure the discrepancy between subjects' *beliefs* about others' contributions and the actual contributions, and observed that this discrepancy decreased with repetition and disappeared in the final round. Therefore, in principle it seems possible to measure whether and how much subjects are 'pessimistic'.

The analysis above suggests that what (M)PD games are not good at measuring is not subjects' beliefs as such, but their *beliefs about others' intentions*. Another way to put the same point is that (M)PD games are not good at examining the *reciprocal* nature of players' choice (e.g., "I choose defect *because* you will do the same"), although these games can show its *conditional* nature (e.g., "I choose defect *if* you do the same"). There are two reasons for this. First, static (or simultaneous-move) games such as the

---

[6] Rabin's original version was intended for normal-form games only, but the model was extended to the analysis of extensive-form games by Dufwenberg and Kirchsteiger (1998) and by Falk and Fischbacher (1998).

[7] In discussing a similar method (the minimal acceptable offer method: MAO) used in Ultimatum games, Camerer (2003: 48-49) suggests that this elicitation method has 'the huge advantage of measuring likely reactions to all possible [decisions by others]', and even wonders why economists are reluctant to use this method. I suspect that economists are reluctant to use more than one elicitation method because they implicitly learned from preference reversals (PR: see chs. 2 and 3) that different elicitation methods may 'reveal' different preferences where they shouldn't. Camerer himself (2003: 49, fn. 2) observes this procedure variance in Ultimatum games, but notes that it is neither well established nor well understood.

PD-material game we have been using as an example do not easily allow inferences about players' intentions. For example, the observation of (*defect, defect*) in a PD-material game cannot tell us whether it is a dominant equilibrium or a 'hostile' fairness equilibrium. Second, players in multi-person games such as public goods cannot easily attribute intentions to other players; even if each player is identified with her strategies, a particular player's intentions to *you* are not entirely clear. For these reasons, some classes of *two-person, sequential* games are considered as 'sharper tools' (Camerer 2003: 46) for measuring social preferences, in particular reciprocal preferences.[8] Three types of such games have been invented. In what follows I will briefly describe these games with stylized experimental results, so that I can refer to them in a later section.

An *Ultimatum game* (Güth, Schmittberger and Schwarze 1982) is a game in which one player (the Proposer) makes a take-it-or-leave-it offer, as a division of some amount of money between herself and another player.[9] If the second player (the Responder) accepts the division, then both players earn the specified amounts. If the Responder rejects it, they both get nothing. The standard prediction (rational play plus selfish preference) is that the Proposer will offer a minimum divisible sum of the money, which will be accepted by the Responder: for the Responder, any positive sum is better than zero (money maximization); since the Proposer knows this, she proposes the smallest amount to maximize her own money. Evidence from experiments shows (i) that Proposers offer on average 30-40% of the money (modal and median offers are 40-50%); and (ii) that Responders reject small offers below 20% about half the time. These results clearly falsify the standard prediction. A *Dictator game* (Kahneman, Knetsch and Thaler 1986) removes from an Ultimatum game the Responder's ability to reject. That is, the Proposer becomes a Dictator whose offer determines the final allocation. In experiments, Dictators' offers are considerably smaller than Proposers' offers in ultimatum games, but still not the minimum amount (the average allocation is about 20%). Another related game is the *Trust game* (Berg, Dickhaut and McCabe 1995), in which an Investor first chooses how much to 'invest' from her endowment into a 'project'; the project is always successful (i.e., the investment is multiplied by $r > 1$), but the investment and its profit are under the control of a Trustee, who allocates the money

---

[8] Sequential two-person PD games (not repeated) satisfy these conditions, and are used in experiments to test social preference models. However, its payoff structure is that of 'mixed-motive', which is a potential problem.

[9] This and the other games described below are thought to be 'models' of strategic interactions in the real world, just like public goods games are thought to be a model of public goods provision in real economic contexts. Since my focus in this chapter is on how these games are used as measuring tools, I will not discuss how well these games model tools to understand real world phenomena. Sugden (2000) argues that modelling real world phenomena with games is possible and discusses how.

between herself and the Investor (i.e., the Trustee is a Dictator whose budget is decided by the Investor). The investor may or may not 'trust' the Trustee, i.e., risk her money in order to increase it, and in turn the Trustee may or may not be 'trustworthy', i.e., make an allocation that is profitable to the Investor. The standard prediction is that the Investor invests nothing, since there is no enforcement mechanisms to guarantee the Trustee's 'trustworthiness'. In experiments, Investors transfer on average about 50% of their endowments; the average amount Trustees return is about 95% of the investment. The fact that the gain from 'trust' is around zero is robust, but there are wide variations in data from experiments with subjects of different nationalities (see Camerer 2003: 86).

These games have sequential moves, but the strategic reasoning involved is not complicated, for there are at most two stages. The second player's move is made after observing that of the first player, making it easy to infer the second player's belief about the first player's intentions. Typically, only two players are involved, which also helps the experimenters to infer the second player's beliefs about the first player's intentions. Players' considerations about equality are also easy to infer because there are only two players whose payoffs are common knowledge. In the next section, I will review the performances of models of social preferences in explaining evidence from these experimental games.

5.1.3 Empirical Assessment

Before starting, we need to ask a preliminary question: When can we say that a particular type of social preference (either distributive fairness, social welfare, or reciprocal fairness) has been observed? We can say that social preference S_1 is detected when model M_1 that presupposes S_1 performs better than other models M_2, M_3, etc. with S_2, S_3, etc. in a 'prediction contest' that is similar to the one between two models of altruism (see chapter 4): that is, the winner M_1 must make severely testable predictions that are in turn confirmed by a wide range of data across different games without arbitrary parameter adjustment (e.g., changing the value of β from positive to negative). Although it is in principle possible to abstain from making an ontological commitment to S_1 (interpreting M_1 as a useful tool for prediction or just a parsimonious way to organize empirical data), behavioural researchers usually assume that M_1 captures some causal properties of human psychology. Rabin (1993) incorporates beliefs into his utility function precisely because he thinks that beliefs about others' intentions are a psychologically realistic causal factor of one's behaviour. Camerer and Fehr (2004: 80) explain Responders' rejection of low offers (such as 20%) in Ultimatum games as caused by hard-wired emotions, which 'can be captured by appropriate formulations of the utility function'. The experimentalists' strategy of modelling social preference is therefore realist, rather than instrumentalist, in spirit. This implies that different models may capture different but more or less real causal factors. With this proviso in mind, we can now ask: Has a real causal preference structure been identified?

Although hasty conclusions should be avoided since the prediction contest is still in progress, an interim report is available (see Camerer 2003: 110-113). To summarize, none of the models mentioned in 5.1.1 has won across different games. For example, Charness and Rabin (2002) conducted a series of two-person Dictator game experiments with variations (adding the possibility of response and a third player). They estimated the relative strength of each preference specification using a statistical model based on the assumption that the subjects consist of one type of individuals with a certain mixture of three motivations (social welfare, inequality aversion, and reciprocal fairness) plus error.[10] [11] Charness and Rabin summarize their main findings as follows: first, social welfare explains their data better than inequality aversion does, but not completely; second, reciprocal fairness explains the data only partially and in an asymmetrical way, i.e., subjects reciprocate negatively to the other player's selfish behaviour ('concern withdrawal'), but not always positively to the other player's 'kind' behaviour. Although there are many interesting issues to discuss (e.g., is Charness and Rabin's assumption of subject homogeneity reasonable given the findings from public goods experiments?), in the following I will focus on two serious conceptual problems that have been discussed in the philosophy literature.

5.1.4 Path Dependency and Norm Exogeny

The first problem concerns the *path dependency* of people's preferences. To put it simply, the problem is that models of inequality aversion cannot capture it, and models of reciprocal fairness cannot measure it. I will show the first point. As noted in 5.1.2, models of social preference are often tested in sequential (extensive-form) games. For example, consider a version of the Ultimatum game depicted in Figure 5.1 (Left):

---

[10] The likelihood of error was assumed to be a decreasing function of the utility cost of an error (Charness and Rabin 2002: 838).

[11] Charness and Rabin (2002) elicited preferences using the decision schedule method. Specifically, a Responder makes contingent choices without being told about the Proposer's decision. The discussion of whether this method yields the same preferences can be found in Charness and Rabin (2002: 828, fn. 17). They believe in procedural invariance.

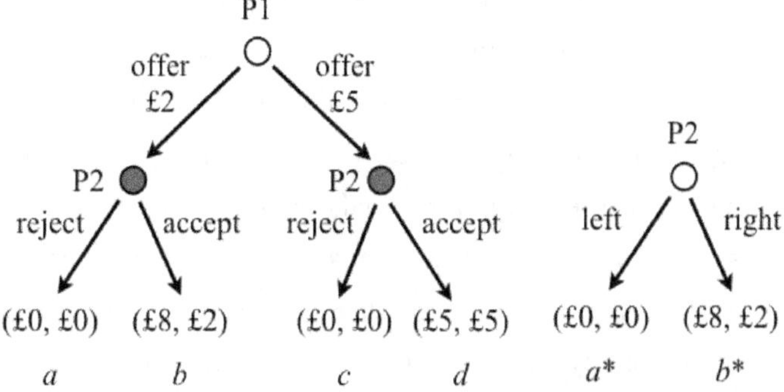

Figure 5.1: Ultimatum game (Left) and Dictator game (Right)

In this Ultimatum game, P1 (Proposer)'s choice is limited to either *offer £2* or *offer £5*. P2 (Responder)'s choice is as usual, *reject* or *accept*. Rational play (best reply and subgame perfection) plus selfish preference predicts that P2 chooses *accept* at both possible decision nodes (black dots); knowing this, P1 chooses her money maximizing strategy, *offer £2*; P2 accepts the offer, and the game ends. We have already seen that this standard prediction is disconfirmed. Models of inequality aversion may predict outcome *d* as a subgame perfect Nash equilibrium if that strikes the players' balance between own money maximization and inequality aversion. What would inequality-aversion predict if P1 chose *offer £2*? Again, the prediction depends on parameters, but if the prediction is outcome *a*, this is because of P2's particular way of weighing inequality (equality vs. £6 more money to self) against own money (£0 vs. £2).

Although reciprocal fairness models make a very similar prediction, they presuppose a different mechanism from inequality aversion. Outcome *a* may be chosen because it is a 'hostile' fairness equilibrium; and outcome *d* may be chosen because it is a 'friendly' fairness equilibrium. It is possible to differentiate these predictions by having subjects play the Dictator game in Figure 5.1 (Right). Inequality-aversion models predict that P2 is likely to choose *a** as much as *a* (and *b** as much as *b*). Reciprocal fairness models predict differently because these games are not identical for Player 2: in the Ultimatum game, P2 perceive P1's *offer £2* as 'mean' because P1 could have chosen *offer £5*; in the Dictator version, by contrast, P2 cannot have the same belief about P1's intentions, since P1 makes no decision in this game. Thus, P2 may reasonably choose (£8, £2) if she wants more money than less. In similar comparisons between the rejection rates in Ultimatum games and their subgame Dictator games, Charness and Rabin (2002) found some evidence that subjects differentiate these two types of games. Inequality-aversion models cannot explain this, since they assume *separability*, i.e., utilities of terminal-node outcomes are separable from the path through the tree and from outcomes on unchosen branches. Although Camerer (2003: 112) also mentions some evidence suggesting that separability is a good approximation (e.g., comparison between Trust games and Dictator games), he admits that some violations of separability have 'plausible psychological interpretations'. Reciprocal fairness provides such interpretation: people's evaluations of outcomes are path-dependent because they care about others' intentions. Inequality aversion cannot capture this intuition.

If models of reciprocal fairness can capture the intuition that intentions matter, can they measure preferences for such concerns? Guala (2006) says *no*. The reason is that the assumption of separability may be incompatible with an important assumption in the standard preference elicitation method. First, as we have seen in the previous chapters, there are two ways of preference elicitation, preference theory (in particular the principle of revealed preference) for riskless choice, and EUT (in particular the Ramsey method) for risky choice. The Dictator game (Figure 5.1 Right) is a riskless choice, so from this choice it is possible to elicit P2's preferences ($a^* \geq b^*$ or $a^* \leq b^*$). However, because separability is empirically violated, we cannot use this 'revealed' preference to infer P2's preference over $\{a$ and $b\}$; instead, what we can elicit from the observation of P2's choice over $\{a$ and $b\}$ is $a \geq b$ or $a \leq b$. Now, since games usually involve strategic uncertainty, we need to use EUT, rather than preference theory, to elicit players' preferences.[12] The Ramsey method (or equivalently, the Savage measurement procedure) I have illustrated in chapter 2 is the standard (and currently the only available) method to operationally measure vNM utilities using EUT. Recall that the Ramsey method first offers an individual different prospects (lotteries, gambles) that specify outcomes for different states of nature, and then infers her cardinal utilities from the observations of her choice behaviour among these prospects. A necessary assumption in this procedure is that the individual has the preference ordering over prospects constructed from *any* combination of an outcome and a state of nature. This assumption is called the *rectangular field assumption* (Broome 1991: 80-81; 115-117), and is represented in Table 5.4.

---

[12] This is the very reason von Neumann and Morgenstern (1947) axiomatized EUT in developing game theory.

Table 5.4: The rectangular field assumption

		States of nature $(N = m)$			
		s_1	s_2	$s_3 \ldots \ldots s_m$	**Outcome sets**
Prospects	p_1	$o_1^{\ 1}$	$o_1^{\ 2}$	$o_1^{\ 3} \ldots \ldots o_1^{\ m}$	O_1
$(N = n)$	p_2	$o_2^{\ 1}$	$o_2^{\ 2}$	$o_2^{\ 3} \ldots \ldots o_2^{\ m}$	O_2
	p_3	$o_3^{\ 1}$	$o_3^{\ 2}$	$o_3^{\ 3} \ldots \ldots o_3^{\ m}$	O_3
	.	.	.	. $\ldots \ldots$	.
	p_n	$o_n^{\ 1}$	$o_n^{\ 2}$	$o_n^{\ 3} \ldots \ldots o_n^{\ m}$	O_n

The assumption says that the individual has a preference ordering over the product of outcome sets (i.e., $O_1 \times O_2 \times O_3 \times \ldots \times O_n$). In other words, the closed rectangular field in Table 5.4 defines how finely outcomes can be individuated. Now, Guala (2006) suggests a tension between this assumption and separability.[13] Separability allows one to individuate outcomes of a game based on considerations of path-dependency: the unchosen paths (what could have happened) may affect one's evaluation of the outcome (what did happen) at the end of the actual path in the game. However, this outcome may not make sense (either causally or logically impossible) in other games that do no have the identical paths. For example, outcome a in the Ultimatum game (Figure 5.1, Left) may be finely individuated for P2 as 'gets offended by an insulting offer (£2) but punishes P1 with rejection and feels better', but this outcome cannot be used to construct a new prospect to measure P2's preferences in some other game, which is required by the rectangular field assumption. The upshot is that although models of reciprocal fairness try to capture the psychologically plausible phenomenon that intentions matter, in doing so the models endanger the Ramsey method by making the rectangular field assumption implausible.[14] Reciprocal fairness is recognized by researchers, but still not measurable at this stage.

The second problem concerns the measurement of *beliefs* in models of reciprocal fairness. Consider for example (*defect, cooperate*) in Table 5.3. I assigned $RFU_1 = 3 - 3 \times 3\beta$ based on the following reasoning. First, P1 got three units of material

---

[13] Loomes and Sugden (1982) and Broome (1991) first noticed this in the context of testing EUT, and Guala (2006) made explicit its implication in the context of testing game theory.

[14] Although regret theory reviewed in chapter 2 has the similar problem ('regret' or 'rejoice' makes sense only in specific decision contexts and outcomes thus individuated cannot be used to construct arbitrary prospects), Loomes and Sugden (1982: Appendix) suggest an application of the Ramsey method to infer the regret utilities (and subjective probabilities) from choice behaviour. No such method is proposed for measurement of intentions in games.

payoff. But by choosing *defect*, he was 'mean' to P2, which is represented by what P2 got ('−1') minus what P2 could have gotten ('2'), that is, −3 (negative). P1 did this while believing that P2 was being 'kind' to P1, which is represented by what P1 got (3) minus what P1 could have gotten (0), that is, 3 (positive). The overall utility to P1 is thus $3-9\beta$. But is this a valid reasoning? In computing P2's 'kindness', P1 used '3' as her material payoff, but it is unlikely that this is what P2 intended to give P1. Unless P2 is a pure altruist, it is more likely that he was having (*cooperate, cooperate*) rather than (*defect, cooperate*) in mind when he played *cooperate*. So P1 should use '2' instead of '3' in computing P2's 'kindness'. But this would mean that P2's guess was wrong, that is, his belief about what P1 would do was not consistent with what P1 actually did ($b_1 \neq a_1$). This violates psychological game theory's requirement that all higher-order beliefs be consistent with actual strategies. So the reasoning process behind calculating P1's total payoff in (*defect, cooperate*) seems to be inconsistent with the theory. Generally speaking, the problem seems to be that *the model's prediction comes directly from the assumption that all higher-order beliefs will be in equilibrium, rather than from the reciprocal fairness utility calculus.* That is, only (*cooperate, cooperate*) and (*defect, defect*) are candidates for equilibria, and the reciprocal fairness calculus is simply endorsing this fact.

This makes one wonder whether reciprocal fairness models are really models about preferences. Do we need to measure preferences in the first place? In Hargreaves Heap and Varoufakis's (2004: 284) words, requiring equilibrium in beliefs prior to the utility calculus in this way 'turns what used to be a simple unidirectional system of causation in game theory, running from utilities to rational beliefs to equilibrium, into a form of circularity'. In other words, the main analysis is done by specifying people's beliefs about what results actually obtain, prior to the utility calculus. This makes the hypothesis that people try to maximize reciprocal fairness utilities rather redundant. Why not simply say that players act as they do because we, the analysts, know that each player has such-and-such true beliefs about the outcome? Another problem is that the reciprocal fairness models became psychologically *more* unrealistic in an attempt to 'incorporate psychology into economics'. Psychological game theory requires the axiom of *consistently aligned beliefs* in a stronger way than standard game theory does, and this reduces the psychological plausibility of the model (Hargreaves Heap and Varoufakis 2004: 279-280). Moreover, people's beliefs regarding outcomes depend on the specification of a reference point, which is not given endogenously within the framework of psychological game theory; it is more plausible that a relevant reference point is defined by some *norm* that players regard relevant in a given interaction. Once such norm is specified, however, the result may be predicted without referring to utilities. To sum up: incorporating beliefs into utility functions makes the role of preferences in the reciprocal fairness models redundant; and the reference points that are crucial for determining beliefs are not specified in the models.

I have pointed out two serious problems which models of reciprocal fairness face, one concerning the tension between the separability of outcomes and the measurability of utilities, the other concerning the tension between a strong role of beliefs and its exogenous nature in the models. Why do we face these problems? I submit that we face these problems probably because choice-relevant causal factors in human psychology cannot be satisfactorily captured by utility functions and equilibrium concepts. We have already seen that behavioural economists are realists abut psychological factors. At the same time, they are nevertheless committed to the economic modelling strategy of representing utility functions and deriving equilibria. Behavioural economists try to reduce tensions between these two commitments by saying that utility functions are 'just a convenient way' of capturing those psychological factors. However, whether or not utility representation is a convenient strategy depends on features of the target system (human psychology) as well as on our cognitive capacity to meaningfully understand these representations. While 'almost anything can denote or even represent almost anything else' (Goodman 1976: 89), scientists are more selective in choosing a model: they use models that are *similar* to the target system in some relevant sense (Giere 1988; Sugden 2000). Therefore, the recalcitrant difficulties in representing decision-relevant human psychology by utility functions must be taken as evidence that these two are not similar in some relevant sense. Camerer (2003: 113), believing that reciprocal fairness models 'get the psychology right', suggests that researchers will learn to use these complex models because reciprocal fairness models 'cannot possibly be more difficult than the incredibly complicated mathematics now being done in areas such as asset pricing, macroeconomics, epistemological game theory, and econometrics'. No doubt, reciprocal fairness models will be useful in some contexts if they do not exceed our cognitive capacity to keep track of them; but what I do doubt is Camerer's optimism that these models get the decision-relevant psychology right. At least I regard the two problems highlighted above as serious enough to justify a search for alternative approaches. Indeed, some alternatives are available. I will examine Bicchieri's (2006) theory of social norm in the next section, and Bacharach's (2006) theory of team reasoning in section 5.4. One important difference between these two theories is their attitudes towards social identification, which will be discussed in 5.3.

5.2 Social Norms

Bicchieri's (2006) theory of social norms can be interpreted as an attempt to overcome the second problem (the exogenous nature of reference points) by explicitly modelling the choice of a reference point. Although her utility representation obscures this fact,[15] Bicchieri's model is a major departure from rational choice theory in that it acknowledges the incompleteness of standard game theory plus the payoff specification approach. The key idea is that social norms are context-specific, in the sense that people infer relevant norms by relying on contextual cues. To the extent that this inference is successful (i.e., others' observed behaviour doesn't contradict such inference), it is said that there is a social norm, in the technical sense of collectively self-fulfilling expectations. To be precise, a behavioural rule R is a *social norm* if and only if:

(1) An individual i knows that a rule R exists and applies to situations of type S (*contingency*);
(2) i prefers to conform to R in S on the condition that (*conditional preference*):
  (a) i believes that a sufficiently large subset of population P conforms to R in S (*empirical expectations*); and
  (b) i believes that a sufficiently large subset of P expects i to conform to R in S (*normative expectations*), possibly with readiness to sanction i (*normative expectations with sanctions*).[16]

(1) distinguishes a social norm from a *universal* one which applies in any situation at any time to anyone, and (2) distinguishes a social norm from a *deontic* one to which people conform because they 'ought to'. People thus conform to social norms essentially because they want to, given their (empirical and normative) beliefs. In this respect Bicchieri's (2006) model is squarely in the tradition of rational choice theory that explains people's behaviour solely based on individual's beliefs and desires (instrumental rationality). What makes it distinct from other rational choice models is its explicit use of resources external to decision and game theory in explaining where

---

[15] For example, in her Appendix to chapter 1, Bicchieri (2006) introduces a general utility function based on norms, in much the same way as I have been introducing other social preference models in 5.1.1, i.e., postulating a utility function consisting of one's material payoff plus some weighted negative psychological payoff resulting from norm violations.

[16] Bicchieri (2006: 11). Pettit (1990) contains essentially the identical formulation.

social norms come from. Specifically, Bicchieri relies on the following cognitive framework from context to norm activation (Figure 5.2):

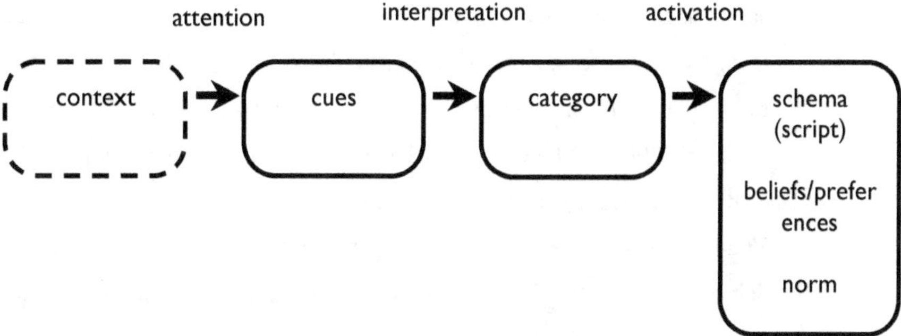

Figure 5.2: Mapping from context to norm (a modified version of Bicchieri 2006: 56)

Roughly speaking, each box represents a cognitive device or template (apart from the first 'context', which is the 'raw' material of cognition), and each arrow represents a cognitive process: first, given a decision context, an individual focuses her attention to certain cues to facilitate the speed and accuracy with which she makes decision independent of task-related motivations (*semantic priming*); second, the individual makes a similarity-based inductive inference to categorize the cues thus highlighted on the basis of her prior experience. Finally, based on this categorization, the individual activates a schema (or script) which gives the context a structure with a set of actions, events, people and roles. Bicchieri (2006: 94) says that '*social norms are embedded into scripts*', meaning that what (the individual believes) is the 'normal' thing to do is naturally determined by a script thus activated. For example, in an abstract public goods experiment the only salient cues are material payoffs. Some individuals may interpret such payoff structure as a context of 'cooperation' in which each would (and should) play a role to achieve a maximum social welfare, while others may interpret it as a context of 'competition' in which each would (and should) maximize her individual payoff. Yet others may see the situation as a 'social dilemma' in which there is a vacillation between the two orientations, just like between the duck and rabbit interpretations in the famous gestalt picture. Once a categorization is given, an appropriate schema will be activated, and will provide each player with instructions regarding what to expect from others and what others will expect from her.

This framework is based on extensive researches in cognitive and social psychology, and the above summary cannot do justice to that rich body of literature (see

Bicchieri (2006: ch. 2) and the references therein). This brief overview, however, enables us to notice the potential benefit of 'incorporating psychology into economics' in this way rather than in Rabin's (1993) way. For example, this cognitive framework enables us to incorporate *framing effects* that are well established in individual decision-making research (see chapter 3) into game theory; 'how a situation is presented or described alters perceptions by guiding the interpretation of cues in a specific direction' (Bicchieri 2006: 87). Indeed, extensionally identical games may be framed differently and played differently by subjects, depending on how these games are described, e.g., a 'fund-raising' vignette elicits more cooperative behaviour while a 'poker' vignette elicits more free-riding in public goods games (see Colman, Pulford and Rose 2008: Experiment 1, described below). Another example of using the idea of framing along these lines is Margolis (2007: chs. 6, 7), who, based on evolutionary psychology, hypothesizes four crude categorizations of social contexts—the 'competitive' branch, which is further broken down into zero-sum type 'games' and positive-sum type 'markets'; and the 'cooperative' branch, which is further broken down into a 'weak' one with free-rider temptations and a 'strong' one of pure coordination. The author then conjectures that some puzzles in public goods experiments, such as the moderate contribution rates in 'easy-rider' games with MRPC>1 (where game theory says everyone should contribute everything; see my discussion of Saijo and Nakamura (1995) in chapter 4), can be explained by the evolutionary fact that it is difficult to move from one frame to another in response to objective changes in context because people evolved in environments which reward speed over accuracy, and favour conservative ('default') behaviour (the 'cascade conjecture').[17] As one can see from these two examples, the framework is indeed useful to map a variety of cognitive processes with different natures underlying final decision making. The question, then, is which process(es) can explain the data from different games in experiments. Bicchieri (2006: ch. 3) puts forward her model against other social preference models and claims that it performs better in explaining the data from Ultimatum and Dictator games. Here I would like to focus on her explanation of stylized fact 3 in public goods experiments, i.e., that face-to-face communication improves cooperation rate. She argues that relevant communication focuses subjects' attention onto social norms of cooperative behaviour, thereby increasing contribution rates. Traditionally, however, social psychologists have offered an alternative explanation.

---

[17] Bicchieri (2006:148) also proposes that, once activated, a social norm becomes the 'default', which cannot be fine-tuned to new situations easily. This rigidity may have some evolutionary origins.

5.3 Group Identification

An alternative explanation to the communication effect is that communication induces individuals to categorize themselves as members of the group, thereby changing the goal of individuals from individual payoff maximization to group payoff maximization. The idea comes from the *minimal group paradigm* in intergroup relations (e.g., Tajfel and Turner 1979), which has accumulated evidence that individuals, when believing that they belong to one group ('in-group') as opposed to another ('out-group'), start to behave in favour of the in-group and against the out-group, even if their membership is based on arbitrary categorizations such as 'those who overestimated the number of dots on a page' vs. 'those who underestimated it'. Although this strong effect and its manipulability suggest that group identity is a cognitive mechanism causing unjustifiable and socially undesirable discriminations, it may also cause individuals' pro-social behaviour if *social identification* is made to 'those aspects of an individual's self-image that derive from the social categories to which he perceives himself as belonging' (Tajfel and Turner (1979), cited in Orbell et al. (1988: 812)). According to this hypothesis, the high cooperation rate observed in the relevant discussion condition in Dawes et al. (1977) would be a result of communication-induced group identification of subjects, and the following payoff transformation.

Experimental economists are sceptical about the group identity explanation,[18] and also pessimistic about the robustness of such an unmeasured effect when institutionalized. While this scepticism may be justified from the mechanism design perspective discussed in chapter 4, there are some good reasons to go beyond such scepticism. For one thing, the discussion effect needs an explanation since it is a fairly replicable phenomenon in the laboratory (in addition to Dawes et al. (1977), reports of the same phenomenon includes at least Caldwell (1976); Edney and Harper (1978); Jerdee and Rosen (1974); Rapoport (1974); van de Kragt et al. (1986);[19] game theory is completely silent about why 'cheap talk' matters. For another thing, it is not so clear why such a well-established effect in the laboratory cannot be relied upon as a lasting organizational feature. In fact, the communication effect was *enhanced* in repeated conditions favoured by experimental economists, whereas repetition *alone* decreased cooperation (see chapter 4). Moreover, relevant discussion is a prevalent feature of

---

[18] 'There may be something here, but it has not yet been isolated, measured, and controlled.' (Ledyard 1995: 165).

[19] My classroom experiment also suggests this. See Appendix to chapter 4.

modern organizations for which cooperation is of crucial importance. In sum, the communication effect's stability needs to be explained, and if possible, exploited in institutional design to achieve high cooperation.

Since group identification is unobservable, the key to understanding whether it is at work in public goods experiments is first to operationalize it, and then to manipulate it, while controlling other factors. The causes and effects of group identification are rather complex (see Bacharach (2006: 76) for a concise summary), but in public goods experiment it is uncontroversial to define the effect of group identification by the increase in cooperation rate. The challenge is rather to discriminate the group identification effect from the same increase in cooperation rate caused by some other mechanisms such as social norm activations. Moreover, is it conceptually possible to distinguish group identification and social norms? For example, Bacharach's (2006: 76) list of the effects of group identification includes 'adopting the group's norms'. So isn't it the case that there is *first* group identification, and *then* social norms are activated based on that? Bicchieri (2006:147) explicitly rejects this hypothesis, arguing that 'it is not group identity, but norms of promise keeping, that explain the high rate of cooperation after a period of discussion'. Her argument is two-fold.

Bicchieri's (2006) first argument concerns the 'carry over effect' of discussion observed in Orbell et al. (1988). These experimenters introduced a two-group design public goods experiment, in which each group of 14 subjects was divided into two sub-groups consisting of 7,[20] and individuals were asked to make a typical public good investment binary decision (between *keep* and *give* \$6, which would double and be distributed equally among 6 other members[21]), but half of the groups were told that the public good would go to the other sub-group instead of their own group, and that their own group's income would depend similarly to the other group's investment decision. Note that this manipulation does not change the MPD payoff structure, since the individuals' dominant strategy is still to contribute nothing (*free-ride*), whereas all the members, either in one sub-group or in the other, benefit most from cooperation. In addition to this condition, Orbell et al. (1988) allowed half of the 7-person sub-groups to engage in a 10-minute discussion regarding which decision to make. Finally, the authors, after the discussion/no-discussion manipulation, announced to half of the sub-groups that now the recipients of the public good investment was changed for

---

[20] The 14-person group was first separated in one room, and then two sub-groups were directed to different rooms on different floors in the same building.

[21] That is, $y_i = \$2 \times n$ where n is a number of those who chose 'give' other than i. $U_i = x_i + y_i$

experimental purposes. Table 5.5 summarizes these three conditions and the resulting cooperation rates in percentage.

Table 5.5: Cooperation in three conditions (from Orbell et al. (1988: 814)).

	Initial belief that benefit from cooperation goes to			
	Own group		Other group	
	Belief at the time of decision-making			
Condition	Own group	Other group	Own group	Other group
No discussion	37.5	30.4	44.6	19.6
Discussion	78.6	58.9	32.1	30.4

The main finding is that discussion promotes cooperation among the members of one's own group, but not toward the other groups. Based on this finding the authors rejected the hypothesis that a generic norm of cooperation, which should not discriminate different groups, was at work. Bicchieri (2006:148), however, insists on the possibility that the norm at work was not a generic but context-specific one of promise keeping. This interpretation is mostly based on the finding from the content analysis of the taped discussion that subjects often promised to cooperate. Orbell et al. also found a 'carry over effect' of discussion, which is highlighted in the table (58.9%): apparently, discussion increased cooperation even after subjects were told that the benefit would go to the other group.[22] Bicchieri argues that this carry over effect is the inertia from the activation of a norm of promise keeping during the preceding discussion period. However, the data is compatible with the group identification hypothesis, if one can say that group identity also has inertia, which is no less *ad hoc* than Bicchieri's explanation.[23] Moreover, looking at the results in the no-discussion condition only, the comparison between the own-own-group condition (i.e., where subjects were told that the benefit goes to the own group and no change was announced) and the other-other-group condition (i.e., where subjects were told that the benefit goes to the other group and no change was announced)—37.5% vs. 19.6%—suggests that merely physically separating individuals into two groups can change cooperation rates somewhat

---

[22] A similar carry over effect was reported in Isaac and Walker (1988) discussed in chapter 4, and used by Bicchieri (2006:149) as evidence for the same conclusion.

[23] In fact, Bicchieri (2006:169) takes the fact that group identity does *not* carry over to a later stage as evidence *against* the group identity hypothesis. That is, she is expecting that carry over effect also happens to group identity.

significantly (almost twice in this case), despite the fact that MPD payoff structure is identical in both conditions. Although it is possible to say that mere formation of a group triggers norms, this explanation is no better than the explanation by group identity.

Bicchieri's second argument seems more plausible. She argues that the social norm hypothesis is compatible with the data from experiments where the topic of discussion was manipulated, while the group identity hypothesis is not. Her inference is that, if group identification is the main cause, it should increase cooperation no matter how group identity is aroused. More specifically, the content of discussion should not change contribution rate (they should equally increase cooperation) as long as group identity is created by such discussion. Although Dawes et al. (1977) showed that discussion needs to be relevant in order to increase cooperation, this may be because irrelevant discussion is not enough to create group identity. Bouas and Komorita (1996) fine-tuned the variable of relevant discussion by introducing a condition in which subjects discuss relevant topics such as the increase of tuition fee in the university where subjects studied, and a condition in which subjects discussed the social dilemma they faced in the experiment. Since both conditions are sufficiently favourable to nursing group identity among the subjects, argues Bicchieri (2006:165), we should observe the same cooperation rate in both conditions, if group identity is the main cause of cooperation. The result is favourable to Bicchieri: the cooperation rate in the dilemma discussion condition was 81%, whereas that in the relevant discussion condition was 17%.[24] This finding suggests that something other than group identification is at work in increasing cooperation. That something is, according to Bicchieri, a norm of promise keeping elicited in the discussion of the dilemma.

The evaluation of Bicchieri's argument above suggests that, while discussion-induced cooperation seems to be caused by a norm of promise-keeping or some such mechanisms (e.g. what Bouas and Komorita (1996) calls 'perceived consensus') rather than group identity, group identity remains as a possible cause of cooperation in non-discussion conditions. I will now turn to an explanation of such cooperation without communication.

---

[24] Bouas and Komorita (1996) actually used another condition ('common fate'), but this didn't have a significant effect on cooperation rate. In addition, they measured the strength of group identity independently based on Hinkle et al.'s Group Identity Scale, according to which group identity was strong in both discussion conditions.

5.4 Team Reasoning

Rather than opposing the group identity hypothesis, Bacharach (2006) bases his theory of *team reasoning* on cognitive mechanisms explicated by the group identity hypothesis. Bacharach, in so doing, modifies standard game theory in significant ways, hence my separate categorization of his theory from those of Margolis (2007) and Bicchieri (2006). First, let us see Bacharach's two ways of exploiting the idea of group identity. The first concerns the causes of group identification, the second its effects.

5.4.1 The Interdependence Hypothesis

Bacharach (2006: 76) points out that there are various causes of group identification, including 'being members of the same pre-existing social group; belonging to an *ad hoc* category; exposure to the pronouns "we", "our", and so on; having "common interests"; being subject to a "common fate"; shared experience; face-to-face contact; and "interdependence", that is, having common interests that can only be achieved together' (references are omitted). Bacharach then focuses on two among these causes, namely, *common interests* and *interdependence*, because these two factors are endogenous characters of payoffs in experimental games. He defines, roughly, that Players 1 and 2 have a *common interest* in one strategy profile (s^*) over another (s) if they mutually know that both prefers s^* to s. The important case of common interests is that of *interdependence*, where s^* can only be achieved by appropriate combination of P1 and P2's actions (P1 and P2 are said to have *copower* for s^* over s). Bacharach understands that P1 and P2 don't have to prefer s^* to all the other outcomes to be interdependent, as in a Prisoner's Dilemma (PD) P1 and P2 prefers (*defect, cooperate*) and (*cooperate, defect*), respectively, to (*cooperate, cooperate*). In a PD, players are said to be *strongly interdependent*, because cooperation from the other player, which is a necessary condition to achieve (*cooperate, cooperate*), seems far from assured (in fact, standard game theory says the opposite is assured by dominance). The first component of Bacharach's theory, the *interdependence hypothesis*, says that group identification is stimulated by the perception of strong interdependence; in game-theoretic form strong interdependence is defined as follows: for some S, S^* (sets of s and s^*) the players have common interest in, and copower for, S^* over S, and the solution set of game G in standard game theory contains outcomes in S (Bacharach 2006: 85). In terms of the cognitive framework outlined in section 5.2, strong interdependence provides players with a cue to interpret a given context as one in which players categorize themselves as members of a group, rather than individual players.

A notable thing about the interdependence hypothesis is that group identification is presumed to be a type of framing effect, but not an irrational one.[25] In the context of individual decision making, framing effects are often thought (by both proponents and antagonists of explanations based on such effects) as irrational because they violate the descriptive invariance principles. It is, however, implicit in Bacharach's discussion that group identification is not necessarily irrational. For one thing, there is a sense in which the cognitive framework in which framing occurs makes people's decision making possible, as well as causes biases. Although in Figure 5.2 I presented 'context' as an objective or 'raw' material of decision making, in games contexts often need to be interpreted for players to be able to make a choice, as the payoff respecification approach would recognize. As the objective standard against which one measures the deviation by framing effects becomes ambiguous, it becomes less clear that framing leads to irrationality. For another, Bacharach emphasizes strong independency (defined by a specific payoff structure) as the presumed cause of the framing effect. One prominent example of such payoff structure is found in PD. Normatively, most game theorists think that choosing a dominated strategy *cooperate* is outright irrational: 'one cannot expect rational agents to succeed in cooperating when constrained by the rules of the Prisoner's Dilemma' (Binmore 1994: 103). At the same time, some people have the opposite intuition that *cooperate* in a PD is the rational strategy. And yet others feel a 'dilemma' between these two answers. The intuition that *cooperate* can be rational comes from the fact that P1 and P2 are both better off in (*cooperate*, *cooperate*) than in (*defect*, *defect*). It is far from obvious that this intuition is irrational (i.e., normatively unjustifiable), given the empirical fact that many people at least feel the force of the 'dilemma', and some people benefit from betting on such intuition (i.e., they are making objectively 'good' game-theoretic reasoning). The notion of strong interdependence tries to capture this normative intuition as an empirical cognitive mechanism of framing. In so far as it tries to incorporate a potentially rational intuition as an empirically plausible cognitive mechanism, Bacharach's theory differs from the cognitive approach, which tends to characterize cognitive mechanisms as something objectively

---

[25] One exegetic point: Sugden and Gold (2006: 23) point out that Bacharach himself was ambivalent about whether his theory is assuming limitations of rationality, citing his aspiration to show 'coordination in favourable cases to be the product of an involuntary processing stage which is neither rational nor irrational, and good game-theoretic reasoning' (unpublished draft). As Sugden and Gold note, the distinction between arational framing and rational reasoning cannot be maintained in some cases. In fact, Bacharach's (2006) emphasis on common interests and strong interdependence suggests that 'good game-theoretic reasoning' and framing are intimately connected.

questionable, such as a source of 'social illusions' (Margolis 2007) and 'psychological essentialism' (Bicchieri 2006).

5.4.2 The Reasoning Effect and Agency Transformation

The second component of Bacharach's theory is the *reasoning effect* to create *agency transformation*. This is not involved in the classical effects of group identification he lists, which reads as follows: 'judging oneself to be more similar to other group members and dissimilar to nonmembers than one really is (accentuation), seeking unanimity at all costs (groupthink), favouring members against outsiders in bestowing benefits and in judging worth (in-group favouritism), using first-person plural pronouns,[26] depersonalization, emotional contagion, adopting the group's norms, being motivated by the group's goals (payoff transformation), and cooperating with fellow members' (Bacharach 2006: 76, original footnotes are omitted). The last item is of course what we want to explain. Payoff transformation is the effect presumed to take place because of group identification in public goods experiments with discussion. It is also a natural candidate of a cause of cooperation in public goods experiments without discussion, if one emphasizes, as Bacharach does, cognitive mechanisms endogenously induced by the payoff structures of games. However, Bacharach conjectures that something more fundamental is going on, namely, *agency transformation*. What is it, and how is it different from payoff transformation? What is the reasoning effect that is said to cause agency transformation?

The reasoning effect is one of the effects of group identification that prompts a specific mode of reasoning called *team reasoning*, which takes place in *coordination contexts*. A *simple coordination context* is defined over a triple (T, O, U), i.e., a set T of *agents* who have a set O of alternative action *options*, and a common ranking by the agents of the profiles made up by these alternatives, captured by a payoff function U (Bacharach 2006: 122). In a simple coordination context, an agent i is said to *team-reason* when she (i) computes o^*, (ii) locates the element o_i^*, and (iii) reasons that she should perform o_i^* because this is the component of the best profile that is under her own control. (i) and (ii) constitute reasoning *at the group level*, in which i reasons based not on alternatives but on profiles, as the director of T would do (What should T do as a group?). (iii) is reasoning *as an individual*, in which i reasons about her best alternative, i-th component, of the best profile (What should i do as an individual?).

---

[26] Unlike other effects, the use of first-person plural pronouns is not supported by empirical studies but by Bacharach's introspection and his reading of Gilbert's (1989) notion of joint-intentions. See Bacharach (2006: 91, fn. 5).

Although team reasoning is still a psychological event that can happen only in each individual's head, Bacharach says that some shift in agency is happening in team reasoning. This claim is based on the particular manner in which Bacharach defines an agent as follows: 'an entity that can do alternative things which cause outcomes, which it values more or less' (Bacharach 2006: 135). This is a very thin definition of agent, comparable to Ross's (2005) characterization of an agent as an entity with consistent preferences. While Ross applies his thin concept of agent to each temporal slice of individuals, Bacharach applies his concept to a set of individuals:[27] a 'set of agents defines a set of profiles which cause outcomes', so 'if one entifies the set—thinks of it as a group—and endows it with values, one is thinking of it as an agent' (Bacharach 2006: 135). In a simple coordination context, therefore, '[i]f one entifies T and endows it with U, one thinks of T as a (complex) agent or [...] as an *agency*' (*ibid.*). This process is called *agency transformation* because i 'thinks of her agential self—her doing and causing self—as a component part of T's agency' (p. 136). But is there something in agency transformation that cannot be captured by payoff transformation? In order to see that there is, let us return to the preference for social welfare we reviewed in section 5.1.1. There we have seen an individual's utility function similar to Bacharach's U, which showed that (*cooperate, cooperate*) can be the dominant strategy equilibrium. The difference between payoff transformation and agency transformation becomes transparent by looking at another class of games called *Hi-Lo* games (Table 5.6).

Table 5.6: Hi-Lo game

<table>
<tr><td></td><td></td><td colspan="2" align="center">Player 2</td></tr>
<tr><td></td><td></td><td align="center">A</td><td align="center">B</td></tr>
<tr><td rowspan="2">Player 1</td><td>A</td><td align="center">2, 2</td><td align="center">0, 0</td></tr>
<tr><td>B</td><td align="center">0, 0</td><td align="center">1, 1</td></tr>
</table>

A Hi-Lo game is a pure coordination game in which the PD's mixed motive is completed removed. That is, there is no conflict of interests as (A, A) is preferred to (A, B) and (B, A) by both Players 1 and 2. Perhaps somewhat surprisingly, game theory

---

[27] Bacharach envisioned to provide an analysis of personhood as a special case of team agency of temporal selves, but his death prevented this. John Davis allowed me to read a draft of his new book, which contains a comparison between Ross and Bacharach.

does not predict (A, A) as a unique solution, but allows (B, B) as *equally* likely. P1 is rational (in the sense of best-reply) to choose A, only if P2 also chooses A; P1 is equally rational (in the sense of best-reply) to choose B, only if P2 also chooses B. The same to P2. In a Nash equilibrium the rationality of each player's choice is conditional on the choice of the other player (unlike in a dominance equilibrium). Can payoff transformation help? The answer is *no*.

Table 5.7: Hi-Lo-material game played by individuals with preference for social welfare

Player 2

		A	B
	A	2+2, 2+2	0, 0
Player 1			
	B	0, 0	1+1, 1+1

Table 5.7 is the Hi-Lo game in Table 5.6 after payoff respecification with a social welfare utility function (see section 5.1.1).[28] The payoff structure remains exactly the same, and therefore both (A, A) and (B, B) remains two Nash equilibria of the game. Not only does game theory's prescription conflict with our intuition about what one should do in such games (*judgemental fact*), but also its prediction fails both in the field and in the lab (*behavioural fact*). Team reasoning gives a straightforward solution to this *Hi-Lo Paradox*. Each player computes the best profile (2, 2), locates its elements (A and A), and then reasons that she should play the component that is under her own control (A) (and executes it): each player is thinking as a member of a group qua an agency with T (P1 and P2), O ([A, A], [B, B], [A, B] and [B, A]), and U ([A, A] > [B, B] > [A, B] ≈ [B, A]). Bacharach proposes his theory of team reasoning as a general theory of games that can explain not only the fact that people are remarkably good at solving this type of pure coordination problems (simple coordination contexts), but the fact that people often achieve common interests despite the presence of 'mixed motives' in games such as Stag Hunts, Battles of the Sexes, bargaining games, and Prisoner's Dilemmas. Its wider scope is one of Bacharach's arguments for the superiority of team reasoning vis-à-vis other theories ('transcendental evidence'): '[t]he team-reasoning theory reaches parts that no other theory can reach' (Bacharach 2006: 146). I'm not sure

---

[28] The term for own money is omitted, but this does not change the analysis.

if such an inference to the best explanation lends any *evidential* support to a theory. In particular, what Bacharach calls a 'modest' version of this inference seems unwarranted. Even if he is right in concluding that existing theories that purport to explain the behavioural fact either beg the question or change the subject or appeal to irrationalities, thereby failing to explain the judgemental fact, he cannot exclude that there is a theory that explains these facts at least as well as his theory of team reasoning. (By contrast, what Bacharach calls the 'grandiose' argument that there could possibly be no theory yielding A-choice in Hi-Lo games that does not imply team reasoning can be sound, because this can be deductively shown.) Let us then look at what the empirical evidence says about the theory of team reasoning.

5.4.3 Experimental Tests of Team Reasoning

In this section, I will first review Bacharach's own experiments on Hi-Lo games, and then other experiments performed recently to test the theory of team reasoning.

Let me reconstruct the reason why Bacharach uses Hi-Lo games to test his theory of team reasoning (cf. Bacharach 2006: 147). First, consider a two person PD-material game. Although preference for social welfare transforms the game into one in which *cooperate* dominates *defect*, this prediction is falsified by the fact that the typical cooperation rate is a little short of 50% (the standard prediction that *defect* dominates is falsified by the same evidence, of course). The problem seems to be the assumption that players rank (*cooperate, defect*) and (*defect, cooperate*) as higher than (*defect, defect*) simply because the former is Pareto-superior to the latter. But players may have some other motives as suggested by models of social preference (inequality aversion, reciprocal fairness, etc.). For example, inequality aversion plus social welfare may define *social welfare distributive fairness* utility function as follows:

$$SWDFU_i \equiv \sum[i{=}1 \to N]\$_i - \beta|\$_i \ - \${-}_i|$$

Table 5.8: PD-material game played by individuals with *SWDF* preferences

		Player 2	
		cooperate	*defect*
Player 1	*cooperate*	4, 4	2-4β, 2-4β
	defect	2-4β, 2-4β	0, 0

Table 5.8 shows a PD-material game transformed with this utility function. If $\beta > 1/2$, this is a game of Hi-Lo, in which both (*cooperate, cooperate*) and (*defect, defect*) are Nash equilibria.[29] However, this is as far as the payoff respecification or transformation approach can go, *viz.*, to make games with 'mixed motives' into a pure coordination game. Using a Hi-Lo game to test the theory of team reasoning against others, therefore, makes it possible to control for the effect of payoff transformation. The problem, however, is that in unambiguous Hi-Lo games almost 100% of the subjects choose A, making it difficult to measure the effect of group identification in such situations. Moreover, a prominent hypothesis by Harsanyi and Selten (1988) makes the same prediction based on an individualistic mechanism, i.e., that people choose A in Hi-Lo games *because its Pareto-optimality makes it salient*. Thus Bacharach and Guerra designed a Hi-Lo matching experiment (unpublished but summarized in Bacharach (2006: 147-149)) to discriminate between these two hypotheses, adding an equilibrium strategy set that is *salient but not Pareto-optimal*, and crossed it with two group identity conditions (with and without manipulations such as the use of group-oriented language 'your partner' instead of 'the other person' and imposing a common fate). The basic findings are: (i) when equilibrium is not unique, a salient but Pareto-inferior equilibrium was often observed (without group identity manipulations, such equilibrium strategy was chosen by 26-44% of the subjects); but (ii) group identity manipulations shifted the balance toward a strategy in Pareto-optimal equilibrium (16-28%). They observed a range of figures for each action probably because some games had two alternative strategies and others three, thereby making different games more or less cognitively demanding for subjects. Or perhaps these are simply due to random error as the sample size was rather small. In any case, though preliminary, these results seem to suggest that Bacharach's theory, in particular the hypothesis concerning the reasoning effect of group identity, may be capturing something real. However, the first part of Bacharach's causal hypothesis, from strong interdependency to group identification, is not tested here.

Recently, Colman, Pulford and Rose (2008) report two experiments designed to test the theory of team reasoning directly against standard, individualistic game theory. Since this is the first experimental study that addresses team reasoning (apart from

---

[29] Bacharach starts from a Stag-Hunt game (in which there are asymmetries in payoffs for P1 and P2 at (C, D) and (D, C)) and then transforms it into a Hi-Lo game. My reconstruction is meant to be equivalent to such transformation, but presented slightly differently in order to make it consistent with my focus on the PD in chapter 4.

Bacharach's own study), I will analyze the designs and results of their experiments in detail. Unlike Bacharach and Guerra's, these experiments are not immune from the argument from payoff transformation. Rather than trying to create a situation in which payoff transformation does not make a difference, Colman et al. (2008) explicitly crafted strategy profiles in such a way that each profile would be chosen by individuals with a specific preference. Table 5.9 summarizes these options in Experiment 1:

Table 5.9: Strategy-profiles 'customized' for different types of individuals (made from Colman et al. (2008: 391-392); each set of pounds sterling represents money to self and other, respectively.)

Prediction	Maximizing: Vignette	A other's £	B equality	C collective £	D own £	E £ difference
G-oriented	Fund-raising	£1, £7	£3, £3	£5, £6	£6, £4	£4, £1
	GM site	£1, £7	£4, £5	£4, £6	£6, £3	£4, £0
I-oriented	Prize draw	£3, £7	£4, £4	£5, £6	£6, £2	£5, £0
	Poker	£1, £6	£2, £2	£4, £5	£5, £2	£4, £0

The table also shows that these profiles are embedded in four life-like vignettes made for framing manipulations; two are predicted to elicit group-orientation, the other two to elicit individual-orientation. For example, the 'GM site' vignette reads as follows: 'You are involved in a group of people who are against a proposed test site for genetically modified crops. You and another group member spend half an hour in the local town collecting money for publicity opposing the new test site', followed by the above options labelled neutrally in alphabet. The players were told that the verbal contents of the vignettes were merely to help their understanding of the payoffs and that each will receive own payoff plus the amount of money her partner (anonymously assigned) assigned to other (e.g., if an individual chooses A in 'GM site', while her partner chooses B, then the former receives £6 (£1 plus £5) and the latter receives £11 (£4 plus £7)). Table 5.10 below summarizes the result in percentage of each option chosen by the subjects (N=81), who played in groups of approximately 30. The money was paid after the experiment according to the result of one game randomly chosen from the four that were played (participants earnings ranged from £4 to £13; mean= £9.48; standard deviation=£1.89).

Table 5.10: Results of Experiment 1 (from Colman et al. (2008:393); numbers are in (rounded) percentage of the subjects who chose options

prediction	Label: maximizing: vignette	A other's £	B equality	C collective £	D own £	E £ difference
G-oriented	Fund-raising	0.0	4.9	59.3	34.6	1.2
	GM site	2.5	11.1	49.4	35.8	1.2
I-oriented	Prize draw	1.2	16.1	23.5	54.3	4.9
	Poker	1.2	6.2	22.2	59.3	11.1

After some statistical analysis (in particular the significance of C-D difference highlighted in the table), the authors concluded that 'the interpretive framing of the games had a moderately powerful effect on the outcome preferences and mode of reasoning adopted by the players, with predominantly collective rationality and team reasoning only in the vignettes designed to prime it' (Colman et al. 2008: 393). One problem the authors are vaguely[30] aware of is that this experiment does not test Bacharach's *interdependence hypothesis*, because it does not control for the possibility that vignette manipulations cause group identification in some other ways (e.g. 'same category', 'same social group', 'competing group' and so on). More generally, the data do not eliminate an individualistic hypothesis like Bicchieri's (2006) norm-based explanation, which does not even presuppose group identification in the first place.[31]

---

[30] I say 'vaguely' because Colman et al. (2008: 393) talk only about their inability to measure quantitatively the framing effect within group-oriented vignettes. My point is rather that their design does not allow them to differentiate qualitatively different kinds of framing effects, such as the framing effects that are endogenous to games and those that are exogenous.

[31] Colman et al. (2008) elicited beliefs by asking subjects 'What do you expect the other person to choose?' and infer that the fact that a large majority (77.1%) of the players who chose C expected their co-players to choose it also supports the team-reasoning hypothesis. Bicchieri would say that this suggests empirical expectations on the part of the players, which is consistent wish her definition of social norms.

Since group identification is an important mediating cognitive mechanism of which team reasoning is presumed to be one effect, this design needs to be improved. Another problem, of which the authors are unaware, is that the large percentages of C-choice in group-oriented vignettes (50-60%) may be a result of *individual reasoning* based on preference for social welfare (Pareto-optimality). Sugden (2008: 403) points out that this indeterminacy results from the use of *decomposable games* in Experiment 1, plus the assumption that *utility is linear*. Another potential problem is more serious, however, because even if games are non-decomposable, there is always in principle a possibility that payoff transformation (by some utility like *SWDFU*) explains the data as a result of individual reasoning, everywhere except in Hi-Lo games. Let us now examine whether Experiment 2 improves on these points.

Experiment 2 consists of five abstract one-shot two-person 3×3 normal-form games, each with one Pareto-optimal profile and one Nash equilibrium profile (played by the same subjects N=81 immediately after Experiment 1; participants' earnings ranged from £5 to £9; mean=£6.54; standard deviation=£1.18). Figure 5.3 shows the five games' payoffs in normal form, although decision problems were presented to subjects not in normal form but in sentences like 'You choose X; the other person chooses Y. You get £x, the other person gets £y, etc.

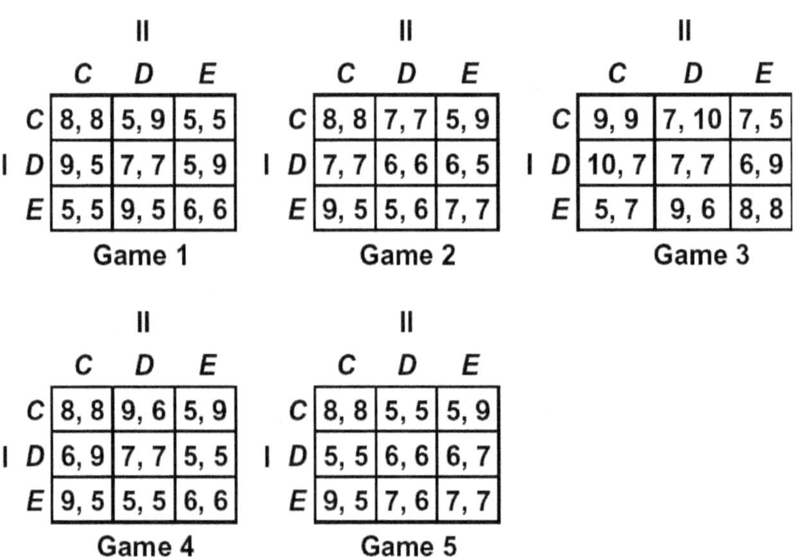

Figure 5.3: Five PD games, in each of which (E, E) is a unique Nash equilibrium, which is strictly Pareto-dominated by (C, C) (reproduced from Colman et al. 2008: 393).

Table 5.11: Results of Experiment 2 (from Colman et al. (2008: 394))

Game	Strategy chosen			$\chi^2(2, N=81)$	p
	C: pro-Pareto	D	E: Nash		
1	53.1	32.1	14.8	17.9	<0.001
2	56.8	3.7	39.5	35.6	<0.001
3	55.6	39.5	4.9	32.5	<0.001
4	86.4	6.2	7.4	102.7	<0.001
5	54.3	0.0	45.7	41.4	<0.001

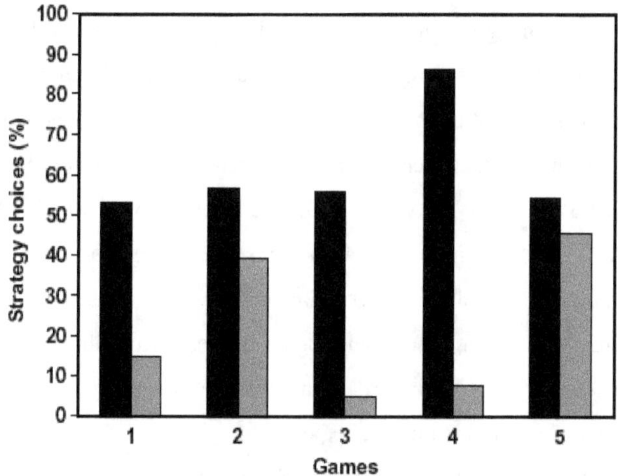

Figure 5.4: C-choice (dark bars) versus E-choice (light bars) in five experiments (*ibid.*)

Table 5.11 and Figure 5.4 summarize the result. The major finding is that in all five games, more than half of the subjects (53%-86%) chose C, a necessary component strategy of the Pareto-optimal outcome (C, C), despite the presence of a unique Nash equilibrium strategy. Thus Colman et al. (2008: 395) conclude that 'team reasoning predicted strategy choices more powerfully than game theory'. Do the data justify this conclusion?

Sugden (2008: 403) expresses some reservation: he suggests that it is 'now widely accepted that the standard assumptions of [best-reply] rationality and common knowledge do *not*, in general, imply Nash choice in one-shot games' (original italics), because the necessary presupposition for this proof—that every game has a unique rational solution (as claimed by e.g. Harsanyi and Selten 1988)—is ungrounded. Because of the controversial status of Nash choice, Sugden proposes to look at games in which each player has a strictly dominant strategy. Game 5, the only game in which E is a dominant strategy, yielded the closest match between C-choice and E-choice (54% vs. 46%). Sugden interprets this as showing that the subjects are almost equally divided into two types, team reasoners and individual-payoff-maximizing players. Further, Sugden proposes that the individuals of the latter type are prone to cognitive limitations and random error, as hypothesized by *level-n theory* or *cognitive hierarchy theory* (Camerer, Ho and Chong 2004; Stahl and Wilson 1995). Cognitive hierarchy theory says that each player is modelled as having a particular *level* of strategic reasoning: Level 0 players simply choose among strategies randomly; level 1 players maximize their expected payoffs given the belief that their opponents are at level 0 or 1, and so on. This theory relaxes the best-reply rationality assumption, which requires unlimited depth in this reasoning. It turns out that, *ex post*, the data summarized in Figure 5.4 can fit very well with a model which assumes that about 50% of the subjects are team reasoners, 10% are level 0 players, and 40% are level 1 players (Sugden 2008: 401, Table 1). Although Sugden admits that such *post hoc* explanation is not a serious explanation of this particular set of experimental data, he suggests that this idea makes intuitive sense, since team reasoning is cognitively less demanding (compute s^*, and then locate s_i^*, and just do your part!) than individual reasoning (maximize own payoff, given others do the same) in this 3×3 experiment.

I am interested in the *ad hocness* of Sugden's suggestion, rather than its *post hocness*: in particular, can cognitive hierarchy theory be non-*ad hoc$_3$* in Lakatos's sense, that is, is it consistent with the spirit of some research programme? The answer seems to be yes, because various cognitive limitations are well supported in the context of individual risky decision making. To the extent that behavioural decision research is not *ad hoc$_3$*, as I have argued in chapter 3, applying this approach in the context of game theory is not *ad hoc$_3$* either. One might argue that Bacharach's theory of team reasoning is more in line with the spirit of game theory, i.e., theorizing strategic interactions as games among *rational* agents. Sugden's intuitive suggestion, however, nicely reminds us that team reasoning itself presupposes a particular framing effect (the reasoning effect), which makes team reasoning cognitively less demanding and thus more available. In this sense, the theory of team reasoning and theories of cognitive limitations are not necessarily incompatible. The evidence of subject heterogeneity reviewed in chapter 4 also supports such co-existence.[32]

One possibility discussed by neither Colman et al. (2008) nor Sugden (2008) is that the subjects in Experiment 2 have preferences for social welfare.[33] The prediction of payoff transformation with a simpler SWU may be made consistent with the data. A problematic case is Game 3, where payoff transformation makes (C, C) and (E, E) both Nash equilibria, with the former Pareto-dominating the latter (18>16). The low percentage of E-choice (5%) compared to that of C-choice (56%) might be explained by the salience of Pareto-optimality à la Harsanyi and Selten (1988), but this leaves the very large percentage of D-choice in this game (almost 40%) unexplained. Colman et al. (2008: 395) interpret the result of Game 3 in terms of (C, C)'s *risk dominance* over (E, E), but this doesn't explain the high rate of (D, D) either. Sugden's cognitive hierarchy model explains (D, D) well, as well as (D, D) in Game 1. All in all, I suggest that the heterogeneity hypothesis that the subjects consist of team reasoners and individual reasoners (both with cognitive limitations) is more plausible than the homogeneity hypothesis that they are all individual reasoners with one type of social welfare preference, mainly because the former, but not the latter, is consistent with the findings from the public goods experiments that strongly suggests subject heterogeneity.[34]

To sum up the discussion of this section, I will list what has been shown so far and what has to be shown in future research on team reasoning. Bacharach (2006) has made a conceptually compelling case for team reasoning, by making it as non-mysterious as it can be. In a nutshell, the theory of team reasoning is a psychological theory of how reasoning—*qua* part of cognitive causal processes—interacts with other cognitive mechanisms such as group identification and framing. The *empirical* case for team reasoning, by contrast, is not adequate yet. Although group identification seems to elicit team reasoning, team reasoning purely triggered by strong interdependence has not yet been clearly observed, even in Colman et al. (2008). In order to investigate

---

[32] An interesting question is whether the relative cognitive demand of an individual frame makes team-frame more available to players. Such interaction has not been studied yet.

[33] I won't consider here the possibility of inequality aversion, because Experiment 2 consists of abstract games without cues that could activate such preference. The verbal explanation was rather against such preference: 'You are now going to make [several] decisions, from which you can earn money. There are no scenarios with these—they are purely cash decisions' (Colman et al. 2008: 394). The authors explicitly deny the possibility of carry-over effects from Experiment 1.

[34] There is a question about what exactly is heterogeneous. Most likely both preferences *and* cognitive limitations are.

whether and how payoff structures influence framing, other frames (such as different vignettes) should be controlled for; how cognitively demanding each game is must be explicitly taken into account in designing experiments, and should be measured if possible; subject heterogeneity (and what the heterogeneity is about) must be measured instead of assumed in statistical models; different preference elicitation methods (such as the decision schedule method) must be explicitly compared.

5.5 Conclusion

In this chapter, I carefully evaluated several recent approaches in behavioural economics to explain anomalies in game theory experiments. Models of social preference are admittedly more sophisticated than those of altruism reviewed in the last chapter, but these models reveal the limits of the payoff respecification approach, which presupposes that game theory works well once we get the payoffs right. The problems of this approach were highlighted in the fact that psychologically most 'realistic' models of reciprocal fairness make the measurement of preferences itself either implausible or redundant. On this basis, I contended that alternative approaches should be informed by the literatures of evolutionary, social and cognitive psychology, instead of further complicating utility functions and equilibrium concepts with intuitive folk psychology. I have examined two prominent approaches, theories of social norms and of team reasoning. Although both keep some aspects of the rational choice tradition, they depart from the standard economic approach in a number of ways. In particular, social norms are not endogenous in models, and team reasoning allows (technically defined) group agency; it is easy to criticize these models for these 'heterodox' characteristics, but the available evidence suggests that crossing the traditional boundaries of economics and psychology and exploring new theories may be more fruitful than 'incorporating psychology into economics' à la Rabin (1993). One obvious direction is to explicitly model the cognitive processes studied by psychologists, as exemplified by social norms and cognitive hierarchy theory. Another approach, which I find promising, is to reinterpret reasoning explicitly as a cognitive process that is genuine and therefore interacts with other cognitive processes such as framing. This may require serious modifications to the concepts of rational play in game theory, but may result in a surprisingly simple but potentially powerful theory, as exemplified by the theory of team reasoning. Keeping these points in mind, we may be able to create experimental paradigms that could move behavioural research in new directions.

Chapter 6

Neuroeconomics and the Unity of Science

In the previous chapters, I have been examining several approaches to explain anomalies in individual decision making. Observations of inconsistent choices under uncertainty have led to the multiple-self approach and the procedural approach (chapter 3). Observations of cooperative and reciprocal strategies in games have led to the payoff respecification approach and the extended rational choice approach (chapters 4 and 5). In either case, some mental processes (evaluative, cognitive, or emotional) are inferred from the observation of subjects' choice behaviour. This inference from behaviour to mental processes makes both theory and experimentation crucial for behavioural economics: theories (such as preference theory, EUT and game theory) give formal structures to the empirical system under study, thereby enabling precise measurement and severe test. In turn, experiments provide artificial but transparent situations in which predictions of different models can be discriminated in a sharp manner. Innovations in behavioural economics have been thus both theoretical and experimental. Recently, however, another kind of innovation that took place in different contexts has had an impact on behavioural economics. The innovation is a development of brain-imaging techniques such as functional magnetic resonance imaging (fMRI) in clinical and cognitive psychology. *Neuroeconomics* combines these techniques with standard behavioural decision-making experiments, and aims to gain new insights that were unavailable with behavioural observations alone.[1]

Neuroeconomics has caused a lively controversy among economists as to whether such measurement of brain activities is relevant to economics in the first place, even if technology allows it. This debate is a good opportunity to make explicit and evaluate economists' scepticism about the relevance of psychology to economics. I will do this and argue that economists should be realists about mental processes. Moreover, I will analyze some real examples from neuroscientific research in order to see different degrees to and senses in which scientists can be realists about decision-relevant mental processes. This exercise will reveal the importance of metaphysical commitments underlying the different models of decision making we have been reviewing.

---

[1] Ross (2008) calls this research programme 'Behavioural economics in the scanner (BES)', and distinguishes it from what he calls 'Neurocellular economics (NE)', another programme to employ economic theories (e.g., EUT) to model behaviour of brain parts, not of individual economic agents. Although these programmes are intimately related, I shall focus in this chapter on the former, and call it *neuroeconomics*.

The chapter proceeds as follows: First, I will revisit the classic debate on reductionism in 6.1 as a general framework of the discussion. Then, in 6.2, I will examine the recent controversy on the prospect of neuroeconomics. I will critically analyze in particular one conceptual and one methodological critiques of neuroeconomics by economists. This examination will suggest two distinctive metaphysical stances underlying the debate, mechanism and functionalism, which will be discussed at length in 6.3. In 6.4 I shall turn to some examples from cognitive neuroscience, and show how the functional stance is 'at work' in actual research. I will suggest that the radical replacement of standard economics by a totally new neuroeconomic model is unlikely, based on this examination. Some conclusions follow (6.5).

6.1 The Metaphysical Turn in the Unity of Science Debate

After the demise of the logical positivists' project to formally reduce all statements about inferred, theoretical entities into empirically verifiable sentences,[2] the modern debate on reductionism has become 'openly metaphysical' (Trout 1991: 388). Take Oppenheim and Putnam's (1958) classic argument for microreductionism—the thesis that it is possible and desirable to reduce one theory into another by replacing the vocabulary of a 'higher'-level theory with that of a 'lower'-level theory if the explanatory power of the reducing theory is stronger than that of the reduced. This microreductionism is based upon a particular metaphysical picture that there be levels in ontology such that a thing belonging to one level is composed of things that belong to the next level below, and so on, leading down to the lock-bottom level which is composed of things that cannot be decomposed any further. Fodor (1974) convincingly argues that an appeal to such mereological metaphysics does not imply that microreduction is even in principle possible (let alone desirable): *if* a generalization (or law-like statement) about things, events, properties, phenomena, etc. at a 'higher' level (e.g. Gresham's law[3]) is physically realized by heterogeneous things, events, etc. at a 'lower' level (e.g., coins, notes, cheques, electronic data, etc.), *then* theoretical reduction will result in an unsystematic disjunction of the kind-terms of the 'lower' level(s) which has less cognitive value than the original generalization. Fodor (1974:

---

[2] Recently, this interpretation of logical positivism has been criticized as misrepresenting what some logical positivists (in particular Carnap in *Aufbau*) were trying to accomplish. See e.g. Friedman (1999).
[3] Gresham's Law states that 'bad' money drives out 'good', i.e., if coins containing metal of different value have the same value as legal tender, the coins composed of cheaper metal ('bad' money) will be used for payment, while those made of more valuable metal ('good' money) will be kept and exported, thereby disappearing from circulation. This is Fodor's (1974) example.

113) contends that the antecedent is probably true because 'the way the world is put together' is such that the kind-terms in the special sciences *'cross-classify'* the physical natural kind-terms. This is to say that what makes microreduction very unlikely is not our limited epistemic ability to make sense of the disjunction, but rather the world itself.

After the 'metaphysical turn', philosophers of science started to look at both the contents and activities of different sciences for evidential support of claims either for or against reductionism. For metaphysical doctrines regarding the nature of material world such as reductionism must at least be consistent with the sciences as they are at present (Ladyman and Ross 2007). Naturally, the two classic papers mentioned above draw on theories and developments of various sciences to support their claims. But where Oppenheim and Putnam (1958) find the evidence for microreduction, Fodor (1974) sees the opposite: first, the successful theoretical reductions cited by Oppenheim and Putnam[4] are not a goal of science in itself, but rather a byproduct of scientists' primary concern to explicate the physical mechanisms which bring about phenomena conforming (or failing to conform) to 'higher'-level generalizations. Second, the special sciences are proliferating, rather than converging to physics, suggesting that the world is heterogeneous in the sense explicated above.

Fodor's metaphysical picture (which was mainly motivated by his concern about some psychologists' confused commitment to physiological reductionism) has gained some support from the studies of diverse sciences such as biology (Dupré 1993), physics and macroeconomics (Cartwright 1999). The lesson I'd like to draw from this debate is, however, not the plausibility of one comprehensive worldview over another, but rather the basic point that whether or not kind-terms in different sciences are heterogeneous is ultimately an empirical matter. Indeed, Fodor does not deny that a particular attempt to elucidate the physical mechanisms of a phenomenon may result in microreduction. Thus if scientists suggest a possibility of microreduction, we need to carefully assess its empirical success, rather than its affinity with the predominant metaphysics. Let us then look at the attempt of microreduction that is most relevant to our concerns, namely, *neuroeconomics*.

6.2 The Neuroeconomics Controversy

6.2.1 The Promise of Neuroeconomics

Paul Zak (2004: 1737) characterizes *neuroeconomics* as 'an emerging transdisciplinary field that uses neuroscientific measurement techniques to identify the neural substrates

---

[4] Of course, another problem is that, as Trout (1991: 390) rightly points out, Oppenheim and Putnam (1958) have not shown that these episodes of reduction satisfy their criteria of theoretical microreduction.

associated with economic decisions', where 'economic decisions' are broadly interpreted as 'any (human or non-human) decision process that is made by evaluating alternatives'. This characterization suggests an instrument- or technology-driven approach: neuroeconomics is possible because technology enables a new measurement that was theretofore impossible. The sense of excitement generated by this technological innovation is well expressed by Camerer, Loewenstein and Prelec (2005), who promote neuroeconomics as a natural extension of successful behavioural economics. Just like economics has been informed by behavioural decision research, which is a branch of psychology, they argue, behavioural economics will benefit a lot by learning from other areas of psychology such as the rapidly growing field of cognitive neuroscience. More specifically, Camerer et al. (2005) propose two ways in which neuroscience can inform economics, namely, *incremental* and *radical*. The incremental approach 'adds variables to conventional accounts of decision-making or suggests specific functional forms to replace "as if" assumptions' (p.10). The radical approach, by contrast, 'points to an entirely new set of [theoretical] constructs to underlie economic decision-making' (*ibid.*). While acknowledging the incremental approach as one way to 'enhance the realism of existing models' (p.55), the authors conjecture that the radical approach becomes compelling in the long run. In particular, Camerer et al. point to the limits of traditional economic concepts such as preferences, beliefs and constraints in capturing causal roles of *automatic* and *emotional* mental processes interacting with deliberate decision-making processes. They thus propose to explain economic decision-making as a result of the interaction of the four types of neural functioning that are yielded by crossing two dimensions, *cognitive/affective* and *controlled/automatic*.

In light of the discussion in 6.1, Camerer et al. (2005) can be interpreted as advancing a kind of microreduction. Of course, as working scientists, Camerer and colleagues are primarily concerned with what Fodor (1974) calls the explication of physical mechanisms, a form of reduction that does not necessarily make a 'higher'-level generalization false or redundant. Their description of the incremental approach is consistent with this interpretation. Moreover, quotes such as 'thinking about the brain does not so much "falsify" rational choice theories as suggest *entirely new distinctions and questions*' (Camerer et al. 2005: 55, my italics) indicate that they are trying to *add* another layer to economics, rather than to *replace* economics with neuroscience. In this sense, they differ from the 'confused' neuropsychologists whom Fodor (1974) had in mind. However, in an important sense Camerer and colleagues are serious about microreduction. That is, they insist on the *necessity* of taking the radical approach in the long run. In an empiricist mood, they contend that there is no reason to stick to the old models of constrained optimization if a radically different neuroscientific model predicts economic behaviour narrowly construed *as well as* a broader range of behaviours (p. 55). In a realist mood, they hint that the '*direct measurement* of thoughts and feelings' made possible by the recent development of neuroscience is 'leading to new theoretical constructs and *calling old ones into question*' (p. 10; my italics). In either mood, the authors are envisioning a *replacement* of the economic theories of choice by neuroscientific theories that explain decision-making not only better, but also in an entirely different way. It may be said that Camerer and colleagues' version of reductionism is even more radical than that of Oppenheim and Putnam's (1958), in the sense that the former skips the process of finding out kind-terms at a 'lower'-level (i.e. neural functions) that correspond to co-extensive kind-terms at a 'higher'-level (i.e. preferences, etc.). It suggests the possibility of simply restarting theorizing from scratch, based on totally different grounds.[5]

Camerer et al.'s (2005) advertisement of neuroeconomics was successful enough to cause a controversy in the economic profession (see Caplin and Schotter (2008); the 2008 special issue of *Economics and Philosophy*; and the forthcoming special issue of the *Journal of Economic Methodology*). I will start from reviewing Gul and Pesendorfer's (2008) response to Camerer et al. (2005), as it states explicitly some general reservations about psychology that are rarely voiced by economists in their writings.[6] After that, I will examine a more methodologically oriented critique by Harrison (2008).

6.2.2 Gul and Pesendorfer's Conceptual Critique

A first thing to note is that Gul and Pesendorfer (2008: 1)[7] define neuroeconomics not by its use of brain-imaging techniques as Zak (2004) does, but by its presuppositions of (i) the direct relevance of psychological and neural[8] evidence to economic theories and/or (ii) the divergence of 'choice utility' and 'experienced utility'. Because of this

---

[5] Camerer et al. (2005: 11) ask the rhetorical question: 'how economics might have evolved differently if it had been informed from the start by insights and findings now available from neuroscience'.
[6] At a conference on neuroeconomics, Ariel Rubinstein reported that no colleagues in their economics department entirely agree with Gul and Pesendorfer. If this is true, their response to neuroeconomics is not representative of the economic profession (or at least not of the department of economics at Princeton). Nevertheless, they are not straw men but highly respected scholars in one of the world's leading economics departments.
[7] Page references are to their working paper.
[8] Although Gul and Pesendorfer (2008) use the term 'physiology' instead of 'neurology', I stick to the latter term. This does not change their argument substantially.

definition, the scope of their critique is very broad, involving 'research that makes no specific reference to neuroscience and is traditionally referred to as psychology and economics'.[9] Although such broad definition is not in itself problematic, their critique is indeed problematic, or so I shall argue. In what follows I will focus on their critique of presupposition (i), and will not discuss presupposition (ii), which mainly concerns their defence of welfare economics. Nor shall I discuss their lengthy comparison of the standard economic model and what they call a neuroeconomic model, because the only point of their comparison is to make the wrong observation that the success of the neuroeconomic model is judged by its agreement with psychological evidence, while that of the standard model is solely judged by its congruence with behavioural evidence (see later for the falsity of this claim).[10]

Briefly, Gul and Pesendorfer's (2008) argument can be reconstructed as the following syllogism:

1. Economics equates preference with choice behaviour (revealed preference theory, or RPT), which has been proven useful for predicting economic phenomena (prices, quantities, etc.) as the aggregate of choice behaviour.
2. RPT does not refer to any psychological or neural process.
3. Therefore, psychological or neural evidence is irrelevant to economics, i.e., it can neither refute nor improve economics.

We have already seen that Premise 1 is false in chapter 4. Moreover, Conclusion 3, even if established, does not imply that *psychology* or *neuroscience* can neither refute nor improve economics, since these disciplines also may provide *behavioural* evidence, which can be relevant to economics (Wilkinson 2008: 19). Behavioural decision research (and also neuroeconomics) is concerned with the inaccuracy of behavioural predictions of standard economics as well as its assumptions' unrealisticness. In fact, many economists (including Gul and Pesendorfer) acknowledge that the main contribution from behavioural decision research to economics is the accumulation of 'experimental evidence that challenges behavioral assumptions of economic models' (Gul and Pesendorfer 2008: 1). But we have also seen that such evidence was

---

[9] Gul and Pesendorfer (2008) use 'psychology and economics' as equivalent to what I call behavioural economics in this thesis. While it is possible to adopt their terminology (as 'law and economics'), I prefer behavioural economics, and reserve 'psychology and economics' or 'economics and psychology' to refer to the conjunction of the two disciplines.

[10] For a more informative comparison of standard economic modeling and its psychological counterpart in the case of intertemporal decision making, see Ross (forthcoming).

accumulated not only because of the development of experimental methods in economics but also because of their adoption of well-developed mental models (cognition, information processing, etc.) in psychology. It is therefore unfair to trivialize this contribution from psychology as 'the common practice of economists to use psychological insights as inspiration for economic modeling' (Gul and Pesendorfer 2008: 1). We have seen in the previous chapter that this is easier said than done. The quote above reveals another point that is more important: behavioural researchers, either economists or psychologists, must presuppose *some* model about internal processes when they make behaviourally testable models. The only difference is that psychologists have explicit models in mind while economists don't. This point has been shown as the limits of the 'usefulness' of economic modelling in the previous chapters. Economic models can be and have been made incrementally more realistic.

Gul and Pesendorfer's (2008) argument cannot deny the possibility of the radical approach, either. Consider Premise 2, namely, the claim that revealed preference theory does not refer to psychological or neurological processes. First of all, even if economics referred to completely different things from the things to which psychology and neuroscience refer, it is not a problem for Camerer et al.'s (2005) version of reductionism, because reduction would be complete if a radically different psycho-neurological model explained economic decisions and aggregate data better than traditional economic theory does (e.g., by having a wider scope, by predicting more accurately, etc.). Whether this can be achieved is an empirical question, which cannot be answered by an *a priori* argument about reference. Second, economic theory refers to 'the same things' as psychology and neuroscience do, in the uncontroversial sense that all particular events, processes, objects, properties, states, etc. that the sciences talk about are nothing but *physical* (this is a thesis known as 'token physicalism', the default position in the philosophy of mind: see e.g., Carruthers 2000, ch. 1).[11] For example, in criticizing Camerer's claim[12] that neuroeconomics will show that EUT is too simplistic a model of decision making under uncertainty, Gul and Pesendorfer (2008: 25) note that '[t]he conceptual separation between probabilities and utilities is very important for expected utility *theory*' (original italics), and that the separation 'need not have a physiological counterpart'. Gul and Pesendorfer can, in line with token physicalism, be interpreted as saying that kind-terms in economics and physiology may 'cross-classify'

---

[11] Although externalism about intentional states (beliefs and desires) may be used to defend the disciplinary autonomy of economics, Gul and Pesendorfer (2008) do not mention it.

[12] Gul and Pesendorfer are referring to a short article on neuroeconomics published on Camerer's webpage. See http://www.hss.caltech.edu/~camerer/web_material/n.html

(Fodor 1974), not that they refer to different things.[13] [14] However, as I have noted in 6.1, the possibility of cross-classification is contingent, as Fodor himself admits. On the one hand, if the mapping of subjective probabilities and utilities into physiology succeeds, that fact may be used as an explanation of why EUT works at all, or it may give economists some confidence in talking about mental properties more publicly, or it may lead economists to stop using belief/desire terms altogether; on the other hand, if the mapping doesn't work, that fact may be relevant to the explanation of the anomalies of EUT. In either case, it will be of great interest for economists. The upshot is that Gul and Pesendorfer's (2008) argument for the complete irrelevance of psychological and neurological evidence to economics fails (i) to appreciate the actual incremental contribution of psychology to economics; and (ii) to deny the possibility that the radical approach may succeed.

So far, I have been arguing that Gul and Pesendorfer's (2008) negative argument for the irrelevance of psychology and neuroscience is unsuccessful. Now I will turn to the problems of their positive argument for the 'flexibility' of economic methodology. They say: 'Many situations in which agents systematically make mistakes can be interpreted as situations where agents face subjective constraints on the feasible strategies that are not apparent from the description of the decision problem' (p. 26). There are at least two problems here: first, the notion of 'systematic' mistakes cannot be worked out in Gul and Pesendorfer's (2008) framework. Of course, we can make sense of the distinction between systematic and non-systematic mistakes intuitively; some mistakes are systematic if we can find a pattern in it, and non-systematic if they are random. The problem arises, however, when we try to translate this intuition into a way of testing economic theory, because 'we have virtually no systematic theory of how to relate errors in the implications of revealed preference to a degree of belief in [testing] the validity of the underlying theory' (Harrison 2008: 323-324). Given the lack of the universally accepted empirical criterion concerning how many errors falsify revealed preference theory, one thus needs at least an explicit hypothesis regarding error in order to talk about systematic/unsystematic mistakes by experimental subjects, as several statistical models mentioned in chapters 4 and 5 do. Gul and Pesendorfer (2008: 6-7) happen to have such an explicit hypothesis, namely, that the theory is either confirmed

---

[13] Note that economics and psychology need not use common terms; all that is needed for cross-classification is that the two disciplines *refer to the same objects, but classy them in different ways.*

[14] Another interpretation is that Gul and Pesendorfer think that EUT does not refer to anything. Their emphasis on 'theory' renders some support for this reading. See also Gul and Pesendorfer's (2008: 30) defence of the notion of 'welfare' in economics as a mere *definition* that cannot be challenged empirically (while claiming that it is *not* a normative notion, either!: see p. 35).

when no errors are observed, or refuted otherwise. It is clear, however, that this hypothesis prevents Gul and Pesendorfer (2008) from distinguishing systematic from non-systematic mistakes in observed choice behaviour, for there is simply no room for mistakes, according to this all-or-nothing hypothesis.[15] Therefore, their talk about 'systematic' mistakes is incoherent.

Second, Gul and Pesendorfer's (2008) interpretive strategy is too flexible. Granted, the general importance of identifying agents' subjective perspectives in economics is undeniable. Economic choice is about something, and that something is usually a result of subjective interpretations of the situation. So finding out how agents frame the world (e.g., in which contexts they find themselves, which alternatives are salient to them, etc.) is important for economics. Economics, however, is not unprincipled hermeneutics, but a systematic empirical study of choice behaviour. Thus, choice theory needs an explicit auxiliary theory of agents' subjective interpretation of the situation. Regarding the lack of such a theory in economics, McCabe (2008: 347-348) worries about, rather than being proud of, the fact that 'economics can already explain just about any kind of behaviour', referring to Ledyard's (1986) proof that 'almost any profile of strategies can be [a] Bayesian equilibrium of some game'. Harrison (2008: 323-324) also notes that the principle of revealed preference is 'practically useless as an empirical tool', referring to Varian's (1988) proof that 'revealed preference places essentially no restrictions on [predicted choice] behaviour' when the observed choices are over a subset of the larger set of goods among which a decision maker chooses. These remarks suggest that the 'flexibility' of revealed preference is a methodological weakness, not a virtue. Given the lack of agreement concerning a generally acceptable theory of error, what experimental psychologists and behavioural economists have been doing is to make EUT *less* flexible, not more. Bragging about the flexibility of economic methodology without proposing any substantial hypothesis about error is equivalent to giving up empirical testing altogether. The upshot is that Gul and Pesendorfer (2008) do not succeed in making the promises of neuroeconomics (broadly construed by Gul and Pesendorfer, i.e., including the relevance of psychology) less likely; on the contrary, their defence reveals the empirical weakness of theoretical economics.

---

[15] For a substantial discussion of possible theories of error, see Harrison (2008: 323-328, in particular fn. 24).

6.2.3 Harrison's Methodological Critique

While Harrison's (2008) tone is no less harsh than Gul and Pesendorfer's (2008), his critique of neuroeconomics is more methodological and substantial than conceptual. Harrison's (2008) critique is two-fold, focusing on (1) statistical inferences involved in the use of brain-imaging techniques, and (2) experimental designs for controlling confounds. I will discuss each in turn.

(1) Statistical inferences: Harrison's (2008) critique regarding the statistical practices of neuroeconomists is (i) that their statistical inferences are not disclosed to the reader for examination and (ii) that there is no agreement among neuroscientists as to which inferences are best for which purposes. The first point is clear enough, and I just agree with Harrison (2008: 315) that we should make sure that 'this unfortunate professional habit ends quickly'. The second point needs some unpacking. Statistical issues in studying brains arise both in inferring about a single brain from its magnetic data and in inferring about an 'average brain' from a sample of brains thus constructed. Each inferential process involves a host of 'open issues of validation and interpretation', which points to 'the extremely limited extent to which modeling and estimation errors are correctly propagated throughout the chain of inferences' (Harrison 2008: 313-314). Then, especially if one considers the 'unfortunate professional habit' of keeping neural data in a black box, it is natural for Harrison to worry that 'there is likely a significant *understatement* of standard errors on estimate of effects, implying a significant *overstatement* of statistical significant differential activation' in brains (*ibid.*, original italics). Kenning and Plassmann (2005) similarly warn that one should be well aware of the long chain of inferences full of unwarranted presuppositions involved in neural imaging data. The introduction of new technology does not necessarily enable the 'direct measurement' (Camerer et al. 2005) of unobservable quantities. A new method or technique makes it possible to measure quantities that are otherwise unmeasurable, but the method itself is based upon theories that are not reliable. 'Brain scans do not light up like Xmas trees' (Harrison 2008: 314). This is a sound methodological caution, but it cannot be a decisive argument against the use of brain-imaging technique. After all, if that is the only measurement method available, we have no choice but to use it (if we want to know how the brain works).

(2) Experimental design: Regarding the experimental design of neuroeconomics, Harrison (2008) has more substantial criticisms, regarding several studies in neuroeconomics. I will discuss the first example in some detail, and the second and the third ones briefly. His first example concerns McClure et al.'s (2004) study of

intertemporal choices, which I have mentioned in section 3.2.2. There I cited McClure et al.'s (2004) fMRI study on brain activities during subjects' intertemporal choices as a study suggesting the existence of two distinct neural systems physically corresponding to two 'selves', *viz.*, the short-run, 'impatient' self and the long-run, 'rational' self. The 'quasi-hyperbolic' discounting function that fits well with behavioural evidence has two parameters, β which represents 'the special value placed on immediate rewards relative to rewards received at any other point in time', and δ which is 'simply the discount rate in the standard exponential formula' (McClure et al. 2004: 504). So first McClure and colleagues hypothesized the correspondence between the short-run interest represented by β and the lymbic system on the one hand (they call this and related areas 'β areas' or the 'β system'), and secondly between the long-run self represented by δ and the lateral prefrontal cortex, on the other ('δ areas' or 'δ system'). To test these correspondences, the authors measured (using fMRI) the brain activity of subjects as they made a series of intertemporal choices between early monetary rewards ($\$R$ available at delay d) and later monetary rewards ($\$R'$ available at delay d'), where $\$40 > \$R' > \$R > \$5$ and 6 weeks $> d' > d \geq 0$ day. The two options were separated by a minimum time delay of two weeks. McClure and colleagues made two types of choice pairs, (a) one in which the early option was available without delay (i.e., $d=0$, the money was given immediately after the scan session), and (b) the other in which even the early option was available only after some delay (i.e., $d>0$). The monetary rewards were paid to the subjects by a random selection procedure (i.e., they received a randomly chosen reward among those they chose in the experiment). McClure et al.'s (2004) predictions were as follows: (i) the lymbic structures will be activated more during (a)-type choices than during (b)-type choices; (ii) lateral prefrontal areas will be activated equally in both (a)- and (b)-type choices; (iii) lateral prefrontal areas will be more activated than the lymbic structures during (b)-type choices in which subjects choose the later reward. After some statistical analysis and further examinations of the relation between the brain activity and decision difficulty, McClure et al. (2004) conclude that all of their predictions are confirmed by the data. From this and other independent considerations, they further conclude that the limbic system (the β system) causes 'passions' for immediate rewards, whereas the prefrontal cortex and related structures (the δ system) are in charge of the discounting calculus which tends to counter passions in intertemporal choices.

Harrison (2008) poses an alternative hypothesis that subjects choose immediate rewards ($d=0$) based on the rational consideration that these rewards are more credible (or equivalently, subjectively felt as imposing less 'transaction costs') than later rewards. Harrison (2008: 318-319) criticizes McClure et al. (2004: fn. 29) as failing to eliminate this possibility, specifically pointing out that McClure et al. make the implicit assumptions that 'unless subjective value gets above some threshold, the reward regions of the brain will not differentially fire, and that the only reason they did fire with immediate payments is because of the higher subjective value'. The suggestion seems to be (i) that either variables for neural activities of the reward regions are continuous, rather than discrete, or they are discrete but with a different threshold from the one assumed by McClure et al. (2004); and (ii) that there may be other causes of these neural activities than subjective value. Regarding the assumption that all subjects had the same discount rate of 7.5% per week, Harrison (2008: 319) does not seem to be satisfied with McClure et al.'s (2004: fn. 29) explanation that this value was estimated based on expressed preferences.

Notice that these are all relevant issues, which are typically mentioned in the 'Discussion' or 'Conclusion' section of a scientific paper. Harrison here can be seen as engaging in neuroeconomic research himself, rather than rejecting it in the way Gul and Pesendorfer (2008) do. In fact, Harrison (2008: fn. 14) constructively considers a possible experimental design that could discriminate between this 'credibility' effect and the effect of 'passions' (although he notes that his design is difficult to implement in practice).

What is rather surprising is Harrison's (2008: 319) contention that McClure et al. (2004) represent a 'pattern' of neuroeconomic research in which '[t]he use of neural data does not provide any insight in relation to the hypotheses being proposed, but is used to promote one favoured explanation even if it does not provide evidence that favours it in relation to known alternative explanations'. Although other neuroeconomic researches might exhibit such a pattern, Harrison cannot justify his attribution of this pattern to McClure et al. (2004). First, the specific alternative proposed by Harrison concerns only an interpretation of the data regarding Prediction (i), and he does not provide any alternative to the interpretations of the data regarding Predictions (ii) and (iii). In particular, (iii) seems to provide reason to believe in some sort of dual system in the brain. At least, one cannot say that it 'does not provide any insight in relation to' the hypothesis. Second, Harrison completely ignores McClure et al.'s (2004) reference to various studies of human and other mammalian brains that presumably support their claim for the existence and the causal efficacy of the 'β system' in the choices of immediate rewards. Although there are difficult issues involved in extrapolating from animal to human brains, Harrison's neglect of these studies does not seem to be motivated by such worry. In sum, Harrison's (2008) critique does not establish his conclusion that neuroeconomics is telling just-so stories. Indeed, his critique demonstrating that inferences in neuroeconomics can be improved as any inference in the sciences.

In discussing the second example of neuroeconomic experiments, Trust games (see section 5.1.2) in the scanner, Harrison (2008: 319) continues to ask in a similar fashion: 'Does neuroeconomics improve on [current practice]?'—i.e., does it help tease out the confounds involved in behavioural experiments? He seems to want to say no, but his examination points toward the opposite answer. Suppose that Player 1 (the Investor) transferred the whole endowment, say $10 to Player 2 (the Trustee). Is it because she is altruistic? Or because she is a risk lover? Or because she is framing her decision as one of a series of encounters, whereas in fact the game is one-shot? Kosfeld et al. (2005) and Zak et al. (2005) found that dosing *oxytocin* (a neurally active hormone associated with social bonding) enhances trust and trustworthiness. In finding this, they controlled for risk considerations and altruism (Zak et al. 2007). Still Harrison (2008: 320) says that 'there are no controls for other known confounds'. He mentions in particular the possibility of 'repeated' framing in discussing another study by DeQuervain et al. (2004), citing Binmore (2007): 'people are habituated to playing the fair equilibrium in repeated versions of the game' (cited in Harrison 2008: 321). While denying that he's saying that Binmore is right, Harrison concludes that 'we have conceptual work to do before we fire up the scanner' (*ibid.*). This is an odd conclusion to draw. First, the issue is clearly *empirical* rather than conceptual. Binmore's view is an empirical hypothesis, and I have examined some empirical evidence against the unnatural habitat hypothesis in chapter 4. Second, Harrison admits that at least two confounds (risk perception and altruism) were controlled for in the experiments by Zak and others. While these are not the direct results of 'firing up the scanner', the oxytocin administration with crossing game design (Trust game vs. Dictator game) controlled for altruism. This is an innovation of neuroeconomics.[16] Harrison does not provide reason to avoid brain imaging other than his worries about statistical inferences discussed above.

The third and final example Harrison mentions is a study by Rilling et al. (2004), which investigated the function of so-called 'mind-reading' systems—brain regions involved in the interpretation of other's intentions, also known as a 'theory of

---

[16] The control of risk was done behaviouralistically. Harrison (2008: 320) calls this 'a nice control', which seems to reveal his unjustified favouritism for traditional control methods against methods introduced by neuroeconomists.

mind' module—as subjects played Ultimatum and Prisoner's Dilemma games. The control groups included (a) subjects who played against a computer programme, but were deceived by the experimenter to think that they were playing with real humans (pictures of those 'humans' were displayed on the screen during the game) and (b) subjects who were truthfully told that they were playing against the computer. Rilling et al. (2004) found that the 'theory of mind' areas were activated more in condition (a) than in (b). While this greater activations in condition (a) might suggest that the presumed areas are responsible for mind reading specific to strategic situations *vis-à-vis* other humans, there are several confounds: subjects might have shown greater *cognitive* engagement (not specific to mind reading) because (i) they were told they had a human opponent; because (ii) they were shown the pictures of 'humans' changing in every round, whereas in condition (b) they were shown the same boring image of a computer. Here Harrison (2008: 321) is simply repeating Rilling et al.'s (2004) reservations, without making the case that neuroeconomics cannot deal with confounds better than behavioural experiments. The upshot is that, although Harrison's (2008: Section 2) methodological critique as such is well taken, it does not make the promise of neuroeconomics (either incremental or radical) less likely. There is even a sense in which he is making the case *for* neuroeconomics by taking it so seriously and making substantial contributions to improving it. Still, his harsh tone suggests the opposite. What makes Harrison (2008), then, so critical about neuroeconomics? In order to answer this question, we must uncover the underlying philosophical disagreements. In the next section, I will point out two distinctive metaphysical stances, to one of which Harrison (2008) subscribes.

6.3 Metaphysics That Matters to Science

6.3.1 The Mechanistic Stance
As noted in 6.1, the metaphysical turn in philosophy of science made it inevitable for philosophers to talk about 'the way the world is', or to put it more subjectively, 'a way of viewing the world', or 'a stance on the world'.[17] I have noted that metaphysics in this sense must be consistent with scientific evidence and practices, but the relation between metaphysics and science is not one-directional; since the two are continuous, it is possible, based on some metaphysical view about the world, to make a prediction

---

[17] I think 'attitude' or 'stance' is more appropriate in this context than 'view', for metaphysics provides us with not only a way of seeing the world, but also a whole range of ways of dealing with it. See also Kuhn's (1962) distinction between cognitive and regulative functions of a paradigm.

about how science as a whole or a particular discipline will develop, or to give a recommendation about how research should be done. This is exactly what Craver and Alexandrova (2008) do when they recommend economists (including neuroeconomists) to adopt a 'mechanistic' stance on the world, which is a version of scientific realism. The first component of this view, which I call *mechanistic realism*, maintains an ontological picture that is not dissimilar to Oppenheim and Putnam's (1958) hierarchical mereology: according to mechanistic realism, a phenomenon at one level is realized by mechanisms that 'frequently span multiple levels'; 'components and activities at one level can often themselves be decomposed into organized entities and activities at a lower level, which can themselves be decomposed into organized entities and activities at still lower levels' (Craver and Alexandrova 2008: 397). Based on this picture, the authors infer that the relation of mechanistic composition dictates the direction of explanation: 'As a general sketch: the behaviour of populations might be explained in terms of the aggregation of or interaction among individual agents, whose behaviour can be explained in terms of cognitive mechanisms, which are in turn explained in terms of underlying interactions among brain regions, cells, molecules, and so on' (*ibid.*). Although Craver and Alexandrova (2008: fn. 16) do not deny the possibility of a higher-level phenomenon explaining a phenomenon at one level below (e.g. individual decisions may be explained by environmental and social contexts), they do not provide a *reason* to believe in this possibility (apart from citing Clark 1997). Their claim for the mechanistic composition of the world, by contrast, is put forward as a reason to believe a success of explanation of higher-level phenomena by lower-level phenomena. To put simply, their argument seems to be this: to explain is to identify mechanisms; since mechanisms extend over multiple levels, economists need to be informed by studies of other levels such as psychology and neuroscience in order to explain. Their argument from mereology to a desirable scientific practice comes very close to Oppenheim and Putnam's (1958), although here the recommended practice is not theoretical microreduction but explanation *qua* explication of lower-level mechanisms, which Fodor (1974) identifies as the goal of scientific reduction.

Since it is a metaphysical but scientific stance, Craver and Alexandrova's (2008) recommendation seems to be based upon the extrapolation that mechanistic realism will make economics more successful because other sciences such as neuroscience, cognitive science and biology have enjoyed a great success by adopting it. In addition to this 'inference to the best explanatory strategy', they explicitly provide another reason why economics should learn from psychology and neuroscience. That reason also concerns scientific realism, but of a weaker kind called *measured realism* (Trout 1998). Measured realism states that one can make an inference that a certain quantity (e.g., temperature) exists if different instruments (e.g., alcohol, mercury, air, and electronic thermometers) point to the similar value, despite the fact that these instruments are based on different physical principles and theoretical assumptions. Craver and Alexandrova (2008: 394) are generalizing measured realism when they claim that interdisciplinary integration 'brings constraints from multiple independent perspectives to bear upon a single phenomenon and so gives it a kind of robustness or claim to reality not shared by phenomena that are not detectable from multiple independent perspective' (Craver and Alexandrova 2008: 394).[18]

Anticipating economists' reply that they are interested in neither explanation nor reality but only *prediction*, Craver and Alexandrova (2008: 398) provide a pragmatic argument to the effect that adopting mechanistic realism will provide (i) a more effective heuristic for building *successful predictive* models than instrumentalism (the thesis that a scientific theory or model is a mere tool for prediction without any commitment to its reality or truth) and (ii) the knowledge of 'the causal structures' behind economic decision making that is necessary for *successful intervention*, whose importance for policy purposes is difficult to deny. To sum up, they are arguing that the goal of economics—whether it is prediction, explanation, or intervention—is likely to be better achieved by adopting mechanistic realism and embracing psychology and neuroscience than by remaining separated and endorsing instrumentalism.

Craver and Alexandrova's (2008) argument for the mechanistic stance is actually preceded by their critique of the instrumentalist defence of revealed preference theory and its use for separating economics from psychology and neuroscience.[19] Their argument (in particular pp. 392-393) is essentially the same as my critique of Gul and Pesendorfer (2008) in section 6.2.2, namely, that economists presuppose internal processes both in theory and in practice anyway, so they better be explicit and get the psychology right. However, if, as I would suggest, this critique is sufficient for the claim that economists should study psychology and physiology, then why do they have to go further and argue in favour of a specific metaphysical stance? I suspect that this is because they are aware (at least implicitly) that their stance does not follow from the

---

[18] Zak (2004: 1745) also makes the same point by emphasizing the importance of 'convergent evidence' more generally.

[19] They target Harrison (2008) rather than Gul and Pesendorfer (2008). This is understandable because Harrison (2008) was one of the target articles of the symposium in *Economics and Philosophy*. Still I think Craver and Alexandrova's (2008) attribution of RPT to Harrison (2008) is misplaced, because Harrison explicitly admits RPT's limitations.

negation of instrumentalism:[20] in principle one could endorse another kind of realism, to which I shall be turning presently.

6.3.2 The Functional Stance

I defined the *functional stance* as a metaphysical attitude which presupposes some purpose(s) behind an object being studied. The functional stance metaphorically sees the object (or system) as an artefact or machine which has been designed to play some function(s). While the mechanistic stance presumes that how the system works is explicable in terms of its mechanistic composition, the functional stance has no such presumption. Instead, the functional stance presumes that there must be some reason *why* the system exists and works as it does. Some methodological implications of the functional stance to the study of human brains can be found in the computer scientist David Marr's (1982) posthumous book on vision.[21] In response to the diminishing success of the classical Cartesian-Sherringtonian approach in physiology that had tried to understand brain functions by studying reflexes in isolation, Marr (1982) claimed that clarifying *the information-processing tasks that a system is trying to accomplish* is essential for understanding the function of the brain and its components. Marr schematically explained this point as the relation of three levels of understanding. The first, *computational*[22] level concerns understanding the goal of the system under study, or what function the system is serving. The goal is to be formally specified as a *function* in the mathematical sense (a mapping from one kind of information to another). The second, *representational and algorithmic* level concerns how this function is represented and solved algorithmically. The third, *hardware implementation* level concerns the details of how the representation and algorithm are implemented physically. For example, consider *economic man* as a system. The computational level specifies its goal as the maximization of his material interests. This can be formally defined as a mapping from consumption to utility. Next, the algorithmic level specifies the mathematical details (EUT, rank-dependent utility theory, regret theory, prospect

---

[20] Craver and Alexandrova (2008) choose *design economics* (the part of economics intended to further the design and maintenance of markets and other economic institutions) as an example that suggests economists are in practice realists. Design economists are indeed realists, but it is not clear if they are *mechanical* realists. Accordingly, it is not obvious if design economics is a case in which economists learned a lot from psychology (while my example, behavioural economics, is such a case). Later I will discuss the possibility that design economics may be indeed an unfavourable example for mechanistic realism.

[21] See Glimcher (2003: ch. 6) for a detailed commentary; for a shorter exposition see Dennett (1987: 74-76).

[22] Dennett (1987: 75-76) rightly points out this term is misleading since this level 'is in fact not at all concerned with computational process'. I will follow Marr's original terminology to avoid further confusion.

theory, etc.) of this function. Finally, the hardware level specifies how the brain physically implements this mathematical representation and algorithm.

Marr's (1982) functional stance can be analyzed into two theses. The first thesis concerns the *relative independence* of each level: although these three levels have to be 'consistent with one another', 'the explication of each level involves issues that are rather independent of the other two' (cited in Glimcher 2003: 140-141). Marr's second thesis has to do with the *top-down nature* of the levels of analysis: 'an algorithm is likely to be understood more readily by understanding the nature of the problem being solved than by examining the mechanism (and the hardware) in which it is embodied' (cited in Glimcher 2003: 142). While the independence thesis is consistent with Craver and Alexandrova's (2008) mechanistic stance, the top-down thesis is somewhat in tension with it. I will discuss these points in turn.

Notice first that the functional stance does not necessarily imply instrumentalism, but is consistent with scientific realism. To begin with, Marr proposed it neither as a metaphysical claim nor as an epistemic principle, but as a 'strategic maxim' (Dennett 1987: 75) (note that the three levels are levels of *analysis* or *understanding*, not of *things*).[23] In addition, his remark that the three levels must be 'consistent with one another' suggests that Marr assumed some constraints imposed upon each level by token physicalism and measured realism. Thus, his independence thesis should be understood as Fodor's (1974) point that the kind-terms of these levels may cross-classify the world. Second, the point of dividing analysis into three levels is not to argue for the *autonomy* of some scientific discipline associated with one level or another, as Craver and Alexandrova (2008: 394) erroneously interpret; Marr's point is rather the opposite, namely, to argue for the disciplinary *integration* (i.e., of computer science into physiology and neurobiology). Marr's independence thesis is thus consistent with realism in the sense of token physicalism and measured realism, and to that extent it is consistent with the mechanistic stance.

Where the functional stance diverges from the mechanistic stance is in its emphasis on a sort of *hermeneutic* approach to the system in question. Both stances share the analogy between machines and biological organisms. But while the mechanistic stance appeals to the analogy only to evoke some image of 'causal structures' or 'how things work' (Craver and Alexandrova 2008: 398), the functional stance goes further, using the analogy to point out a similarity between man-made

---

[23] Unlike Oppenheim and Putnam's (1958) pyramid image, the figure Marr uses (Figure 1-4 cited in Glimcher (2003: 141) as Figure 6.2) is horizontal, not vertical.

machines (artefacts) and living organisms, namely, that both are *designed* to perform some tasks, or to solve some problems.[24] Another way to put the difference is that, while the mechanistic stance assumes that to explain a system is just to understand how it works, the functional stance requires understanding the goal the system serves.

The utility of taking the functional stance on real machines is clear enough, since these artefacts are designed by humans to serve certain purposes, and we usually know what these purposes are. But what are the reasons to assume that this strategy will work in the study of living organisms? If a designer in the supernatural or anthropomorphic sense is nowhere assumed, *design* must be understood *evolutionarily*, i.e., as a result of the interactions between organisms that try to survive and their environments. Concerning this point, Glimcher (2003: 143-144) highlights two problems in Marr's programme. The first problem is methodological: in Marr's scheme, determining a complete unit of organism is equivalent to determining its function, but Marr does not provide us with any guidance regarding how to do this.[25] So the promise of the functional analysis in studying systems *in general* becomes suspect. In the context of economics, defining a limited liability company as some mathematical function of profit-maximization may be reasonable, since it *is* a kind of artefact whose goals typically include profit-maximization (although the company consists partly of employers, stock holders and employees, who are living organisms). In addition, there is market competition driving the company to make more profit, which *is* a kind of evolutionary pressure. But defining a human being as a function of material self-interest maximization may not be equally reasonable, unless we can be confident that the evolutionary process rewards such traits and that such traits are genetically transmitted (the same consideration equally applies to the more abstract definition of economic man as a *consistent* decision maker). The critique is not that the top-down approach is necessarily arbitrary, but that its evolutionary hypotheses need to be empirically well motivated (Sugden 2001).

Which brings us to the next problem of Marr's approach: there are theoretical as well as empirical questions as to whether evolution has moulded the human brain (or the mammalian brain in general) in such a way that its neural architecture is organized by biologically separate units that are definable as computational modules. On the one hand, psychology must provide an empirical ground for mapping behaviour onto

---

[24] Dennett (1987:304) coined the term 'artefact hermeneutics' to refer to the application of the functional stance to machines. This analogy is already found in Simon ([1969] 1996).

[25] Marr's own research adopts the perceptual experience of vision as the computational unit, but this choice is arbitrary because Marr does not explain why the unit is not sensory perception in general or some more specific form of vision (Glimcher 2003: 143; 145).

discrete functional modules; on the other hand, evolutionary biology needs to suggest that evolution tends to produce such modules. Here I cannot go into the details of these tasks (see Glimcher (2003: ch. 7), who claims that these tasks have been accomplished), but must be content with just noting the extent to which the prospect of the functional stance hinges upon actual science. This is only natural for a metaphysical *and* scientific stance. That said, already we can begin to see different implications of the two stances for neuroeconomics.

6.3.3 Implications for Neuroeconomics

What are the implications of these metaphysical stances regarding the prospect of neuroeconomics? First, what about the incremental approach in neuroeconomics, which tries to improve standard economic decision-making models by explicating the underlying brain mechanisms? The mechanistic stance recommends an approach based on mechanistic realism and measured realism. The former boils down to a mereological picture of mechanical composition of things, which I suspect cannot give much reason to believe in the prospect of the incremental approach more than token physicalism does. Measured realism seems to give a stronger reason than token physicalism, but it is not clear that it adds much in the context of neuroeconomics in particular, because there is no guarantee that different levels of analysis refer to the same *phenomenon* which is the target of triangulation. If a phenomenon is cross-classified across different levels, then there may not be a single phenomenon to which we refer from different perspectives (we will see an example of this case in section 6.4.1). Therefore, although the mechanistic stance wholeheartedly recommends the incremental approach, it doesn't give a substantial reason to believe in it, in addition to token physicalism. The functional stance is more nuanced. It is also compatible with the incremental approach, as it endorses token physicalism (i.e., what cannot be implemented physically cannot be performed computationally). At the same time, the functional stance emphasizes the importance of *first* specifying a computational unit, and *then* explicating its neural implementations. As noted in section 6.3.2, the first step cannot be done *a priori*, but must be based on behavioural and theoretical considerations in psychology (including behavioural economics) and evolutionary biology. But these studies must also start with some hypothesis concerning functional units, however arbitrarily defined, and then incrementally improve (or abandon) this hypothesis.

Simon ([1969] 1996: 12) shows that this strategy first supposes that a system has evolved (or been designed) to solve a certain class of tasks, and then infer the system's unobservable properties from the tasks it is not good at performing. That is, the internal mechanisms of a system will 'show through' as its limiting properties. Simon illustrates the fruitfulness of the functional stance by drawing several examples from the psychological research on economic and administrative decision making, problem solving, and memory and learning. Glimcher (2003: 166) suggests a similar strategy in discussing the study of animal evolution: 'it is when animals can be shown to deviate from [specified] optimal goals that we have succeeded in identifying a phyletic or architectural constraint'. McClure et al.'s (2004) study of the dual system (see section 6.2.3) proceeds just as recommended by the functional stance, i.e., first comes a behavioural anomaly (time inconsistency), then a functional (mathematical) elaboration of the model ('quasi-hyperbolic' model), and finally a study of brain implementation (prefrontal cortex and the limbic system). This example indicates the heuristic significance of the functional stance, as pointed out by Simon and Glimcher, as well as Marr (see also Harrison 2008: 331).

The mechanistic stance fails to capture this heuristic role. To the extent that the functional stance is successful in psychology and evolutionary biology—as suggested by these authors—there seems to be a reason to believe in its usefulness for the incremental approach in neuroeconomics. One proviso to this top-down strategy is that its fruitfulness depends on the state of a given discipline. Marr's (1982) proposal was influential given the background that physiology at that time was too narrowly focusing on separate reflexes (see also Harrison 2008: fn. 33). By contrast, economic models of decision-making had already achieved mathematical sophistication more than 50 years ago, and the number of proposed utility functions has been only increasing since. Given this situation, it can be more valuable to understand the implementation level (the brain) that gives empirically well grounded criteria for selecting among proliferating models, than to propose yet another definition of function in *an a priori* fashion. The current practice of neuroeconomists seems to be following this pattern.

Are the recommendations derived from the two stances different concerning the radical approach in neuroeconomics? The mechanistic stance does not have much to say about the prospect of the radical approach. Craver and Alexandrova (2008: 384) maintain that, since 'it is too early to bet', '[t]he question of whether neuroeconomics is revolutionary is […] not nearly as important as the question of how the science should structure itself to maximize its potential for building new and better models and for attracting and retaining converts and graduate students'. This claim is a little puzzling, since the two questions are closely related. On the one hand, to the extent that the second question concerns rhetoric and politics, as Kuhn (1962) suggests, the claim that a scientific revolution is taking place is crucial for it. On the other hand, to the extent that the issue of the re-structuring concerns a kind of metaphysics continuous with science itself, as I suggest, the claim of a scientific revolution should be at least provisionally answered by scientific metaphysics. Mechanistic realism is simply too poor a metaphysics to do this. Hence, the silence of Craver and Alexandrova (2008) on the prospect of the radical approach of neuroeconomics. I am not suggesting that it is inconsistent to advance one type of metaphysics or another, while remaining neutral as to the prospect of a revolutionary change in a particular science. What I am suggesting is only that such metaphysics is redundant. Truly scientific metaphysics must be an engine for scientific enquiry. In contrast, mechanical realism is like an idling wheel in the machine of science.

The functional stance is by contrast relevant to the radical approach, but in rather complicated ways. First, the top-down thesis seems to suggest that some sort of functional definition of an individual decision maker is necessary, and that therefore utility maximization will not disappear from economics. However, the computational unit can be specified not *a priori* but in an empirically and theoretically motivated manner. Thus Ross (2005) criticizes EUT and its variants as 'Ptolemaic', claiming that identifying a whole person as the computational unit has lost its scientific ground.[26] Nor can the goal of the unit be defined *a priori*. I suggested two approaches in behavioural economics, namely, the value-based and reason-based approaches. My critique of Ross (2005) in chapter 3 can be interpreted as a suggestion that seeing the goal of the individual as *reasoning* is at least as good an option as dividing the individual into multiple agents defined by their *utility maximizing properties*. While Ross (2005) might support his theory by saying that evolutionary biology indicates that the whole person is not an appropriate unit of evolution, I might reply by saying that social pressures mould the whole person as a reasoning agent (with which Ross (2005) almost agrees). Notice that this debate revolves around the specification of a goal and a unit in economics, psychology and evolutionary biology. That is, although the functional stance cannot resolve this scientific debate, it is functioning through and through as a heuristic for both Ross's claim and mine. It is not idle like mechanistic realism. Similarly, although the functional stance alone does not decide the prospect of the radical approach in neuroeconomics, we can begin to examine such approach by taking this stance. This is what I am going to do in the rest of this chapter.

---

[26] As I have argued in chapter 3, this accusation doesn't straightforwardly apply to cognitive psychologists.

6.4 The Functional Stance at Work in Cognitive Neuroscience

In this section, I will examine several studies of the neural basis of framing and compatibility effects, in an attempt to evaluate the prospect of the radical approach in neuroeconomics. In chapter 3, I have examined Gold and List's (2004) model of path dependence, which purports to explain the framing effects (Tversky and Kahneman 1981) and the compatibility effects (Lichtenstein and Slovic 1971) in a unifying fashion. I called this a reason-based approach, and suggested that adopting it is a viable alternative to the value-based approach, on which Ross's (2005) multiple-self model is based. Harrison (2008: 337) also notices the viability of the reason-based approach: '[a]n alternative interpretation of the concept "dual selves" would be a single decision maker that has dual cognitive processes that are activated under different conditions'. Can the neurobiological basis of information processing discriminate these alternative ways of modelling?

The study by Gold and List (2004) fits well with the functional stance research strategy. First come behavioural anomalies (framing and compatibility effects), and then a functional representation and algorithm (first-order predicate logic). What is missing is the final stage of checking the neural implementation. I have considered in section 3.6 different implications of the evidence at the implementation level. If a 'decision path'—i.e., the order in which an agent considers propositions in a sequential decision process—is literally interpreted as a *temporal* order, then the hypothesis might be inconsistent with the multiple-self model; if we interpret the decision path actually taken by the agent as a set of the propositions which are *considered heavier* or *more focal* than other propositions, then the hypothesis will be consistent with the fact that different parts of the brain process information in a parallel and simultaneous way, as multiple-self models would suggest (or selves might be playing sequential games). Therefore, which interpretation is more true to the neural implementation seems relevant to the choice between the path-dependence model and the multiple-self model. I will review the neural evidence on framing effects and compatibility effects in turn.

6.4.1 Framing

Kahneman and Tversky (1979) distinguish two phases in the choice process: an initial phase in which acts (e.g., buying or selling), outcomes (e.g., loss or gain) and contingencies (e.g., certain, uncertain, probable, etc.) are framed, and a subsequent phase of evaluation. A framing effect refers to a cognitive bias where different presentations of an extensionally identical judgement and decision making problem induce different ways of framing, thereby changing the evaluation of the problem, which then leads to judgement and choice inconsistencies (Tversky and Kahneman 1981). Although experimental manipulations of presentations causes inconsistencies in a robust way, how exactly a framing effect is implemented at the brain level has been little known. In order to identify the neural mechanisms underlying framing effects, Deppe et al. (2005) conducted a fMRI study with 21 subjects making binary credibility judgment tasks (i.e., answering a question: Is this news (a) true or (b) false?) in different frames (30 normalized news headlines were presented in 4 different German magazines with varying credibility). In addition to fMRI measurement, Deppe et al. also measured, for each individual, the susceptibility to the framing information (magazine logos) in judging the credibility of the news presented. Their basic findings are: (i) that a framing effect is correlated with neural processes within the medial prefrontal cortex, and (ii) that this correlate reflects inter-individual differences in the degree of the susceptibility to framing information. The medial prefrontal cortex is known as playing, among others, a crucial role in assessing and integrating *emotional* and other *implicit* information during decision making. This is explained phylogenetically as a result of the adaptive importance for the individual to assess the relevance of *all* kinds of environmental stimuli and respond flexibly. Deppe et al. (2007) changed the type of material from semantic stimuli (news headlines) to visual stimuli (advertisements of commercial products such as rings), which had to be intuitively evaluated on a participant-specific intrinsic scale ('liking' and 'not liking') in similar framing (magazine logos), and found (i) that a framing effect is correlated with neural processes within the anterior cingulate cortex (ACC: a central node in a neural network responsible for the integration of information about positive or negative reinforcements), and (ii) that this framing-related ACC activity predicts individuals' susceptibility to framing.

De Martino et al. (2006) conducted another fMRI study as subjects made choices over lotteries in different frames (the 'gain' frame and the 'loss' frame). They found (i) that subjects' tendency to be risk-averse in the gain frame and risk-seeking in the loss frame (i.e., tendency to manifest a framing effect predicted by prospect theory) is correlated with increased activation in the amygdala (a part of the limbic system which is responsible, among others, for the detection of emotionally relevant information present in contextual and social emotional cues); (ii) that subjects' countering tendency regarding this risk attitude is correlated with increased activation in

ACC, and (iii) that there is a significant correlation between decreased susceptibility to the framing effect and enhanced activity in the orbital and medial prefrontal cortex (OMPFC). From these findings, De Martino et al. conjecture that economic risky choices are made as a result of the conflict between two systems, one 'emotional' (amygdala) and the other 'rational' (OMPFC), whose interaction can be seen in the activation of ACC. Weber et al. (2007) conducted another fMRI study while subjects made buying and selling decisions in a real-market-type design, and found an activation of the amygdala only in selling decisions. The experimenters interpret this result as loss aversion with respect to prior possessions.

These four fMRI studies of judgment and decision-making mechanisms all seem to identify interactions between different neural functions, in particular affective and cognitive, as hypothesized by Camerer et al. (2005). Although very schematic, such interactions seem to be compatible both with dual-self interactions and with a parallel cognitive process that is activated under different conditions. Alternatively, these two models may not be discriminated by implementation-level evidence. In fact, Don Ross (in personal communication) suggests that these two accounts wouldn't necessarily conflict 'if the dynamics occurred on different scales of phenomenal resolution'. One way to see the comparative merit of each model is to see what one can do with each model, or more specifically, how each model helps one to manipulate choice behaviour. Consider for example two interpretations of a 'decision path' in the path-dependence model, namely, temporal and salient. Although this distinction may not illuminate neural functions very much, it may tell us about different ways of eliciting framing effects. Specifically, people may exhibit susceptibility to framing in response to both (i) the same information in different temporal orders and (ii) the same information in different frames.[27] If this is true, then one can argue that the path-dependence model is useful for manipulation in the sense that the model predicts different conditions (temporal and salience manipulations) under which an expected effect (framing) is elicited. If the model works as a guide for manipulation, this is a good reason to use the model, independently of whether these mechanisms can be mapped onto certain brain regions.

The functional stance suggests an alternative way to compare the multiple-self model and the path-dependence model, namely, to see how useful each model is as a functional heuristic in furthering neuroeconomic research (top-down), rather than to wait until neuroscientific research will tell which model is better (bottom-up).

---

[27] I am not aware of any experimental results in this regard.

Regarding the criteria of usefulness, the brief examination of recent fMRI studies above suggests that a useful heuristic does not necessarily have to be a complete mathematical formula. For example, unlike McClure et al. (2004), who exploit the quasi-hyperbolic function to hypothesize about the corresponding brain systems, De Martino et al. (2006) do not believe in the neural implementation of the function of prospect theory, however accurate and useful it may be as a representation of the existing behavioural data. It is like a phenomenological law, which does not do much work as a functional heuristic for explicating the neurobiological mechanisms. Rather, De Martino et al. believe in some neural correspondence of what psychologists call 'heuristics'[28] or rules of thumb, or the information-processing processes (e.g., framing => response selection => information search).[29] Therefore, we will need to examine whether Gold and List's (2004) model is useful, independently from its algorithmic sophistication and wide scope. The same proviso applies to Ross's (2005) game-theoretic model of multiple selves.[30]

6.4.2 Compatibility

Unlike framing effects, compatibility effects are not regarded as a single unit subject to fMRI studies because presumably their mechanisms involve distinct stages in decision making (after the framing stage), namely, the choice of decision strategies and the search for information. Mechanisms of the former kind are proposed by the strategy compatibility hypothesis (Tversky, Sattath and Slovic [1988] 2000; Fischer and Hawkins 1993), which states that people use two types of decision strategies—quantitative (e.g., anchoring and adjustment) and qualitative (e.g., elimination by aspects, lexicographic ordering, etc.)—in different response tasks (see chapter 3 for how these hypotheses purport to explain preference reversals). Another hypothesis called *expression theory* (Goldstein and Einhorn 1987) states that people evaluate alternatives in the same way for all response modes, determining the unique mental utility scale for a particular set of alternatives (so this theory takes the 'as if' representation of EUT somewhat literally); expression theory instead assumes another stage in decision making, namely, the expression of evaluation. Since these two hypotheses make incompatible assumptions regarding the information-processing processes in the decision maker's brain, in principle we can discriminate them by studying these

---

[28] For human decision-makers in general, not just scientists.

[29] Rabin (1998: 33) similarly suggests that loss aversion and other related biases challenges the very idea of maximization rather than improves upon existing maximization models.

[30] Harrison (2008: 331-332), from a different perspective, considers the epistemic complementarity of 'heuristics' (in the psychology literature) and 'algorithms' (in the computer science literature).

processes. Schkade and Johnson (1989) devised a computer software called Mouselab,[31] which enabled them to measure key variables regarding a decision maker's information processing as she made choices over lotteries appearing on a computer screen. A noticeable feature of this programme is that it hides the relevant information (pay-offs and probability values of gambles) behind labelled boxes that can be opened to reveal their contents by moving the cursor into a box using the mouse (boxes are closed when the cursor is moved away). Another feature is that, for pricing and rating tasks, a scale is displayed on the screen and the desired location can be determined by moving the pointer on the scale using the mouse. These features enabled the experimenters to record several measures that may tell us something about decision-making mechanisms. Schkade and Johnson concentrated on four classes of such measures, (1) total time; (2) attention to stimulus features; (3) patterns of information acquisition; and (4) response activity. Expression theory states that neither response modes (choice and judgment) nor gamble types (H bet and L bet) affect evaluation processes of alternatives. For example, Goldstein and Einhorn (1987) suggest that choice mainly consists of a comparison of two evaluation judgments, one for each gamble. If this is true, the time required to make a choice should be larger (maybe twice or even more) than the time required to make a single judgment, for the former consists of two judgments plus choice among them. This can be tested by comparing the time spent on each type of tasks. Schkade and Johnson (1989) report that choosing between two gambles required significantly *less* time (on average 32.05 seconds) than generating a price for a single gamble (on average 36.80 seconds). This makes more plausible the assumption that different decision strategies are behind choice and pricing tasks than the assumption that different tasks involve the same evaluation process. Further, the evaluation process was found to differ somewhat across gamble types. For example, in pricing tasks, the subjects spent a lot of time (on average 11.7 seconds, or equivalently over 30% of their time) moving the cursor on and near the scale, with a pattern of starting from a certain price and then adjusting it by moving the cursor. It was observed that the subjects used different starting points for L bets (on average $6.10) and H bets (on average $3.19), and then adjusted downwards for both bets (on average $0.19 in each). This supports the anchoring and adjustment hypothesis, while making it unlikely that decision makers evaluate different gamble types in the same manner. Here it was possible to compare two rival models by looking at measures regarding (1) total time and (4) response

---

[31] This software is downloadable from www.mouselabweb.org.

generation activity: taken together, these data confirm the model of anchoring and adjustment and disconfirm expression theory.

The study by Schkade and Johnson mentioned above did not use any neuroimaging technique (which was not available in the first place), and yet managed to discriminate between two rival hypotheses about the information-processing processes involved in risky decision making. Would they have used fMRI or some such technique had it been available with a reasonable cost at that time? Maybe, maybe not. But if they had, they would have benefited from its use only to the extent that their model is useful as a heuristic. Schkade and Johnson (1989) increased this extent by eliminating an extra stage hypothesized by expression theory. In fact, a recent electrophysiological study of the anchor-and-adjustment process (Qu et al. 2008)[32] tries to locate one of the two mechanisms involved (the adjustment process associated with self-generated anchors vs. the accessing process associated with externally provided anchors), based upon the existing behavioural research. A similar example can be found in recent fMRI studies of the stimuli-response (S-R) compatibility, of which the scale compatibility is a type. A current debate in cognitive (neuro)science revolves around whether response selection is a unitary process performed by the same brain region(s), or it is performed by distinct regions depending on the nature of compatibility such as visual and non-visual (numerical, semantic, etc.) (see Schumacher et al. 2003; Schumacher and Jiang 2003). This debate largely presupposes the unit of analysis (S-R compatibility) shared by cognitive scientists and psychologists, and based upon that, tries to explicate finer mechanisms underlying it. These studies all exemplify a kind of *continuity* between behavioural and neuroimaging research, suggesting that neuroeconomics may also follow this pattern, i.e., elaborating on behavioural economics rather than displacing it.

6.4.3 The Functional Stance on What?

At the end of sectioin 6.3.3, I remarked that the functional stance has implications concerning the possibility of the radical approach in neuroeconomics. Here is the result: the studies examined in section 6.4.1 are not relying on economic constructs such as subjective beliefs and preferences in the first place. This is natural because cognitive neuroscience proper is not interested in economic decision-making processes, but in human information processing in general. From the perspective of cognitive neuroscience, there is no such distinct neural process as economic decision making (risky or not). In other words, preferences and beliefs are not neuroscience's 'natural

---

[32] Qu et al. (2008) measured a subject's brain (alpha-band) activity by attaching silver chloride electrodes mounted in an elastic cap directly to 64 scalp sites and above and below the left eye.

kind' terms. The situation is similar in behavioural decision research (BDR), or the behavioural economics inspired by it, for there is no such psychological process as economic decision making. Despite this fact, BDR had an impact on economics, because it constructed and explained *economic* anomalies such as preference reversals, and explained these anomalies by the fact that economic decision making is part of more general human cognitive mechanisms. For example, psychologists constructed the phenomenon of preference reversals using EUT, while being guided by an alternative heuristic and biases approach. That is, they had a sophisticated functional model (EUT) to calibrate an anomaly on the one hand, and a worked out procedural model to explain such an anomaly, on the other. Since fMRI and other electrophysiological studies cited in section 6.4.1 to a large extent confirm or presuppose the information-processing procedural model, one natural task of neuroeconomics will be to see whether and how different implementation mechanisms uncovered by these studies will make a difference to the study of economic phenomena such as preference reversals, loss aversion, framing, etc. This points towards the incremental approach. By contrast, the radical approach advocates the elimination of economic constructs altogether. However, if these constructs disappeared, then there would be no economic anomaly left to explain. Although such a possibility remains conceivable, it is important to remember that the radical neuroeconomist then would not be able to rely on the success model of behavioural economics. He would have to construct a neurobiological theory of economic choice that explains better than the existing theories without using the functional resources of economic modelling. However, it is very difficult to imagine how *economically relevant* neurobiological mechanisms can be explicated without using any *economic* models. Both the logic of the functional stance and its use by scientists suggest that the radical approach is not a good research strategy.

A schematic comparison of the paradigms of experimental economics and experimental psychology (cognitive science) may be useful to understand why the radical approach is not a good strategy (Figure 6.1).

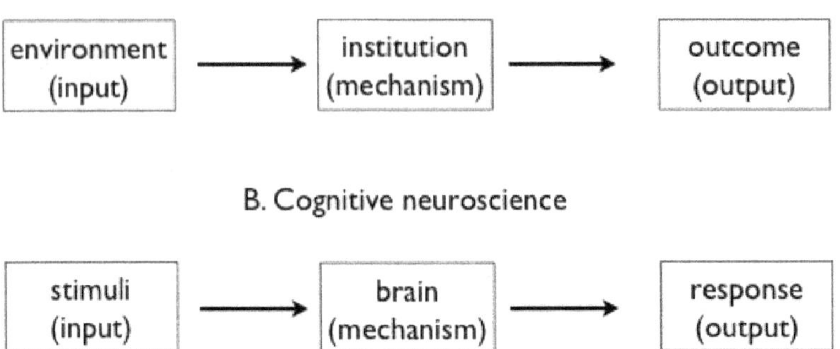

Figure 6.1: Comparison between two experimental paradigms. See also McCabe (2008: 351).

The crucial difference concerns (i) what one takes to be a mechanism, and (ii) what one can do with that mechanism. As explained in 4.2, in experimental economics the mechanism is an institution, which consists of a message space together with governance rules (what messages agents are allowed to send, when they are allowed to send them) and production rules (how the environment changes as a function of the messages sent). The chief goal is to design a mechanism (e.g., a voluntary contribution mechanism with or without communication) whose performance criteria are defined by a function from environment to outcome. The institution is an artefact; the economist wants to know how it works, but ultimately he wants to make it work as he wishes. For this purpose, the economist needs to explicate 'the conditions under which people achieve socioeconomic outcomes that are not part of their conscious intention' (Smith 1991: 893). By contrast, for the psychologist the target mechanism is a single brain *qua* information-processing machine, which she usually cannot manipulate, except in naturally occurring cases (such as brain lesions). The goal is to explicate the mechanism, not to change it. The brain is not an artefact.[33] This contrast makes it clear that the brain is important for the economist as part of the construction material of institutions, not as an ultimate object of investigation. This is probably one reason why many economists are agnostic about the brain. They have to be convinced that the fine-tuned understanding of the brain is important to build good institutions.

---

[33] I am simplifying here. See Simon ([1969] 1996: 76), who stressed 'the artificial character of human thinking'.

At the same time, the parallel is striking. Both economists and psychologists are taking the functional stance on their target mechanisms, despite the fact that these mechanisms are realized with very different materials. This parallel is in fact the basis of both the multiple-self model and the path-dependence model. The former sees a parallel between games among whole persons and games within the brain; the latter sees a parallel between aggregative procedures in social choice and information-processing processes in individual choice. In this way, the functional stance enables researchers to export and import a functional model across ontologically heterogeneous systems.[34] This is no less 'radical' than microreduction, but may prove to be a more plausible approach to finding a unity in economics and psychology.

6.5 Conclusion

This chapter started by noticing that many contemporary philosophers of science have become openly metaphysical in advancing particular views about what the world is like. The examination of the recent neuroeconomics controversy in 6.2 revealed that metaphysical issues are also implicit in this debate, together with methodological issues. Section 6.3 aimed at finding the implications of such metaphysical issues by pointing out two distinct 'stances', mechanistic and functional. I have argued that, while both stances use the analogy of machine, the mechanistic stance is not the metaphysics that is guiding actual research. By contrast, the functional stance turned out to be quite widely used in sciences such as psychology, evolutionary biology and economics. Section 6.4 examined recent studies in cognitive neuroscience in order to see whether this wide use of the functional stance makes the radical replacement of economic constructs by neuroeconomics more likely. There is no knockdown argument against this possibility, but a careful look at cognitive research suggests that it is not happening, and will not happen in the near future. Although economics (represented by experimental economics) and psychology (represented by cognitive science) share the functional stance, both presuppose different paradigms with different goals in mind (institutional design vs. unpacking the brain). To the extent that these goals overlap, psychology will turn out to be useful for economists, whether it is social, cognitive, or evolutionary psychology, and economics will turn out to be useful for psychology, whether it is EUT, social choice theory, or game theory. To the extent that they diverge, however, the two

---

[34] What Ross (2008) calls neurocellular economics (NE) is another example of this practice.

sciences will keep cross-classifying things according to their discipline-specific interests. Such is the present state of the unity of economics and psychology.

Chapter 7

Conclusion

I have begun the present investigation of the boundaries of economics and psychology from the premise that careful analysis of scientific *practice* is the key to understanding their relations and interactions, and evaluating their relative merits for the study of individual decision making (chapter 1). Upon this premise, I have looked at how empirical anomalies have emerged and how economists and psychologists have responded to them. Despite some philosophers' scepticism, Expected Utility Theory (EUT) has been put under severe test, which resulted in the observation of *inconsistent* choice behaviour (chapter 2). In particular, preference reversals (PR) are a more serious anomaly than others, for they challenge the very assumption that there are preferences to be measured in the first place, as assumed by EUT. This challenge has led some cognitive psychologists to propose a constructivist approach to preference measurement, or more specifically, a *procedural* approach to explain how people choose. I have argued that this approach is not *ad hoc* in any sense that has been worked out by philosophers of science, and that it is on a par with the multiple-self approach which has been developed in explaining inconsistent *intertemporal* choice (chapter 3).

In addition to these anomalies in individual risky choice, experimental games have enabled researchers to find anomalies in *strategic* decision making (chapter 4). In particular, the observations of dominated cooperative strategies in Prisoner's Dilemma and Public Goods games have stimulated the payoff respecification approach. Altruism has not been observed in these games; instead, the *conditional* nature of preferences and the *heterogeneity* of subjects have emerged. Behavioural economists have proposed models of *social* preferences to explain these observations, and devised new experimental games that could test these models (chapter 5). However, models of *reciprocal* fairness that try to 'get the psychology right' have faced serious problems: it turned out that the way these models individuate the outcomes of games (i.e., separability) is inconsistent with the framework of expected utility measurement that is indispensable for testing game theory. Furthermore, incorporating *beliefs* into utility functions makes these models psychologically less plausible, and jeopardizes the essential explanatory role of preferences in rational choice theory.

I have argued that the conditional nature of preference is better captured either by incorporating *social norms* explicitly into models, or by extending the concept of agency to *teams*. Both approaches strive to be fully informed by cognitive psychology, and exemplify how game theory can be extended in an empirically plausible way. *Neuroeconomists* however do not stop here: they conjecture that the economic models of rational choice are not only informed by cognitive psychology but will be transformed by innovative brain-imaging techniques (chapter 6). This idea is fiercely disputed by economists. After clarifying some confusions involved in this controversy, I have pointed out two distinctive scientific-metaphysical attitudes presupposed by protagonists and antagonists of neuroeconomics, namely, the *mechanistic* and the *functional* stance. Based upon some case studies of cognitive neuroscience, I have argued that the practice of brain science is more congenial to the functional stance. On this basis, I put some reservations about the possibility of effecting a radical transformation of economics by neuroscience. Both economists and psychologists take the functional stance, but on different things.

I would like to reiterate the fruitfulness of looking at practice, not just theory, in studying science. General patterns in the dialectics of 'crises and responses' in behavioural economics suggest a kind of division of intellectual labour: while economic approaches with rigorous formalism are good at finding out anomalies (if combined with proper empirical tests), psychological approaches are suitable for providing explanations as to why and how these anomalies take place as cognitive and emotional processes. This can be a fruitful pattern of interdisciplinary collaboration, once the relative merit of each discipline is properly recognized. A careful look at practice, however, reveals that even this division of labour is not so clear-cut. For example, some of the mathematical representations are for parsimoniously summarizing data (e.g., prospect theory, social preference models), while others are used to study the brain-level implementation of decision processes (e.g., quasi-hyperbolic utility functions and multiple-selves). Some 'X-effects' are meant to capture the exact way in which decision biases are caused by certain cognitive processes (e.g., compatibility effects), while others are used to refer to the way in which such phenomena can be reliably constructed (e.g., elicitation effects, framing effects). In other words, similar representations may differ in the roles they play in empirical studies (heuristics, cognitive economy, instruments for manipulation, etc.). Therefore, one has to look at ways in which these representational models and labels are employed in the dynamic context of research instead of just focusing on their theoretical properties. Scientists' methodological writings are valuable, but they contain a host of rhetoric and propaganda, which must be always compared with what scientists actually do. I hope that my study has done justice to some of the best practices in economics and psychology, and that it has found some lessons relevant to the methodology and philosophy of science more generally.

I have mentioned in chapter 1 that my interests differ from those of economists and psychologists only in degree of abstraction, not in subject. In particular, I share with economists and psychologists an interest in the concept of *rationality*, which is also an important concept in philosophy. However, I have consciously avoided turning empirical issues concerning human decision making into questions such as: *Are humans rational?* This is because such framing obscures the objects of investigation (i.e., individual decision making and decision-relevant cognitive processes) and criteria of test and measurement (e.g., severity and precision). Talk of rationality raises philosophical, emotional, moral and even political issues, thereby making 'rational' debates difficult. I have thus been employing technically defined terms such as choice consistency, decision strategies, dominance, utility maximization, etc., while using 'rational choice theory' only as an umbrella term for a conjunction of decision and game theory coupled with different application models. Now I would like to relax this constraint and contemplate some implications of the present study to rationality as part of human nature.

An implicit disagreement between the multiple-self approach and the procedural approach in chapter 3 was the locus of *rational agent*. The former says that humans are not rational agents because the maximization principle does not apply to individual human beings. This argument depends on the assumption that rationality can be equated with some technically defined consistency in choice. The reason-based approach points out another possibility: that rationality can be interpreted as an ability to *reason*, which is certainly a whole-person cognitive process (the theory of team reasoning reviewed in chapter 5 even suggests a sense in which reasoning may be a group-level process). Some theorists might prefer the consistency interpretation of rationality because it makes rationality measurable and testable. However, as we have seen, the reason-based interpretation makes rationality neither less testable nor less measurable. The compatibility hypothesis discussed in chapter 3 predicts some effects of unconscious choice of decision strategies, i.e., reasoning about how to make choice. Moreover, substantial evidence suggests that inducing people to consciously think of reasons significantly influences their attitudes, judgments and choices (the 'reason-giving effects').[1] To the extent that these effects are well established, the cognitive significance of reasoning is measurable and measured, and therefore there is nothing to be ashamed of in referring to reasoning *qua* cognitive process in explaining human behaviour.

On the other hand, some might prefer the reason-based interpretation of rationality because consistency is too poor a concept to apply to human behaviour in its entirety. Although I have admitted this in chapter 2 when I highlighted the incompleteness of decision theory, incompleteness in itself is not a problem for science in general, and in particular, the incompleteness of decision theory can be patched up with the cognitive approaches I have been advocating in chapters 3 and 5. Some proponents of the reason-based interpretation of rationality might claim that reason is at odds with nature to begin with, i.e., reason is not part of the natural causal order of objective reality. Something similar to this view was lurking behind the normative critique of decision theory which I rebutted in chapter 2.

Instead of elaborating on my earlier argument against such idealistic views of reason, here I would like to make the uncontroversial sociological observation that reason-giving is deeply embedded in our social practice. From governments and corporations to schools and families, social institutions put people under continuous pressure to give reasons for their attitudes, speeches and actions.[2] Reasoning *qua* individual cognitive process is therefore not causally independent from social processes. This does *not* mean that a science of rationality is impossible; it just means that rationality must be studied not only by the brain and behavioural sciences, but also by the social sciences. I conclude this chapter by noting another platitude, namely, that the practices of these sciences are themselves part of social processes, and thus have an impact on how rationality is understood, aimed for, and exploited. How exactly the sciences of rationality interact with this social process will be studied in another occasion. I hope the present study will turn out to be useful in such investigation.

---

[1] Unfortunately, the effects are not always positive. Explicit reason analysis can increase attitude-behaviour inconsistency (e.g., it can shorten the period of a romantic relationship; Wilson et al. 1984), decrease the accuracy of prediction (Halberstadt and Levine 1999), and cause regret after making choice (Wilson and Schooler 1991). Bortolotti (forthcoming) discusses implications of these reason-giving effects to the authority of self knowledge.

[2] Markets usually ask for money but not reasons for consumption. Although markets are exceptional institutions in this respect, market participants are not free from the pressure of reason-giving. For example, the abstract 'household' in consumer theory has in reality its several constituents (family members), who routinely give each other reasons for particular consumption. Moreover, *De gustibus non est disputandum* is just another *reason*.

Bibliography

Abrams, B. A. and M. A. Schmitz. 1978. The crowding out effect of government transfers on private charitable contributions. *Public Choice* 33: 29-39.

___________ and ___________ 1984. The crowding out effect of government transfers on private charitable contributions: cross sectional evidence. *National Tax Journal* 37: 563-568.

Ainslie, G.W. 1991. Derivation of rational economic-behavior from hyperbolic discount curves. *American Economic Review* 81(2): 334-340.

___________ 2001. *Breakdown of will*. Cambridge: Cambridge University Press.

___________ 2005. Précis of breakdown of will. *Behavioral and Brain Sciences* 28: 635-673.

Allais, M. 1953. Le comportement de l'homme rationnel devant le risque, critique des postulats et axioms de l'école américaine. *Econometrica* 21: 503-46.

Anand, P. 1993. *Foundations of rational choice under risk*. Oxford: Oxford University Press.

Andreoni, J. 1988. Why free ride? Strategies and learning in public goods experiments. *Journal of Public Economics* 37: 291-304.

___________ 1990. Impure altruism and donations to public goods: a theory of warm-glow giving. *Economic Journal* 100: 464-477.

___________ and J. H. Miller 1993. Rational cooperation in the finitely repeated Prisoner's Dilemma: experimental evidence. *The Economic Journal* 103(418): 570-585.

Ashraf, N., C. Camerer and G. Loewenstein 2005. Adam Smith, behavioural economist. *Journal of Economic Perspectives* 19(3): 131-145.

Axelrod, R. 1984. *The evolution of co-operation*. New York: Basic Books.

Bacharach, M. 2006. *Beyond individual choice: teams and frames in game theory*. Princeton: Princeton University Press.

Barnes, B. 1983. Social life as bootstrapped induction. *Sociology* 17(4): 524-545.

Becker, G. S. 1962. Irrational behavior and economic theory. *Journal of Political Economy* 70(1): 1-13.

___________ 1976. *The economic approach to human behavior*. Chicago: University of Chicago Press.

__________ 1991. *A treatise on the family*. Cambridge, Mass.: Harvard University Press.

Becker, G. M., M. H. DeGroot and J. Marschak. 1964. Measuring utility by a single-response sequential method. *Behavioral Science* 9: 226-232.

Bentham, J. [1789] 1843. An introduction to the principles of morals and legislation. In Bowring, J. (ed.) *The Works of Jeremy Bentham Vol. 1*. Edinburgh: William Tait.

Berg, J. E., J. Dickhaut and K. McCabe. 1995. Trust, reciprocity, and social history. *Games and Economic Behavior* 10: 122-142.

Bermúdez, J. L. 2005. *Philosophy of psychology: a contemporary introduction*. Milton Park: Routledge.

Bernoulli, D. 1954. Exposition of a new theory on the measurement of risk. *Econometrica* 22: 23-26.

Bicchieri, C. 2006. *The grammar of society: the nature and dynamics of social norms*. Cambridge: Cambridge University Press.

Binmore, K. 1994. *Game theory and the social contract*. Vol. 2. Cambridge, Mass.: MIT Press.

__________ 1999. Why experiment in economics? *The Economic Journal* 109: F16-F24.

__________ 2005. Economic man—or straw man: a commentary on Henrich et al. *Behavioral and Brain Sciences* 28: 23-24.

__________ 2007. *Playing for real: a text on game theory*. Oxford: Oxford University Press.

Bishop, Michael A., and J. D. Trout. 2005. *Epistemology and the psychology of human judgment*. New York: Oxford University Press.

Bohm, P. 1972. Estimating demand for public goods: an experiment. *European Economic Review* 3: 111-130.

Bolton, G. E. 1991. A comparative model of bargaining: Theory and evidence. *American Economic Review* 81(5): 1096-1136.

__________ and A. Ockenfels 2000. ERC: A theory of equity, reciprocity, and competition. *American Economic Review* 90(1): 166-193.

Borsboom, D. 2005. *Measuring the mind: Conceptual issues in contemporary psychometrics*. Cambridge: Cambridge University Press.

Bortolotti, L. forthcoming. The epistemic benefits of reason giving. *Theory&Psychology*.

Bouas, K. S., and S. S. Komorita 1996. Group discussion and cooperation in social dilemmas. *Personality and Social Psychology Bulletin* 22(11): 1144-1150.

Breiter, H.C., I. Aharon, D. Kahneman, A. Dale and P. Shizgal 2001. Functional imaging of neural responses to expectancy and experience of monetary gains and losses. *Neuron* 30(2): 619-639.

Broome, J. 1991. *Weighing goods: equality, uncertainty, and time.* Cambridge, Mass.: Basil Blackwell.

Brown, H. I. 1993. A Theory-laden observation can test the theory. *British Journal for the Philosophy of Science* 44(3): 555-559.

__________ 1994. Circular justifications. *PSA: Proceedings of the Biennial Meeting of the Philosophy of Science Association* 1: 406-414.

Brunton, D., R. Hasan, and S. Mestelman 2001. The 'spite' dilemma: spite or no spite, is there a dilemma?' *Economics Letters* 71(3): 405-412.

Cabeza, R. and Kingstone, A. 2006. *Handbook of functional neuroimaging of cognition.* 2nd ed., Cambridge, Mass.: MIT Press.

Caldwell, M. 1976. Communication and sex effects in a five-person prisoners' dilemma game. *Journal of Personality and Social Psychology* 33: 273-280.

Camerer, C. 1995. Individual decision making. In J. H. Kagel, and A. E. Roth (eds.), *The handbook of experimental economics.* Princeton: Princeton University Press. pp. 587-703.

__________ 2003. *Behavioral game theory: experiments in strategic interaction.* Princeton: Princeton University Press.

__________, T. Ho and K. Chong. 2004. A cognitive hierarchy model of games. Quarterly Journal of Economics 119: 861-898.

__________, K. Chong and K. Weigelt. 2002. Strategic teaching and equilibrium models of repeated trust and entry games. *Caltech working paper*, October.

__________ and E. Fehr. 2004. Measuring social norms and preferences using experimental games: a guide for social scientists. In Henrich et al. (eds.) *Foundations of human sociality.* Oxford: Oxford University Press. pp. 55-95.

__________, G. Loewenstein and M. Rabin. 2003. *Advances in behavioral economics.* Princeton: Russell Sage Foundation; Princeton University Press.

__________, __________ and D. Prelec 2005. Neuroeconomics: how neuroscience can inform economics. *Journal of Economic Literature* 43: 9-64.

Caplin, A. and A. Schotter. 2008. *The foundations of positive and normative economics: a handbook.* Oxford: Oxford University Press.

Carruthers, P. 2000. Phenomenal consciousness: a naturalistic theory. Cambridge: Cambridge University Press.

Cartwright, N. 1989. *Nature's capacities and their measurement.* Oxford: Clarendon Press; Oxford University Press.

__________ 1999. *The dappled world: a study of the boundaries of science.* Cambridge: Cambridge University Press.

Chang, H. 2004. *Inventing temperature: measurement and scientific progress.* Oxford: Oxford University Press.

Charness, G. and M. Rabin. 2002. Understanding social preferences with simple tests. *The Quarterly Journal of Economics.* 117: 817-869.

Choi, J. J., D. Laibson, B. Madrian and A. Metrick 2006. Saving for retirement on the path of least resistance. In E. McCaffery and J. Slemrod (eds.), *Behavioral Public Finance.* New York: Russell Sage.

Chu, Y., and R. Chu. 1990. The subsidence of preference reversals in simplified and market-like experimental settings: a note. *American Economic Reviews* 80: 902-11.

Chung, S. H and R. J. Herrnstein 1967. Choice and Delay of Reinforcement. *Journal of the Experimental Analysis of Behavior* 10(1): 67-74.

Clark, A. 1997. Being there: putting brain, body, and world together again. Cambridge, Mass.: MIT Press.

Clotfelter, C. T. 1985. *Federal tax policy and charitable giving.* Chicago: University of Chicago Press

Colman, A. M. 1995. *Game theory and its applications in the social and biological sciences.* 2nd ed. Boston: Butterworth-Heinemann.

__________, B. D. Pulford and J. Rose. 2008. Collective rationality in interactive decisions: evidence for team reasoning. *Acta Psychologica* 128(2): 387-397.

Cox, J. C. and D. M. Grether. 1996. The preference reversal phenomenon: response mode, markets, and incentives. *Economic Theory* 7(3): 381-405.

Craver, C. and A. Alexandrova. 2008. No revolution necessary: neural mechanisms for economics. *Economics and Philosophy* 24: 381-406.

Cubitt, R. P., C. Starmer and R. Sugden. 2001. Discovered preferences and the experimental evidence of violations of expected utility theory. *Journal of Economic Methodology* 8(3): 385-414.

Davidson, D. [1974] 2001. Psychology as philosophy. In *Essays on actions and events*. Oxford: Oxford University Press, 229-244.

__________ 1985. Reply to Patrick Suppes. In B. Vermazen and M. B. Hintikka (eds.), *Essays on Davidson: actions and events*. Oxford: Clarendon Press; Oxford University Press, 247-252.

__________ [1995] 2004. Could there be a science of rationality? In *Problems of rationality*. Oxford: Oxford University Press. pp. 117-134.

__________, J. C. McKinsey and P. Suppes. 1955. Outline of a formal theory of value, I. *Philosophy of Science* 22(2): 140-160.

__________ and P. Suppes. 1957. *Decision making: an experimental approach.* Stanford: Stanford University Press.

Dawes, R.M., J. McTavish and H. Shaklee 1977. Behavior, communication, and assumptions about other people's behavior in a commons dilemma situation. *Journal of Personality and Social Psychology* 35(1): 1-11.

__________, and R. H. Thaler 1988. Anomalies: cooperation. *Journal of Economic Perspectives* 2(3): 187-197.

de Finetti, B. 1937. La prévision: ses lois logiques, ses sources subjectives. *Annales de l'Institut Henri Poincaré* 7: 1-68.

De Martino, B., D. Kumaran, B. Seymour and R. J. Dolan 2006. Frames, biases, and rational decision-making in the human brain. *Science* 313: 684-687.

Dennett, D. 1987. *The intentional stance*. Cambridge, Mass.: MIT Press.

Deppe, M., W. Schwindt, J. Krämer, H. Kugel, H. Plassmann, P. Kenning and E.B. Ringelstein. 2005. Evidence for a neural correlate of a framing effect: bias-specific activity in the ventromedial prefrontal cortex during credibility judgments. *Brain Research Bulletin* 67: 413-421.

__________, W. Schwindt, A. Pieper, H. Kugel, H. Plassmann, P. Kenning, K. Deppe and E. B. Ringelstein. 2007. Anterior cingulate reflects susceptibility to framing during attractiveness evaluation. *NeuroReport* 18(11): 1119-1123.

De Quervain, D. J. F., U. Fischbacher, V. Treyer, M. Schellhammer, U. Schnyder, A. Buck and E. Fehr. 2004. The neural basis of altruistic punishment, *Science* 305: 1254-1258.

Dufwenberg, M. and G. Kirchsteiger. 1998. A theory of sequential reciprocity. *Tilburg Center For Economic Research* discussion paper 9837.

Dupré, J. 1993. *The disorder of things: metaphysical foundations of the disunity of science*. Cambridge, Mass.: Harvard University Press.

Edgeworth, F. [1881] 1932. *Mathematical Psychics*. London: London School of Economics.

Edney, J. and C. Harper. 1978. The commons dilemma: a review. *Environmental Management* 2: 491-507.

Edwards, W. 1954. The theory of decision making. *Psychological Bulletin* 41: 380-417.

__________. 1961. Behavioral decision theory. *Annual Review of Psychology* 12: 473-498.

__________, H. Lindman and L. J. Savage 1963. Bayesian statistical inference for psychological research. *Psychological Review* 70: 193-242.

Ellsberg, D. 1961. Risk, ambiguity and the savage axioms. *Quarterly Journal of Economics* 75: 643-669.

Elster, J. [1979] 1984. *Ulysses and the Sirens: studies in rationality and irrationality*. Rev. ed. Cambridge: Cambridge University Press.

Evnine, S. 1991. *Donald Davidson*. Stanford: Stanford University Press.

Falk, A. and U. Fischbacher 1998. A theory of reciprocity. *IEER working paper*, University of Zurich.

Fehr, E. and U. Fischbacher. 2003. The nature of human altruism-proximate patterns and evolutionary origins. *Nature* 425: 785-791.

______, and K. M. Schmidt 1999. A theory of fairness, competition, and cooperation. *Quarterly Journal of Economics* 114(3): 817-868.

Fischbacher, U. and S. Gächter. 2006. Heterogeneous social preferences and the dynamics of free riding in public goods. *CeDEx Discussion Paper No. 2006-01*. The University of Nottingham.

__________, S. Gächter, and E. Fehr. 2001. Are people conditionally cooperative? Evidence from a public goods experiment. *Economic Letters* 71: 397-404.

Fischer, G. W. and S. A. Hawkins 1993. Strategy compatibility, scale compatibility, and the prominence effect. *Journal of Experimental Psychology: Human Perception and Performance* 19(3): 580-597.

Fisher, I. 1892. *Mathematical investigations in the theory of value and price*. New Haven: Yale University Press.

Fodor, J. A. 1974. Special Sciences (Or: The disunity of science as a working hypothesis). *Synthese* 28: 97-115.

Friedman, J. 1996. *The rational choice controversy : economic models of politics reconsidered*. New Haven, CT: Yale University Press.

Friedman, Michael. 1979. Truth and confirmation. *Journal of Philosophy* 76: 361-382.

______________1999. *Reconsidering logical positivism*. Cambridge: Cambridge University Press.

Friedman, Milton. and L. J. Savage 1948. The utility analysis of choices involving risk. *Journal of Political Economy* 56: 279-304.

Fudenberg, D. and D. K. Levine. 2006. A dual self model of impulse control. American Economic Review 96(5): 1449-1476.

Galison, P. 1987. *How experiments end*. Chicago: University of Chicago Press.

Geanakoplos, J., D. Pearce and E. Stacchetti. 1989. Psychological Games and Sequential Rationality *Games and Economic Behavior* 1(1): 60-80.

Giere, R. N. 1988. *Explaining science: a cognitive approach*. Chicago: University of Chicago Press.

Gilbert, M. 1989. *On social facts*. London: Routledge.

Gilovich, T., D. W. Griffin and D. Kahneman (eds.) 2002. *Heuristics and biases: the psychology of intuitive judgement*. Cambridge: Cambridge University Press.

Gintis, H. 2006. Behavioral ethics meets natural justice. *Politics, Philosophy and Economics* 5: 5-32.

Glimcher, P. 2003. Decision, uncertainty, and the brain: the science of neuroeconomics. Cambridge, Mass.: MIT Press.

Gold, N. and C. List 2004. Framing as path dependence. *Economics and Philosophy* 20(2): 253-277.

Goldman, A. I. 1992. *Liaisons : philosophy meets the cognitive and social sciences*. Cambridge, Mass.: MIT Press.

Goldstein, W. M. and H. J. Einhorn 1987. Expression theory of choice and the preference reversal phenomenon. *Psychological Review* 94: 236-254.

Goodman, N. [1954] 1979. *Fact, Fiction, and Forecast*. 4th ed. Cambridge. Mass.: Harvard University Press.

___________ 1976. *Languages of Art*. Indianapolis: Hackett Publishing Company, Inc.

Grandy, R. 1973. Reference, meaning, and belief. *Journal of Philosophy* 70: 439-452.

Green, D. P., and I. Shapiro. 1994. *Pathologies of rational choice theory: a critique of applications in political science*. New Haven: Yale University Press.

Grether, D. M. and C. R. Plott. 1979. Economic theory of choice and the preference reversal phenomenon. *American Economic Review* 69: 623-638.

Grünbaum, A. 1960. The Duhemian argument. *Philosophy of Science* 27: 75-87.

Grüne-Yanoff, T. and P. Schweinzer. 2008. The roles of stories in applying game theory. *Journal of Economic Methodology* 15(2): 131-146.

Guala, F. 2000a. Artefacts in experimental economics: preference reversals and the Becker-Degroot-Marschak mechanism. *Economics and Philosophy* 16: 47-75.

_______ 2000b. The logic of normative falsification: rationality and experiments in decision theory. *Journal of Economic Methodology* 7(1): 59-93.

_______ 2005. The methodology of experimental economics. Cambridge: Cambridge University Press.

_______ 2006. Has game theory been refuted? *Journal of Philosophy* 103(5): 239-263.

_______ 2007. The philosophy of social science: metaphysical and empirical. *Philosophy Compass* 2, 10.1111/j.1747-9991.2007.00095.x

_______ 2008. Experimental economics, history of. In S. Durlauf and L. Blume (eds.), *The New Palgrave Dictionary of Economics.* 2nd ed. Hampshire: Palgrave-Macmillan.

_______ forthcoming. Methodological issues in experimental design and interpretation. In H. Kincaid and D. Ross (eds.), *The Oxford Handbook of the Philosophy of Economics.* Oxford: Oxford University Press.

Gul, F. and W. Pesendorfer. 2008. The case for mindless economics. In A. Caplin and A. Schotter (eds.), *Foundations of positive and normative economics.* Oxford: Oxford University Press.

Gächter, S. 2007. Conditional cooperation: behavioral regularities from the lab and the field and their policy implications. In B. S. Frey and A. Stutzer (eds.), *Economics and Psychology: a promising new cross-disciplinary field.* Cambridge, Mass.: MIT Press. pp. 19-50.

_______ and C. Thöni. 2005. Social learning and voluntary cooperation among like-minded people. *Journal of the European Economic Association* 3: 303-314.

Güth, W., R. Schmittberger and B. Schwarze. 1982. An experimental analysis of ultimatum bargaining. *Journal of Economic Behavior and Organization* 3: 367-388.

Hacking, I. 1983. *Representing and intervening: introductory topics in the philosophy of natural science*. Cambridge: Cambridge University Press.

__________ 1995. *Rewriting the soul : multiple personality and the sciences of memory*. Princeton, N.J.: Princeton University Press.

Halberstadt, J. B. and G. M. Levine. 1999. Effects of reasons analysis on the accuracy of predicting basketball games. *Journal of Applied Social Psychology* 29(3): 517-530.

Hanson, N. R. 1958. *Patterns of discovery; an inquiry into the conceptual foundations of science*. Cambridge: Cambridge University Press.

Hardin, G. 1968. The Tragedy of Commons. *Science* 162: 1243-1248.

Hargreaves Heap, S. H. and Y. Varoufakis 2004. *Game theory: a critical text*. 2nd ed. Milton Park: Routledge.

Harrison, G. W. 2008. Neuroeconomics: a critical reconsideration. *Economics and Philosophy* 24: 303-344.

__________, M. I. Lau and M. B. Williams. 2002. Estimating individual discount rates in Denmark: a field experiment. *American Economic Review* 92(5): 1606-1617.

Harsanyi, J. C. and R. Selten 1988. *A general theory of equilibrium selection in games*. Cambridge, Mass.: MIT Press.

Hausman, D. 1992. *The inexact and separate science of economics*. Cambridge: Cambridge University Press.

__________ 2000. Revealed preference, belief, and game theory. *Economics and Philosophy* 16(1): 99-115.

Hempel, C. G. 1965. *Aspects of Scientific Explanation*. New York: Free Press.

Henrich, J. P., R. Boyd, S. Bowles, C. Camerer, E. Fehr and H. Gintis. (eds.) 2004. *Foundations of human sociality: economic experiments and ethnographic evidence from fifteen small-scale societies*. Oxford: Oxford University Press.

Hicks, J. and R. Allen. 1934. A reconsideration of the theory of value. *Economica* 1: 52-76, 196-219.

Hoch, S. J. and G. Loewenstein. 1991. Time-inconsistent preferences and consumer self-control. *Journal of Consumer Research* 17(4): 492-507.

Holland, J. H., K. J. Holyoak, R. E. Nisbett and P. R. Thagard. 1986. *Induction: processes of inferences, learning, and discovery*. Cambridge, Mass.: MIT Press.

Holt, C. A. 1986. Preference reversals and the independence axiom. *American Economic Review* 76: 508-514.

_________ and S. K. Laury. 1997. Classroom games: voluntary provision of a public good. *Journal of Economic Perspectives* 11(4): 209-215.

Hoover, K. D. 2001. *The methodology of empirical macroeconomics*. Cambridge: Cambridge University Press.

Houthakker, H. 1950. Revealed preference and the utility function. Economica 17: 159-174.

Howson, C. 2001. The logic of Bayesian probability. In D. Corfield and J. Williamson (eds.), *Foundations of Bayesianism*. Kluwer Academic Publishers, pp. 137-160.

Huettel, S. A., A. W. Song and G. McCarthy. 2009. *Functional magnetic resonance imaging*. 2nd ed. Sunderland, Mass.: Sinauer Associates.

Isaac, R. M., K. McCue and C. Plott. 1985. Public goods provision in an experimental environment. *Journal of Public Economics* 26: 51-74.

_________ and J. M. Walker. 1988. Communication and free-riding behavior: the voluntary contribution mechanism. *Economic Inquiry* 26(4): 585-608.

_________ and _________ 1991. Costly communication: an experiment in a nested public goods problem. In T. Palfrey (ed.), *Laboratory research in political economy*. Ann Arbor: University of Michigan Press. pp. 269-286.

_________, _________ and S. Thomas. 1984. Divergent evidence on free riding: an experimental examination of possible explanations. *Public Choice* 43(1): 113-149.

Jerdee, T. and B. Rosen. 1974. Effects of opportunity to communicate and visibility of individual decisions on behavior in the common interest. Journal of Applied Psychology 5: 712-716.

Jevons, W. S. 1871. The theory of political economy. London: Macmillan.

Jezzard, P., P. M. Matthews and S. M. Smith. 2001. *Functional MRI: an introduction to methods*. Oxford: Oxford: Oxford University Press.

Kahneman, D. 2003. Autobiography. In T. Frängsmyr (ed.), *The Nobel Prizes 2002*. Nobel Foundation: Stockholm.

_________, J. L. Knetsch and R. Thaler. 1986. Fairness as a constraint on profit seeking: entitlements in the market. American Economic Review 76: 728-741.

__________ and A. Tversky. 1979. Prospect theory: an analysis of decision under risk. *Econometrica* 47(2): 263-291.

__________ and __________ 2000. *Choices, values, and frames*. Cambridge: Cambridge University Press.

__________, P. Slovic and A. Tversky. 1982. *Judgment under uncertainty: heuristics and biases*. Cambridge: Cambridge University Press.

Karni, E. and Z. Safra. 1987. Preference reversal and the observability of preferences by experimental methods. *Econometrica* 55: 675-685.

Kenning, P. and H. Plassmann. 2005. NeuroEconomics: an overview from an economic perspective. *Brain Research Bulletin* 67: 343-354.

Kim, O. and M. Walker 1984. The free rider problem: experimental evidence. *Public Choice* 43: 3-24.

Kitcher, P. 1981. Explanatory Unification. *Philosophy of Science* 48: 507-531.

Knobe, J., and S. Nichols (eds.) 2008. *Experimental philosophy*. Oxford: Oxford University Press.

Kosfeld, M., M. Heinrichs, P. Zak, U. Fischbacher and E. Fehr. 2005. Oxytocin increases trust in humans. *Nature* 435: 673-6.

Kramer, R. M. and M. B. Brewer 1984. Effects of group identity on resource use in a simulated commons dilemma. *Journal of Personality and Social Psychology* 46: 1044-1057.

Krantz, D. H., R. D. Luce, P. Suppes and A. Tversky. [1971] 2007. *Foundations of measurement*, 3 volumes. Mineola: Dover Publications.

Kreps, D. 1990. *A course in microeconomic theory*. Hemel Hempstead, Hertfordshire: Harvester Wheatsheaf.

__________, P. Milgrom, J. Roberts and R. Wilson. 1982. Rational cooperation in the finitely repeated prisoner's dilemma. *Journal of Economic Theory* 27: 245-252.

Kuhn, T. S. 1962. *The structure of scientific revolutions*. Chicago: University of Chicago Press.

Ladyman, J., D. Ross, D. Spurrett and J. G. Collier. 2007. *Every thing must go: metaphysics naturalized*. Oxford: Oxford University Press.

Laibson, D. 1994. *Essays in hyperbolic discounting*. Dissertation, Economics. Cambridge, Mass.: MIT Press.

Lakatos, I. 1970. Falsification and the Methodology of Scientific Research Programmes. In I. Lakatos and A. Musgrave (eds.), *Criticism and the growth of knowledge*. Cambridge: Cambridge University Press.

Ledyard, J. 1986. The scope of the hypothesis of Bayesian equilibrium. *Journal of Economic Theory* 39: 59-82.

__________ 1995. Public goods: a survey of experimental research. In J. H. Kagel and A. E. Roth (eds.), *The handbook of experimental economics*. Princeton: Princeton University Press. pp. 111-194.

Lichtenstein, S. and P. Slovic. 1971. Reversals of preference between bids and choices in gambling decisions. *Journal of Experimental Psychology* 89: 46-55.

__________ and ______ 1973. Response-induced reversals of preference in gambling: an extended replication in Las Vegas, *Journal of Experimental Psychology* 101:16-20. Reprinted in *The construction of preference*, chapter 4.

__________ and ______ (eds.) 2006. *The construction of preference*. Cambridge: Cambridge University Press.

Lindman, H. R. 1971. Inconsistent preferences among gambles. *Journal of Experimental Psychology* 89: 390-397.

Loewenstein, G. 1999. Experimental economics from the vantage-point of behavioural economics. *The Economic Journal* 109: F25-F34.

__________ 2007. *Exotic preferences: behavioral economics and human motivation*. Oxford ; New York: Oxford University Press.

Loomes, G and R. Sugden. 1982. Regret theory: an alternative theory of rational choice under uncertainty. *Economic Journal* 92: 805-824.

__________ and __________ 1983. A rationale for preference reversal. *American Economic Review* 73(3): 428-432.

__________, C. Starmer and R. Sugden. 1991. Observing violations of transitivity by experimental methods. *Econometrica* 59(2): 425-439.

__________ and C. Taylor. 1992. Non-transitive preferences over gains and losses. *Economic Journal* 102: 357-365.

Luce, R. D. and H. Raiffa. 1957. *Games and decisions: Introduction and critical survey*. New York: Dover Publications, Inc.

__________ and Tukey, J. W. 1964. Simultaneous conjoint measurement. *Journal of Mathematical Psychology* 1: 1-27.

Machamer, P., L. Darden, C. F. Craver. 2000. Thinking about Mechanisms. *Philosophy of Science* 67(1): 1-25.

Machina, M. J. 1982. "Expected utility" analysis without the independence axiom. *Econometrica* 50: 277-323.

MacKenzie, D. 2006. *An engine, not a camera : how financial models shape markets, Inside technology.* Cambridge, Mass.: MIT Press.

Mandler, M. 1999. *Dilemmas in economic theory: persisting foundational problems of microeconomics.* Oxford: Oxford University Press.

Margolis, H. 1982. *Selfishness, altruism, and rationality: a theory of social choice.* Chicago: University of Chicago Press.

__________ 2007. *Cognition and extended rational choice.* Milton Park: Routledge.

Markowitz, H. 1952. The utility of wealth. *Journal of Political Economy* 60: 151-158.

Marr, D. 1982. *Vision: a computational investigation into the human representation and processing of visual information'*, New York: W. H. Freeman & Company.

Marwell, G. and R. E. Armes. 1979. Experiments on the provision of public goods. I. Resources, interest, group size, and the free-rider problem. *The American Journal of Sociology* 84(6): 1335-1360.

__________ and __________ 1980. Experiments on the provision of public goods. II. Provision points, stakes, experience, and the free-rider problem. *The American Journal of Sociology* 85(4): 926-937.

Mayo, D. G. 1996. *Error and the growth of experimental knowledge, Science and its conceptual foundations.* Chicago: University of Chicago Press.

McCabe, K. A. 2008. Neuroeconomics and the economic sciences. *Economics and Philosophy* 24: 345-368.

__________, D. Houser, L. Ryan, V. Smith and T. Trouard. 2001. A functional imaging study of cooperation in two-person reciprocal exchange. *Proceedings of the National Academy of Sciences of the United States of America.* 98:11832-11835.

McClure, S. M., D. I. Laibson, G. Loewenstein and J. D. Cohen. 2004. Separate neural systems value immediate and delayed monetary rewards. *Science* 306: 503-507.

Menger, Carl [1871] 1981. *Principles of economics.* New York: New York University Press.

Michell, J. 1999. *Measurement in psychology: A critical history of a methodological concept*. Cambridge: Cambridge University Press.

Mill, J. S. [1836] 2000. On the definition of political economy; and on the method of investigation proper to it. *London and Westminster Review*. Reprint, Mill, *Essays on some unsettled questions of political economy*. 2nd ed. Reprint. Kitcher, Ontario: Batoche Books.

__________ [1843] 1974. *A system of logic: Rationcinative and inductive*. Reprint. *The Collected Works of John Stuart Mill, Volume VIII*. ed. John M. Robson, Toronto: University of Toronto Press.

Mirowski, P. 2002. *Machine dreams : economics becomes a cyborg science*. Cambridge ; New York: Cambridge University Press.

Monroe, K. R., and A. Downs (eds.) 1991. *The Economic approach to politics : a critical reassessment of the theory of rational action*. New York: HarperCollins.

Mosteller, F. and P. Nogee. 1951. An experimental measurement of utility. *Journal of Political Economy* 59:371-404.

Myerson, R. B. 1991. *Game theory: analysis of conflict*. Cambridge, Mass.: Harvard University Press.

Mäki, U. (ed.) 2001. *The economic world view : studies in the ontology of economics*. Cambridge: Cambridge University Press.

__________ (ed.) 2002. *Fact and fiction in economics: models, realism and social construction*. Cambridge: Cambridge University Press.

Nisbett, R. E. and T. D. Wilson. 1977. Telling more than we can know: verbal reports on mental processes. Psychological Review 84(3): 231-259.

Olson, M. 1965. *The logic of collective action; public goods and the theory of groups*. Cambridge, Mass.: Harvard University Press.

Orbell, J. M., A. J. C. van de Kragt and R. M. Dawes. 1988. Explaining discussion-induced cooperation. *Journal of Personality and Social Psychology* 54(5): 811-819.

Oppenheim, P. and H. Putnam. 1958. Unity of science as a working hypothesis. In H. Feigl, M. Scriven and G. Maxwell (eds.), *Minnesota Studies in the Philosophy of Science*. Vol. 2. Minneapolis: University of Minnesota Press. pp. 3-36.

Palfrey, T. and J. Prisbrey. 1997. Anomalous behavior in public goods experiments: how much and why? *American Economic Review* 87: 829-846.

________ and H. Rosenthal. 1991. Testing game-theoretic models of free-riding: new evidence on probability bias and learning. In T. Palfrey (ed.), *Laboratory Research in Political Economy*. Ann Arbor: University of Michigan Press.

Pareto, V. [1909] 1971. *Manual of Political Economy*. New York: Augustus Kelley.

Persky, J. 1995. Retrospectives: The ethology of homo economicus. *Journal of Economic Perspectives* 9(2): 221-231.

Pettit, P. 1990. Virtus Normativa: Rational Choice Perspectives. *Ethics* 100(4): 725-755.

________ [1991] 2002. Decision theory and folk psychology. In *Rules, reasons, and norms*. Oxford: Oxford University Press.

Phelps, E. S., and Pollak, R. A. 1968. On Second-Best National Saving and Game-Equilibrium Growth. *Review of Economic Studies* 35:185-199.

Phillips, L. D. and D. von Winterfeldt. 2007. Reflections on the contributions of Ward Edwards to decision analysis and behavioral research. In W. Edwards et al. (eds.), *Advances in Decision Analysis: From Foundations to Applications*. Cambridge: Cambridge University Press.

Plato, and H. D. P. Lee. 2003. *The Republic*. 2nd ed, Penguin classics. London; New York: Penguin Books.

Plott, C. R. 1996. Rational individual behavior in markets and social choice. In K.J. Arrow, E. Colombatto, M. Perlman and C. Schmidt (eds.) *The Rational Foundations of Economic Behaviour*, Basingstoke: Macmillan, pp. 225-50.

Plutchik, R. 1968. *Foundations of experimental research*, 2nd ed. New York: Harper & Row, Publishers, Inc.

Popper, K. R. [1967] 1995. Models, instruments, and truth: The status of the rationality principle in the social sciences. In *The Myth of the framework: In defence of science and rationality*, edited by M. A. Notturno. Milton Park: Routledge. pp. 154-184.

Qu, C., L. Zhou and Y. Luo. 2008. Electrophysiological correlates of adjustment process in anchoring effects. *Neuroscience Letters* 445:199-203.

Quine, W. V. O. 1960. *Word and object*. Cambridge, Mass.: MIT Press.

Rabin, M. 1992. Incorporating fairness into game theory and economics. *Department of Economics working paper No. 92-199*, University of California-Berkeley, July.

_________ 1993. Incorporating fairness into game theory and economics. *American Economic Review* 83(5): 1281-1302.

_________ 1998. Psychology and economics. *Journal of Economic Literature* 36: 11-46.

_________ 2002. Alfred Marshall Lecture: A perspective on psychology and economics. *European Economic Review* 46: 657-685.

Ramsey, F. P. [1926] 1988. Truth and probability. Reprinted in *Decision, Probability, and Utility: Selected Readings*, edited by P. Gärdenfors and N. Sahlin. Cambridge: Cambridge University Press, 19-47.

Rapoport, A. 1974. Prisoners' Dilemma: recollections and observations. In A. Rapoport (ed.), *Game theory as a theory of conflict resolution*. Dordrecht: Reidel. pp. 18-34.

Read, D., and Read, N. L. 2004. Time discounting over the lifespan. *Organizational Behavior and Human Decision Processes* 94(1): 22-32.

Rilling, J. K., A. G. Sanfey, J. A. Aronson, L. E. Nystrom and J. D. Cohen. 2004. The neural correlates of theory of mind within interpersonal interactions. *NeuroImage* 22: 1694-1703.

Robbins, L. 1935. *An Essay on the Nature and Significance of Economic Science.* 2nd ed. London: Macmillan.

Rosenberg, A. 1992. *Economics: mathematical politics or science of diminishing returns?* Chicago: University of Chicago Press.

_________ 1995. *Philosophy of social science.* 2nd ed, *Dimensions of philosophy series.* Boulder: Westview Press.

Ross, D. 2005. *Economic theory and cognitive science: microexplanation.* Cambridge, Mass.: MIT Press.

_________ 2008. Two styles of neuroeconomics. *Economics and Philosophy* 24: 473-483.

_________ forthcoming. Economic Models of Procrastination. In C. Andreau and M. White (eds.), *The Thief of Time*, Cambridge, Mass.:MIT Press.

Roth, A. E. 2002. The economist as engineer: game theory, experimentation, and computation as tools for design economics. *Econometrica* 70(4): 1341-1378.

Rubinstein, A. 2003. "Economics and psychology"? The case of hyperbolic discounting. *International Economic Review* 44(4): 1207-1216.

__________ 2006. A sceptic's comment on the study of economics. *Economic Journal* 116(510): C1-C9.

Saijo, T. and H. Nakamura. 1995. The "spite" dilemma in voluntary contribution mechanism experiments. *Journal of Conflict Resolution* 39(3): 535-560.

Sally, D. 1995. Conversation and cooperation in social dilemmas: a meta-analysis of experiments from 1958 to 1992. *Rationality and Society* 7: 58-92.

Samuelson, L. 2005. Foundations of human sociality: a review essay. *Journal of Economic Literature* 43: 488-497.

Samuelson, P. 1938. A note on the pure theory of consumer's behavior. Economica 5: 61-72.

__________ 1954. The pure theory of public expenditure. *Review of Economics and Statistics* 36(4): 387-389.

Satz, D., and J. Ferejohn. 1994. Rational choice and social theory. *Journal of Philosophy* 91(2): 71-87.

Savage, L. J. 1954. *The foundations of statistics*. New York: Wiley.

Savoy, R. L. 2005. Experimental design in brain activation MRI: Cautionary tales. *Brain Research Bulletin* 67: 361-367.

Schelling, T. C. 1960. *The Strategy of conflict*. Cambridge, Mass.: Harvard University Press.

__________ 1978. *Micromotives and macrobehavior*. New York: Norton.

Schkade, D. A. and E. J. Johnson. 1989. Cognitive-processes in preference reversals. *Organizational Behavior and Human Decision Processes* 44(2): 203-231.

Schumacher, E. H., P. A. Elston and M. D'Esposito. 2003. Neural evidence for representation-specific response selection. *Journal of Cognitive Neuroscience* 15(8): 1111-1121.

__________ and Y. Jiang. 2003. Neural mechanisms for response selection: representation specific or modality independent? *Journal of Cognitive Neuroscience* 15(8): 1077-1079.

Segal, U. 1988. Does the preference reversal phenomenon necessarily contradict the independence axiom? *American Economic Review* 78: 233-236.

Selten, R. 1965. Spieltheoretische Behandlung eines Oligoplmodells mit Nachfrageträgheit. *Zeitschrift für die Gesamte Staatswissenschaft* 12: 301-324.

Sen, A. 1971. Choice functions and revealed preference. *Review of Economic Studies* 38: 307-317.

Shafir, E., I. Simonson and A. Tversky. [1993] 2000. Reason-based choice. *Cognition* 49: 11-36.

Shogenji, T. 2000. Self-dependent justification without circularity. *British Journal for the Philosophy of Science* 51(2): 287-298.

Simon, H. A. [1969] 1996. *The sciences of the artificial*. 3rd ed. Cambridge, Mass.: MIT Press.

Slovic, P. 1964. Assessment of risk-taking behaviour. *Psychological Bulletin*, 61220-61233.

__________ 1975. Choice between equally valued alternatives. *Journal of Experimental Psychology: Human Perception and Performance* 1: 280-287.

__________ 1995. The construction of preference. *American Psychologist*, 50: 364-371.

__________, D. Griffin and A. Tversky. [1990] 2002. Compatibility effects in judgements and choice. Edited and reprinted in T. Gilovich, D. W. Griffin and D. Kahneman (eds.), *Heuristics and biases: the psychology of intuitive judgement*. Cambridge: Cambridge University Press.

__________ and S. Lichtenstein. 1968. Relative importance of probabilities and payoffs in risk taking. Journal of Experimental Psychology Monograph 78(3): Part 2: 1-18.

Smith, V. L. 1991. Rational choice: the contrast between economics and psychology. *Journal of Political Economy* 99(4): 877-897.

__________ 2003. Constructivist and ecological rationality in economics. In Frängsmyr, T. (ed.), *The Nobel Prizes 2002*. Nobel Foundation: Stockholm. pp. 502-561.

Stahl, D. O. and P. Wilson. 1995. On players' models on other players. Games and Economic Behaviour 10: 218-254.

Starmer, C. 2000. Developments in non-expected utility theory: the hunt for a descriptive theory of choice under risk. *Journal of Economic Literature* 38: 332–382.

Stich, S. 1990. *The fragmentation of reason: Preface to a Pragmatic Theory of Cognitive Evaluation*. Cambridge, Mass.: The MIT Press

Strotz, R. H. 1955. Myopia and inconsistency in dynamic utility maximization. *Review of Economic Studies* 23: 165-80.

Sugden, R. 1982. On the economics of philanthropy. *Economic Journal* 92(366): 341-350.

__________ 1988. The role of inductive reasoning in the evolution of conventions. *Law and Philosophy* 17(4): 377-410.

__________ 1993. Thinking as a team: Towards an explanation of nonselfish behaviour. *Social Philosophy & Policy* 10(1): 69-89.

__________ 2000. Credible worlds: the status of theoretical models in economics. *Journal of Economic Methodology* 7(1): 1-31

__________ 2001. The evolutionary turn in game theory. *Journal of Economic Methodology* 8(1): 113-130.

__________ 2002. Beyond sympathy and empathy: Adam Smith's concept of fellow-feeling. *Economics and Philosophy* 18: 63-87.

__________ 2008. Nash equilibrium, team reasoning and cognitive hierarchy theory *Acta Psychologica* 128: 402-404.

__________ and N. Gold. 2006. Introduction. In M. Bacharach, *Beyond individual choice: teams and frames in game theory*. Princeton: Princeton University Press.

Suppes, P. 1951. A set of independent axioms for extensive qualities. *Portuguliae Mathematica* 10: 163-172.

__________ 1954. Some remarks on problems and methods in the philosophy of science. *Philosophy of Science* 21: 242-8.

__________ 1985. Davidson's ideas. In *Essays on Davidson: actions and events*, edited by B. Vermazen and M. B. Hintikka, Oxford: Clarendon Press; Oxford University Press, 183-194.

__________ and Winet, M. 1955. An Axiomatization of utility based on the notion of utility differences', *Management Science* 1(3/4): 259-270.

__________ and Zinnes, J. 1963. Basic measurement theory. In Luce, R. D., Bush, R. R. and Galanter, E. (eds.), Handbook of mathematical psychology, Vol. I. New York: Wiley. pp. 1-76.

Swedberg, R. 1990. *Economics and sociology: redefining their boundaries: conversations with economists and sociologists*. Princeton: Princeton University Press.

Tajfel, H. and Turner, J. 1979. An integrative theory of intergroup conflict. In W. Austin and S. Worchel (eds.), *The social psychology of intergroup relations*. Monterey: Brooks/Cole. pp. 33-47.

Thaler, R. H. 1980. Toward a positive theory of consumer choice. *Journal of Economic Behavior & Organization*, 1(1): 39-60.

__________ 1992. *The winner's curse :paradoxes and anomalies of economic life.* Princeton, N.J.: Princeton University Press.

Trout, J. D. 1991. Introductory essay (Part I, Section III). In R. Boyd, P. Gasper and J. D. Trout (eds.), *The philosophy of science.* Cambridge. Mass.: MIT Press. pp. 387-392.

__________ 1998. *Measuring the intentional world: Realism, naturalism, and quantitative methods in the behavioral sciences.* Oxford: Oxford University Press.

Tversky, A. 1972. Elimination by aspects: A theory of choice. *Psychological Review* 79: 281-299.

__________ and D. Kahneman. 1974. Judgement under uncertainty: heuristic and biases. *Science* 185: 1124-1131.

__________ and __________ 1981. The framing of decisions and the psychology of choice. *Science* 211:453-8.

__________ and __________ 1992. Advances in prospect theory: Cumulative representation of uncertainty. *Journal of Risk and Uncertainty* 5:297-323.

__________ , Sattath, S. and Slovic, P. [1988] 2000. Contingent weighting in judgement and choice. *Psychological Review* 95(3): 371-384.

__________ , P. Slovic and D. Kahneman 1990. The causes of preference Reversal. *The American Economic Review* 80(1): 204-217.

__________ and R. Thaler. 1990. Anomalies: Preference Reversals. *The Journal of Economic Perspectives* 4(2): 201-211.

Udehn, L. 1996. *The limits of public choice: a sociological critique of the economic theory of politics.* New York: Routledge.

van de Kragt, A. J. Orbell, R. Dawes, S. Braver and L. Wilson. 1986. Doing well and doing good as ways of resolving social dilemmas. In H. Wilke, D. Messick and C. Rutte (eds.), *Experimental social dilemmas.* Frankfurt am Main, FRG: Verlag Peter Lang. pp. 177-203.

van Fraassen, B. C. 1977. The Pragmatics of Explanation *American Philosophical Quarterly* 14: 143-150.

Varian, H. R. 1988. Revealed preference with a subset of goods. *Journal of Economic Theory* 46:179-85.

__________ 2003. *Intermediate microeconomics: a modern approach.* 6th ed. New York: Norton.

von Neumann, J. and O. Morgenstern [1944] 2004. *Theory of games and economic behavior*, 60th anniversary ed. Princeton: Princeton University Press.

von Winterfeldt, D. 1999. On the relevance of behavioral decision research for decision analysis. In J. Shanteau, B. A. Mellers and D. A. Schum (eds.), *Decision science and technology: reflections on the contributions of Ward Edwards*. New York: Springer. pp. 133-154.

Walras, L. [1874] 1954. *Elements of pure economics*. Cambridge, Mass.: Harvard University Press

Weber, B., A. Aholt, C. Neuhaus, P. Trautner, C. E. Elger and T. Teichert. 2007. Neural evidence for reference-dependence in real-market-transactions. *NeuroImage* 35: 441-447.

Weintraub, E. R. 2002. How economics became a mathematical science. Durham: Duke University Press.

Wilkinson, N. 2008. *An introduction to behavioral economics*. New York: Palgrave Macmillan.

Wilson, T. D., D. S. Dunn, J. A. Bybee, D. B. Hyman and J. A. Rotondo. 1984. Effects of analyzing reasons on attitude-behavior consistency. *Journal of Personality and Social Psychology* 47(1): 5-16.

__________ and J. W. Schooler. 1991. Thinking too much: introspection can reduce the quality of preferences and decisions. *Journal of Personality and Social Psychology* 60(2): 181-192.

Wimsatt, W. C. 2007. *Re-engineering philosophy for limited beings: piecewise approximations to reality*. Cambridge, Mass.: Harvard University Press.

Woodward, J. 2008. Social preferences in experimental *economics. Philosophy of Science* 75: 646-657.

Zak, P. J. 2004. Neuroeconomics. *Philosophical Transactions of the Royal Society: B* 359: 1737-1748.

__________, R. Kurzban and W. T. Matzner. 2005. Oxytocin is associated with human trustworthiness. Hormones and Behavior 48: 522-7.

__________, A. A. Stanton and S. Ahmade. 2007. Oxytocin increases generosity in humans. *PloS ONE* 11(e1128): 1-5.